Citizen Azmari

Ilana Webster-Kogen

CITIZEN AZMARI

Making Ethiopian Music in Tel Aviv

Wesleyan University Press   Middletown, Connecticut

Wesleyan University Press
Middletown CT 06459
www.wesleyan.edu/wespress
© 2018 Ilana Webster-Kogen
All rights reserved
Manufactured in the United States of America
Designed by Mindy Basinger Hill
Typeset in Minion Pro

Grateful acknowledgment is made for support
from the AMS 75 PAYS Endowment of the American Musicological Society,
funded in part by the National Endowment for the Humanities and the
Andrew W. Mellon Foundation.

Library of Congress Cataloging-in-Publication Data

Names: Webster-Kogen, Ilana, author.

Title: Citizen Azmari: making Ethiopian music
in Tel Aviv / Ilana Webster-Kogen.

Description: Middletown, Connecticut:
Wesleyan University Press, [2018] | Series: Music/culture |
Includes bibliographical references and index.

Identifiers: LCCN 2018003966 (print) | LCCN 2018008560 (ebook) |
ISBN 9780819578341 (ebook) | ISBN 9780819578327 (cloth: alk. paper) |
ISBN 9780819578334 (pbk.: alk. paper)

Subjects: LCSH: Music—Social aspects—Israel—Tel Aviv. | Ethiopians—
Israel—Tel Aviv—Music—History and criticism. |
Jews, Ethiopian—Israel—Tel Aviv—Music—History and criticism.

Classification: LCC ML3917.I77 (ebook) |
LCC ML3917.I77 W43 2018 (print) | DDC 781.62/92805694—dc23

LC record available at https://lccn.loc.gov/2018003966

5   4   3   2   1

CONTENTS

*Audio files can be found at http://wesleyan.edu/wespress/citizen_azmari/
for this book. Files available at that address are labeled consecutively
through the book as (Audio file).*

ILLUSTRATIONS

FIGURES

TABLES

ACKNOWLEDGMENTS

The majority of my research partners remain anonymous in this book because of issues connected to religion and migration in the state of Israel. I wish I could thank them individually, but hope it will suffice to offer this book in gratitude and mutuality. I name musicians with public profiles like Ester Rada, Axum, and Dejen Manchlot, and artists connected to the community like Dr. Ruth Eshel and The Idan Raichel Project. Many thanks are due to the musicians, audience members, and community workers who gave me their time.

I gratefully acknowledge the institutions that have funded my research since 2008. The Jewish Music Institute (JMI) in London supported my PhD fieldwork, the basis for four chapters. Special thanks go to Geraldine Auerbach and Jennifer Jankel, past and current chairs of the JMI. The University of London's Central Research Fund and the Israel Institute offered further research support that made it possible to complete this work. Chapter 3 is derived, in part, from an article published in *Ethnomusicology Forum* on March 11, 2014, available online: http://wwww.tandfonline.com/ 10.1080/17411912.2013.879034. I also thank Marla Zubel of Wesleyan University Press for her work on the manuscript in its early days, Jaclyn Wilson, and Suzanna Tamminen for seeing the project through with utmost patience, as well as the anonymous reviewers whose comments I greatly appreciate. Susan Abel at the University Press of New England made the editorial process extremely smooth, together with David Hornik, whose meticulous work has so greatly benefited this project.

I have presented the material in this book across the UK and Europe, the United States, Israel, and Ethiopia. I have workshopped chapters at the SEM, BFE, and AAA annual conferences, and at the Universities of Oxford, Manchester, Birmingham, and Cardiff (special thanks to John O'Connell), as well as at King's College London and at SOAS's School of Arts, Anthropology Department, and

Centre for Jewish Studies, and I thank the participants in each forum for their suggestions. I completed most of the book's new, post-PhD material during a year at New York University, at its Abu Dhabi campus, and in New York. I owe special thanks to Judith Miller for enabling this to happen, to Zev Feldman and Carlos Guedes for welcoming me into the Music Department, and especially to Nasser and Laila Isleem for their friendship and hospitality in Abu Dhabi. Many thanks are also due to Virginia Danielson, who was so helpful as a mentor there. I have benefited greatly from reading some outstanding works on Jewish music and music in Israel/Palestine, and I thank Amy Horowitz, Edwin Seroussi, Jeffrey Summit, and especially the formidable Kay Kaufman Shelemay for important efforts that I admire. Special thanks go to Francis Falceto and Ben Mandelson for helping with many and sundry questions about the Ethiopian recording industry.

Most of this project was completed during my time at SOAS, and I thank everyone who was involved there. First and foremost, Abigail Wood supervised my dissertation and supported the project from the beginning. Angela Impey has been my most important mentor, and Lucy Duran and Rachel Harris are dear colleague-friends. Caspar Melville and Simon Webster read significant portions of this book, and I am extremely grateful for their editorial eye. I have benefited from guidance and collegiality over the years from Carli Coetzee, Yair Wallach, Mehmet Izbudak, Jaeho Kang, Gil Karpas, Richard Widdess, Owen Wright, Nick Gray, Keith Howard, Tom Selwyn, and Miia Laine. Many thanks go to Yoseph Mengistu for Amharic lessons. I was fortunate to have a distinguished group of people in or around my PhD cohort—Moshe Morad, Sabina Rakcheyeva, Chris Mau, Shzr Ee Tan, Chloe Alaghband-Zadeh, and Joe Browning are dear colleagues, as are Anna Morcom, Oliver Shao, and Phil Alexander, with whom I almost overlapped. I am always inspired by the energy and creativity of my wonderful PhD students Clara Wenz, Robbie Campbell, Rasika Ajotikar, and Vicky Tadros. Special appreciation goes to Mehryar Golestani (Reveal), working with whom has been life-changing.

I am grateful as well to those who helped make fieldwork and writing run smoothly. Sam Thrope has been my launchpad in Israel for many years, and Joyce Klein has always made me feel more comfortable in Jerusalem. I always look forward to meeting with Tamar Warburg, Varda Makovsky, Navah and Seffi Kogen, and Herb Rosenblum when we overlap in Tel Aviv. I would not have embarked on this project without the crucial music education I received from Isaac Malkin. Closer to home, Katherine Williams and Tim Schaap, Virina Laskaridou, Vanessa Springer-Treiber, Arash Yomtobian, Brian Lobel, Tina Elliott, Ben Mandelson, Donna Aranson, Barbara and Ish Rosenblit, and Howard Ellison have been supportive throughout this project. I am particularly grateful to Katie Allen and Stephanie Wells for taking such good care of my young daughter Mika during its last stages.

And finally, thanks are due to my family. My grandparents David and Dina Kogen and Eugenia von Valtier were instrumental in my education; my grandfather understood better than anyone what it took for immigrants to succeed. Catherine and Richard Webster, Anthony Webster, and the late Louise Harries tolerated my working on this project through many visits over the years, and accompanied me to hear a lot of Ethiopian music. My cousins Mira and Josh Resnick, Dov Kogen and Rebecca Shapiro, William Schlanger, and Karl and Fritz von Valtier know this project extremely well by now. Aunts and Uncles Bill and Cheryl von Valtier and Herb and Sheila Rosenblum have been constant sources of encouragement in my life, especially in the areas of music and Hebrew. Isaac and Shaya Woloff have been wonderful companions, and Isaac made my last week of fieldwork especially memorable. My father, Rabbi Judah Kogen, has always been ready to offer assistance on this project, driving me to an interview at an absorption center, and instilling in me a love of ancient text. My mother, Lisa Kogen, has been my lifelong role model in curiosity, resilience, and empathy. Together they have been my most important teachers, and my sisters Shira Kogen and Abigail Woloff have been my dearest friends. Simon Webster has shared his life with this project and with me since the project's inception, and I am so grateful for his editorial contributions and moral support, for sharing my interests, for helping with the book title and tracking down sources when I need them, and for always finding new music for me. It's hard to believe that this research was completed before Mika came into the world, and I'm so delighted that she already loves books!

NOTE ON TRANSLITERATION

In transliterating Hebrew, I have generally adopted the Library of Congress system. In the case of proper nouns for people, places, and musical ensembles, I use their preferred nonstandard spelling. In some cases I add an *h* at the end of a word that ends in the letter hay, and sometimes I transliterate the letter *ayin* as *a* instead of '. The letters "ḥ" and "kh" make basically the same sound in English but represent different letters in Hebrew. I sometimes separate syllables surrounding the sound "ai" with a single prime ('). I have also adopted the Library of Congress system for Amharic words.

INTRODUCTION

Symbolic Codes of Citizenship

Jerusalem Promenade, November 27, 2008

Amid the joyous tumult of the crowd assembled on the promenade (*tayelet*), a lone voice of disapproval cuts stridently through the bustle. "Disgrace, disgrace!" (*Bizayon, bizayon!*), shouts a middle-aged black man in a white shirt, black trousers, and a Jewish skullcap (*kippah*). He has jumped up on a column, where all the revelers can see him, and where he proceeds to declaim, "Long live the nation of Israel!" (*Am Yisrael Ḥai!*), before shouting his disapproval again. The crowd ignores him. This is Jerusalem, after all; ostentatious finger-wagging by the religious is hardly unusual. But to the student of Ethiopian-Israeli[1] culture, this public display of anger on the promenade reveals a deep fracture among Ethiopian-Israelis in their relationship to the state, religion, and their bodies.

Today is Sigd, a pilgrimage festival and the most important day on the Ethiopian Jewish calendar (Abbink 1983, Ben-Dor 1987), and it is being celebrated as a national holiday in Israel. Ethiopian-Israelis, Israeli citizens of Ethiopian lineage from across the country, have traveled to Jerusalem by bus to celebrate together, first praying in the direction of the Old City and then dancing Eskesta, the Ethiopian national shoulder dance, in the afternoon. Both halves of the day express the ambivalence of the Ethiopian experience in Israel: the first half, consisting of centuries-old ritual, gives voice to collective relief at having been brought back from exile; the second, secular part of the day epitomizes the otherness of the Ethiopian in a predominantly white country. Moreover, the state's sponsorship of the afternoon entertainment (the stage and sound system have been set up for dancing) can hardly erase the memory of such fraught episodes as the "blood affair," the mass disposal by the Israeli Blood Bank of Ethiopian donations revealed in 1996;[2] likewise, the rabbinate's refusal to recognize Ethiopian clergy (the Qessim in Hebrew, or Qessotch in Amharic) or to license their ordination (Kaplan 2005: 391, 2010: 82). Thus this moment of joy, solidarity, and appreciation for official recognition is tinged with an awareness of the distance still remaining toward the goal of full equality.

The aforementioned self-appointed critic, however, objects to none of these complex dynamics of integration and inclusion. His harangue is directed at the mixed dancing (men and women together), at the Ethiopian (rather than Israeli) music, and at the public display of an unusual and not widely accepted form of Jewish practice. The critic is himself well integrated into Israel, practicing a kind of normative Ashkenazi Orthodoxy prevalent across the nationalist (*dati le'umi*) community of religious Zionists. This group, associated in the media with the settler movement and its supporters, is often branded as intransigent because of its absolute rejection of dialogue with Arab neighbors, and of the very idea of a Palestinian state. Yet in one of the great many ironies of Israeli society, the national-religious population often welcomes Ethiopians into its midst, the criterion for membership being ideological and political (and religious) rather than strictly race-based. Together with its affiliate youth group, B'nei Akiva, the national-religious movement hosts a disproportionately high number of Ethiopian-Israelis, people who are happy to integrate even when the ideology they are joining is resolutely opposed to inclusion of certain other minorities.

How paradoxical, then, that the most vocal objection to the afternoon's festivities comes from the exceptional example of an Ethiopian who has managed, against the odds, to find a cohort of Israelis that welcomes him into their religious-nationalist community. But this embrace comes at a price: he has to shed the distinct Judaism of his preimmigration life in the rural Ethiopian highlands. He has to discard the secular music of his country of birth, instead embracing the biblically inspired and frequently militant music of religious Zionists. And indeed, despite the legendary "humility" of his kin group (see Salamon 2010: 165), he is sufficiently alienated from them that the behavioral norms of his rural ancestors now appear "immodest." And all of this tension erupts from music and dancing, which embody signals and sounds that, as I shall show, function as political statements in the public sphere. Race may render Ethiopian-Israelis instantly recognizable in Israel, but their complex integration into Israeli society rests on more than skin color. Whether it is in the thousands of celebrants or in the private thoughts of this individual, the soundworlds[3] of Ethiopian-Israelis have become an alternative political framework for articulating and contesting their relationships among themselves and with broader Israeli society.

———

Tower of David, Jerusalem, September 4, 2015

Ester Rada is currently Israel's most celebrated musical export and the first Ethiopian-Israeli international celebrity. Yet it is with a modest "Thank you" that she steps quietly offstage and into the DJ booth, surprising me along with much of the audience. Israelis are accustomed to hearing emotional explanations of the symbolic meaning and historical weight of a performance, especially when staged in a highly charged locale such as the Tower of David in Jerusalem's Old City.[4] I cast my mind back and remember Ron Huldai, the mayor of Tel Aviv, saying, "I was asked to give a blessing, but I already feel blessed being here" (*aval ani kvar margish mevorakh*) on the steps of the Tel Aviv Opera House in August 2008. Or the sentimentality of the performance by the pop star and conscientious objector Aviv Geffen on the banks of the Dead Sea in April 2000. When Israeli musicians and politicians perform in locations with historical significance, they tend to testify to the personal and historical significance the location and performance have for them. Not so with Ester Rada. Against a backdrop of the Tower of David and the Old City's Jaffa Gate, Rada closes her performance at the Jerusalem Sacred Music Festival without fanfare.

As the daughter of Ethiopians who risked their lives to journey to Israel in the 1980s and raised her within the religious-Zionist movement, Rada could hardly have been unaware of the ideological and religious significance of being invited to perform in the Old City. It is by virtue of this vivid personal history that she serves as a sort of informal Israeli ambassador to African and Afrodiasporic culture, introducing both Ethio-color, a performance troupe from Addis Ababa, and an encore performance of reggae star Max Romeo at the festival's closing celebration. Thus Rada has every reason to invoke the symbolic meaning of performing at the citadel. Yet, for her, speeches are invariably de trop. Her musical style, the vehicle of her worldview, conveys her ambivalence toward Israel. She sings almost exclusively in English, even at this venue, while her band plays a combination of soul, 1970s Ethio-jazz,[5] funk, and reggae, excluding the Israeli popular music that was the repertoire of her musical training. For source material she draws heavily from the work of Nina Simone, the African American composer and performer who stood at the forefront of the civil rights movement. Indeed, Rada's musical style is so heavily influenced by the lyricism and pathos of the African American experience that it is impossible not to discern in her repertoire and throaty vocal style a form of social commentary on Israeli society and politics, even though she shies away from explicitly political statements. Rada's musical style fills the void left by her discursive silence—as she declines to make speeches about how moved she is to be there—and encourages her audience to listen for clues in her music. The bodily and sonic codes of her performance replace speech as political statement in this particular—national—public sphere. Taken alone, this nongesture means little, but as I describe a pattern of public Ethiopian-Israeli behavior, I will portray a dynamic that is, in the words of the folklorist Hagar Salamon, "coded and indirect" (2010: 165). A listener paying attention to the use of silence would see this as a moment laden with meaning.

―――

These two contrasting episodes provide an aperçu into the constructed sound-worlds of Israel's others. This book argues that soundworlds are central to the process of establishing an alternative framework of citizenship for Ethiopian-Israelis, the 135,000 "Ethiopian Jews" who have migrated to the State of Israel over the past forty years, and whose integration into Israeli society is consensually considered unfinished and uneasy (Kaplan 2005, Parfitt and Trevisan Semi 1999, 2005, Weil 2004). And among the musicians who inform this research, the Azmari features prominently. In Ethiopia, the Azmari is a self-accompanied folk-poet, often described in the literature as a "wandering minstrel" (Kebede 1975). Although Israeli anxiety over the integration of Ethiopian immigrants is characterized in the impression, widespread among the Azmaris and other folk musicians I worked with, that Israelis think that they "came without culture" (ba'u bli tarbut),[6] in this book I focus on the transformation of the rich musical cultures Ethiopian-Israelis brought with them. I describe how these have been enlarged and adapted by creating unique soundworlds through which this Ethiopian-Israeli population has explored the fraught dynamics of citizenship and developed new ways of being black and Israeli. Whereas sociologists and psychologists occupy themselves with the question of why Ethiopians do not integrate into Israel[7]—and attempt to explain why male unemployment has reached 85 percent (Kaplan 2010: 78)—I draw from the methods of ethnomusicology to propose an alternative perspective.

My approach investigates how Ethiopian-Israelis mobilize their soundworlds as a means of proposing alternative political frameworks that serve them as Israeli citizens. Looking at cultural life reveals dynamics and influences that all too often fall outside the scope of studies focused on social pathologies and their attendant data sets. Investigating the sensory experience, and particularly the soundworld, through music but also ritual, dance, and soundscape provides a better understanding of how Ethiopian-Israeli citizenship works, rather than rehashing debates over why integration has failed.

Working primarily with source material from traditional and popular music (like Herman 2012, Shabtay 2001, or Tourny 2007), and drawing from the invaluable resources of the work of Ezra Abate (2007), Francis Falceto, and Kay Kaufman Shelemay, this book analyzes musical sources to clarify a political repositioning that is under way of Ethiopian-Israelis as active citizens in contemporary Israeli society. Whereas the secondary literature mainly considers music in Ethiopia, or music from Ethiopia that has been transplanted to Israel, I focus primarily on new musical styles being generated by the Israeli-born Ethiopians who are embedded in Israeli society. In insisting on the centrality of music in establishing alternative frameworks of immigrant rights and responsibilities, I engage in a similar mode of cultural analysis to some of the outstanding research about music among Israeli minorities (Brinner 2009, Horowitz 2010, McDonald 2013, Regev and Seroussi 2004). Yet this book represents a departure from a heavily liturgy-focused body of scholarship about Ethiopian-Israeli/Jewish music. The work of ethnomusicologists Alvarez-Pereyre and Ben-Dor (1999), Arom and Tourny (1999), Atar (2005), and Tourny (2010) follows from Kay Kaufman Shelemay's groundbreaking analysis of Beta Israel (a term for Ethiopian Jewry) liturgy (1986). But with the gradual integration of Ethiopians into Israeli society, and the tendency to join mainstream Orthodox synagogues, soon the Jewish liturgical music of Ethiopia may be little more than an artifact in Israel, and the analysis of liturgy a final phase of research into a nearly extinct musical culture.

Looking at how Ethiopian-Israelis experience music today as Israelis, my research engages the most important principle of Ethiopian musical aesthetics, the concept of *sem-enna-werq* or "wax and gold," the impulse to hide meaning in plain sight. The literary term refers to the technique of lost-wax casting in which wax is poured over gold and then chipped away, revealing the gold beneath (Levine 1965). The technique is employed most notably by the Azmari, who uses dual meaning to praise and lambast patrons succinctly (Kebede 1977), and I mobilize the concept to address what is perhaps Shelemay's underlying assertion: that music is the key to understanding Ethiopian (Jewish) culture.

This book reports on how Ethiopian-Israelis leverage music as participation in national life and the public sphere in the absence of what were once the primary routes into Israeli society: religion and the military (see Shabtay 1999: 176, who argues that military service has been successful for integration, especially where religion has failed). The troubles of Ethiopian integration came to the fore in the 1990s, after 1991's Operation Solomon rendered Ethiopian-Israelis a permanent visible minority in Israeli society, the first major population group in Israel who could lay claim to being both black and Jewish. This historical moment coincided with Paul Gilroy's (1993) exposition of the black Atlantic (the transnational circuit of the slave trade that facilitated cultural exchange across Africa, Britain, the Caribbean, and the Americas) as an alternative public sphere represented through music. Meanwhile, multiculturalism and the fall of the Eastern bloc facilitated sociological interest in citizenship and identity-based analyses within ethnomusicology. For Ethiopian-Israelis, the legacy of this period has been a search for black consciousness as an alternative to assimilation into an Israeli national identity from which they found themselves largely excluded. Accordingly, over the past twenty years, scholars in the subdiscipline of Beta Israel studies (the study of Ethiopian-Israeli history, religion, and culture) have couched much of their work in the conceptual language of identity. Yet Ethiopian-Israeli social problems emanate from a fundamental rupture in the social contract: that the rights and privileges of citizenship have been compromised by a public consensus, reported across this book, that renders Ethiopian-Israelis a special, sometimes disadvantaged category of citizen.

The sociologist T. H. Marshall argues that the twentieth century's framing of citizenship is based on an economic and social contract that guarantees the rights of the welfare state, or what he calls social citizenship. He explains that social citizenship derives from older models of political citizenship (the right to participate in public life and decision-making) and civil citizenship (the right to liberty and property) (1949: 10–12). Jürgen Habermas expands on Marshall's formulation by broadening the rights and responsibilities of citizenship beyond "political membership" (1994: 24) to "active participation" (ibid.) in "deliberative democracy" (1994: 32). For Ethiopian-Israelis, Habermas's formulation of rights (the right to immigrate to Israel because of Jewish ancestry) and responsibilities (serving in the military, making a discernible contribution to the state's security) has not yielded the opportunity for active participation in deliberative democracy. More specifically, while participating in state institutions (like the military) might help to integrate young Ethiopian-Israelis, that integration does not automatically lead to upward mobility.

Ethiopian-Israeli citizenship might be better understood in the context of newer articulations of citizenship that have emerged since the 1990s with the fall of the Soviet Union, the breakup of the Balkan states, and the rapid globalization of migration flows. Bart van Steenbergen (1994:151) surveys the emerging ideas of neorepublican citizenship (considering each individual as officeholder), cultural citizenship (the ability to participate in national culture), global citizenship (participation beyond the boundaries of the nation-state), and ecological citizenship of the earth citizen. All of these configurations of the individual's relationship to the nation-state, based on the global flows of migrants and the reformulations of national boundaries, apply to some degree to Israel's idiosyncratic political history as an ethnic democracy (Smooha 1997) that is composed primarily of the descendants of immigrants, and favors Jews over its non-Jewish (Arab, Bedouin, Druze, etc.) constituents. Fundamentally, though, the Ethiopian-Israeli case is sui generis because of religious baggage (antisemitism in Ethiopia being contrasted with religious delegitimization in Israel), racial elements (blackness in a "white" society), and the diasporic imaginings of being part of the Jewish community-in-exile in the past, and, currently, at least for young people, part of the African diaspora.

In this book, I unpack the Ethiopian-Israeli relationship with the state, but I do so through the back channel of musical style. I argue that Ethiopian-Israelis use wax and gold to navigate the rights (to immigrate) and responsibilities (military service) of citizenship, effectively behaving like Azmaris. I call this process Azmari citizenship, and following from Hagar Salamon's description of Ethiopian-Israeli folk stories that are "coded and indirect" (2010: 165), I demonstrate that a widespread wax-and-gold musical habitus navigates Ethiopian-Israeli exclusion and belonging. Since political activism—public protest, formation of political parties—has yielded few tangible victories for this population, music offers an alternative political framework whereby nonspeech can be performed and interpreted as political statements. Musical style thus constitutes an alternative argument for civil rights, whether through Azmari music, Eskesta dance, hip-hop, soul, reggae, or fusion projects. Across musical styles, musical acceptance in the broader Israeli mainstream translates quite directly into civil rights and even the right to immigrate. Hence musicians and their audiences use music (and sound more broadly) as a forum for establishing political principles about how to vote, where to live, and how to react to top-down state initiatives.

My analysis of these musical strategies rests on a series of myths, mobilized and reconfigured through music and sound, and I dedicate a chapter to each of the myth clusters before presenting their reconfiguration in targeted Israeli contexts. Each myth cluster comprises a variety of cultural touchstones, clichés, and narratives whose imagery (sometimes visually, but more often through sonic references) can—notwithstanding Steven Feld's labeling of these references as "schizophonic" (1996)—be as richly evocative as they are succinct. I frame aesthetic choices through the terminology of myths because conventions of tonality, instrumentation, and repertoire are often clustered together seemingly indiscriminately, without necessarily considering original source material. This is not a criticism; indeed, musicians creatively reappropriate schizophonic sounds that signal blackness, Ethiopianness, or Israeliness as a mechanism for framing themselves within an idealized tradition. An accordion implies Israeli folk song; a "Yo" indicates debt to African American culture; and ululation signals an Ethiopian wedding. Working through the way these myths inform the construction of a soundworld to compensate for an unstable immigrant identity, Ethiopian-Israelis navigate their uncertain status in Israeli society through sound with an effectiveness notably lacking in political organization and community work.[8]

AZMARI CITIZENSHIP: WAX AND GOLD AS THEORY AND METHOD

I take the figure of the Azmari as point of departure for this study of music and citizenship. The Azmari lives in perpetual debt to patrons, who can revoke lodging and financial support at any time; hence the folk-poet must recognize the boundaries of acceptable speech. Critical lyrics that mock patrons demonstrate the Azmari's virtuosity, but a critique that is too biting or disrespectful can find the musician out of work immediately (Kebede 1977). For an Azmari, caustic critique is often obscured through humor or flowery language, suggesting a larger truth: that hidden within (any kind of) musical texts are messages and meanings that are subtle and obscured but that might be poignant critiques of power.

In his classic study of Amhara culture, Donald Levine explains the mechanism of wax and gold in detail, based on the flexibility of the Amharic language. He offers the following couplet as an example: "Ya-min tiqem talla ya-min tiqem tajji / Tallat sishanu buna adargaw enji" (1965: 6). He translates the couplet as: "Of what use is beer, of what use is honey-wine? / When seeing an enemy off, serve him coffee." But he explains that when the second line is said aloud, "buna adargaw" is elided and pronounced as "bun adargaw" (reduce him to ashes). He argues that in wax and gold, we find a key to understanding northern Ethiopian culture: the possibility of communicating in several, perhaps opposing registers at once.

The sociopolitical dynamics of Azmari norms are familiar even to the Israeli-born generation, since the State of Israel requires certain behaviors as a precondition for immigration and the benefits of citizenship (see Seeman 2009: 28, 91, for the religious preconditions today). One of these implicit behaviors is obedience, and Ethiopian-Israeli social protests are frequently reactions to governmental strictures on further Ethiopian (Falash Mura) immigration. As a result, many Ethiopian-Israelis, known to Israelis as "shy and quiet" (Seeman 2009: 25) behave, whether individually, collectively, or inadvertently, like Azmaris: they learn quickly which kinds of critique of the state apparatus are acceptable and which will cause them trouble with the authorities. Therefore, as I build the concept of Azmari citizenship, or a mode of relating to the state modeled after an Azmari's awareness of boundaries, I argue that many Ethiopian-Israeli musicians—as prominent spokespeople and social critics—take on the social characteristics of the Azmari without saying so explicitly.

Following from the work of Don Seeman (2009: 102) and Shalva Weil (1995: 3), I posit that Ethiopian-Israelis engage in wax and gold (sem-enna-werq) regularly, and that musicians make aesthetic choices according to the acknowledged parameters of critique. As I explore the different Ethiopian musical genres being created in and around Tel Aviv, I present these aesthetic choices as implicit signals that reorient Ethiopian-Israeli citizenship away from the top-down integration framework, and toward alternative narratives that build a collective sense of contribution to Israeli society based on tangible achievements and repositioning in the context of global migration flows.

I frame the Azmari figure and the technique of wax and gold as a key theoretical strand in this book, but wax and gold was also a crucial element of my fieldwork experience in Tel Aviv in 2008–2009. Working with Ethiopian-Israelis required constant navigation of taboo, veiled opinions and self-censorship because the stakes of representation were so high. In his outstanding book on the Falash Mura's return to Judaism, *One People, One Blood*, anthropologist Don Seeman frames wax and gold, in effect, as etic versus emic knowledge: "The term *wax and gold* also stands for a pervasive cultural aesthetic that applies equally to a form of prose in which meaning is elusive and masks are common. It can take a real virtuoso to crack the code of *semana worke* when it is well performed, because the surface meanings themselves contain multiple levels to confuse or misdirect those who lack the perspicacity to see what lies beneath" (2009: 74).

My fieldwork experience transpired much as Seeman describes: people were willing to talk to me, but the content of what they said was often less useful than the dynamics driving what they did not say at first. The everyday practice of wax and gold as Seeman frames it is indeed partially due to a "pervasive cultural aesthetic," and it is widespread because the stakes of working with Ethiopian-Israelis are so high.

Scholarly representation has affected Ethiopian-Israelis' legal and immigration rights since long before they were called Ethiopian-Israelis (which is to say, back in Ethiopia). As early as the nineteenth century, the claim of Jewish ancestry, along with its endorsement by respected Jewish scholars like Jacques Faitlovitch (see Trevisan Semi 2004), has affected the group's right to religious legitimacy and, later, Israeli citizenship. In his compelling analysis of conversion, Seeman explains that rabbinic or governmental authorities often appropriate researchers' assertions about Ethiopian-Israeli status to determine religious legitimacy, as they did with Kay Kaufman Shelemay's findings (1986, 1991). In an especially poignant case, Hagar Salamon offers a moving explanation of her personal battle over whether to expose the practice of slavery (*barya*) among Ethiopian Jews in Ethiopia (see 2002 for an intense ethnographic account). Ethiopian-Israelis are aware of this dynamic of scholarly research and often exercise reserve accordingly.

By the time I began my fieldwork in summer 2008, these issues of representation and fieldwork ethics were already well-known in the subdiscipline of Beta Israel studies, which focuses on Ethiopian Jews in Ethiopia and Israel. I embarked on fieldwork aware of the potential appropriation of research findings by interested parties. Hence at every stage I have taken issues of anonymity extremely seriously, offering often-minimalist details about my informants, some of whom are engaged in legal battles against the Israeli state. Unless an interviewee is a public figure whose identity cannot reasonably be shielded, I have anonymized all of my informants, as well as some details like the town where they live.

As I carried on my fieldwork, exercising what might be characterized as extreme caution, I soon became aware of the limitations of the semistructured interview in the context of everyday practice of wax and gold. Shalva Weil's article "It Is Futile to Trust in Man" (1995) speaks for itself in this respect, and Seeman confirms that interviews are conducted with the wax-and-gold dynamic in the background (2009: 100–102). Recognizing that my own interview material was clouded by guarded speech, and an overwhelming hesitation among many informants about criticizing the State of Israel explicitly, I soon realized that musical style and text itself might be a site where the "gold" emerges. Therefore, this book offers far more analysis of musical text and style than it does of direct quotation of interview material. For an anthropologist left uncomfortable with my reliance on musical source material rather than the words exchanged in interviews, I contend that musical style is an area where unguarded attitudes toward the State of Israel emerge. If this book is read as especially musicological, then, it is because my analysis delves into musical style and genre as a response to what I perceive as a wax-and-gold dynamic in everyday speech about controversial issues.

It is not an overstatement, then, to say that I rely on wax and gold as a main theory and a key method in this project. I look to some of the extraordinary work done with Ethiopian-Israelis by anthropologists and folklorists as a model for using alternative forms of communication as source material. In addition to Don Seeman's work (2009), and his outstanding recent article on the moral judgments of coffee rituals and possession among Ethiopian-Israelis (2015), I look to Hagar Salomon's work on dream analysis (2002) and jokes (2011). Both scholars nimbly use their extensive interview material to derive their conclusions, but they also draw from a variety of nonverbal and intangible aspects of interpersonal exchange. Itsushi Kawase's stunning documentary film work in Ethiopia on Azmaris (2010) further demonstrates the probative value of musical performance in its own right. My discussion of Azmari citizenship, then, relies primarily on analysis of musical style that engages in critique of the state, when individuals might not do so in their everyday speech.

I should add as a caveat that the concept of Azmari citizenship is inherently paradoxical: some Ethiopian-Israeli musicians would hesitate to say explicitly that their musical style is coded political statement, so overt confirmation of my interpretation is limited by the very social conventions I describe. Ultimately, though, I posit the Azmari figure, and the practice of wax and gold, as an effective way of understanding how Ethiopian-Israelis—even those too young to remember the institution of the Azmari from Ethiopia—relate to Israeli society.

MUSIC AND MYTH, MUSIC AS MYTH

Throughout this book, I describe schizophonic, decontextualized, individual sonic references as invoking Afrodiasporic, Ethiopianist, or Zionist myths. I adopt the terminology of myth as one conceptual framework for understanding sound because I interpret these decontextualized sounds as what the religious-studies scholar Ivan Strenski terms "a dramatic development of dogma" (1992: 117, dogma being understood as religious doctrine or moral code). Only a short time after beginning my fieldwork, I came to recognize that certain performance practices represent social or political positionings that, whether intentionally or not, invoke narrative tropes of inclusion that are recognizable to most Ethiopian-Israelis. Many, like dreadlocks or biblical references in lyrics, are easy to discern as appealing to histories of blackness or Jewishness, but are only interpreted as advocating a method of integration by active listeners who are attuned to the narrative and dramatic power of performing these disembodied schizophonic sounds. Therefore, I suggest that sounds themselves, rather than (or in addition to) speech and stories, constitute a kind of multisensory myth that invokes and articulates etiologies and ideologies of belonging.

Ivan Strenski derives his definition of myth from Bronisław Malinowski's work, rather than through the prism of folklore and comparative religion.[9] Malinowski's ethnographically informed interpretation contrasts with the work of religion scholars like Robert Segal who more or less ignore political motives underlying form insofar as they maintain that the form of myth derives from the social function it performs in society. As Strenski articulates the position of anthropology, myth is "a story which is told in order to establish a belief" (1992: 121). Malinowski thus takes the perspective that, insofar as myths address power relations within a social group, they constitute the public performance of ultimately political narrative tropes. That definition provides the theoretical underpinning of myth as I define it in this study, as does Michael Jackson's assertion about the exchange of rumors and folktales: "It is in this two-way transformation of private into public personae, and shared worldviews into personal allegories, that narratives attain their power" (2013: 227).

I propose that the common definition of myth as a narrative espoused by an imagined community that explains origins or values, and that promotes social cohesion, may be expanded to include nonspeech elements of storytelling. The consensual definition that myths are transmitted verbally (including song and epic) excludes nonspeech sounds and individual musical characteristics. Where my definition of myth adapts and expands that which is generally offered by folklore and comparative religion is in my association of performance style, often divorced completely from lyrics, with etiologies and social history. These individual performative elements (instrumentation and tonality in addition to lyrics) and often-decontextualized sounds (ululation, accordion, reggae beat) invoke Afrodiasporic, Ethiopianist, and Zionist ethnohistories. My proposed, expanded definition of myth provides a conceptual mechanism by which to discuss the competing, interpolating claims being made about Ethiopian-Israelis: myths of Zionism, of Ethiopianism, and of the African diaspora.

Each of these three narratives carries discrete historical baggage. When I explore Zionist myths of home and return in chapter 3, I review the already-accepted terms of the Israeli school of historiography, which has for the past thirty years worked to debunk many of Zionism's sacred cows by calling them myths (see Morris 1988 for the launch of this line of inquiry, or Raz-Krakotzkin 2013 for a good contemporary example). In the case of Israeli history, key narratives of social cohesion are already called myths, and I borrow terms that are already widespread. In the case of Ethiopian studies, scholars are consensually aware of a narrative of Ethiopian exceptionalism hinging on religion, imperial governance, and language, but their awareness that these narratives only appeal to a minority of Ethiopia's diverse society stops short of explicitly calling the narratives myths. So when I refer to Ethiopianist myths, I refer to a common set of narratives familiar to students of Ethiopian history, but I am applying the label "myth" myself. In the dramatic case of the African diaspora, the terms on which any sense of group cohesion was established were driven by external forces practicing systemic violence and injustice. For that reason, some readers might find the term "myth," which may imply untruth, somewhat harsh. I engage fully with the history of violence that created the black Atlantic and its attendant narratives of black solidarity, and it is not my intention to call any of these narratives unreal or illegitimate. Indeed, it is my position that a myth can make legitimate truth claims; that is the essence of a wax-and-gold approach to narrative.

My criticism is reserved for the institutions that impose a top-down integration strategy on an immigrant population for whom it is unsuited. State support for Ethiopian-Israelis is abundant but often ineffective, and musicians frequently step into the breach to produce alternative citizenship narratives. Through musical style, their narratives mobilize cultural myths from three main sets of sources. First, the Zionist myths describe return from exile and rootedness in the land (Raz-Krakotzkin 2013; Regev and Seroussi 2004 from the musical perspective; or BenEzer 2002 for emphasis on the journey to Israel as a formative communal process). Second, Ethiopianist myths reorient Ethiopia as a key theological and anticolonial site of African independence and exceptionalism (Levine 1965, 1974). Third, Afrodiasporic myths (see Gilroy 1993, Hebdige 1987, Mintz and Price 1992), the invented traditions of the black Atlantic, bind together the descendants of the Middle Passage, and insert black minorities in white societies into those narratives. Aesthetic choices in language, instrumentation, tonality, and vocal style represent the perpetual reconfiguration of Ethiopian-Israelis in their local and national contexts, and their place in the wider world.

BECOMING ETHIOPIAN-ISRAELIS

The place of Ethiopian-Israelis, whether in Israeli society today or back in rural Ethiopia before immigration, has been in a near-perpetual state of flux for the better part of five hundred years. The people I describe in this book have been known as Ethiopian-Israeli only in the twenty-first century, and that title represents a centuries-long dynamic process of consistent identity re-formation. They have been known, over the past five centuries, as Ayhud, Falasha, Ethiopian Jews, Beta Israel (or for some, Falash Mura), and Etyopim, and each name reveals the constantly shifting social status of the world's best-known "black Jews." Each name — apart from the self-designation of Beta Israel — reveals the disjunction of being Jewish in Ethiopia, or black and Jewish, and some understanding of what to call this group offers a window into the group's complex history and social status.

Many of the details of Ethiopian Jewish history, immigration, and life in Israel are known outside of the Ethiopian-Israeli population because of the work of ethnomusicologists, folklorists, and anthropologists, and I touch on the main ideas in Beta Israel studies throughout this book. The main scholars of the subdiscipline whom I cite at length are Lisa Anteby-Yemini, Gadi BenEzer, Steven Kaplan, Tudor Parfitt, Hagar Salamon, Don Seeman, Kay Kaufman Shelemay, Emmanuela Trevisan Semi, and Shalva Weil. These scholars document the religious and social history of this group, their religious rites and everyday customs, personal narratives of immigration to Israel, and experience of marginality once settled in Israel. As these scholars' work is often referenced by the authorities when the government is debating whether to allow a new wave of Ethiopian immigration to commence, their research has clear implications for Ethiopian-Israeli life.

The history of Ethiopian Jewry is peppered with dramas over religious authenticity and racial difference. The first references to Jews in Ethiopia mention the Ayhud, a South Semitic cognate of the Hebrew word for Jew (Quirin 1995: 57). This term gave way around the seventeenth century to "Falasha" (wanderer), which implied religious otherness (Shelemay 1986: 209–11) since Jews (non-

Christians) were forbidden to own land. In contrast, people who claim Jewish roots in Ethiopia call themselves Beta Israel (House of Israel). These three terms vary in meaning and connotation, but they all designate Jews as outsiders in Ethiopia to some degree.

Until the later twentieth century, Beta Israel lived in villages in northern Ethiopia, where they survived as smiths and potters and maintained extended family units. As ironworkers who transformed objects through the use of fire, they were often cursed by their Christian neighbors as *buda*, or semihuman sorcerers capable of transforming themselves into hyenas (Salamon 1999, Seeman 2009: 69). They were indeed different both from their neighbors and from world Jewry, as they followed biblical law meticulously without reference to the rabbinic Judaism practiced across the Jewish world. By the time they were "discovered" by Jewish scholars from around the world like the Polish-French Zionist Jacques Faitlovitch, they lived immersed in distinct ritual, family life, and folklore (see Trevisan Semi 2004 for an excellent Hebrew-language biography of Faitlovitch).

The Beta Israel musical tradition is unique in Jewish liturgy. The Torah (Orit) is written in the South Semitic language of Ge'ez, and some passages of liturgy are in Agau because of links to the Agau peoples of Ethiopia (according to Don Seeman, Beta Israel spoke Agau in the nineteenth century and Amharic in the twentieth century before learning Hebrew when they moved to Israel). Being nonrabbinic, they did not adopt the laws of the Talmud and thus do not observe some key practices that unite rabbinic Jews worldwide (Shelemay 1986: 56). The differences include but are not limited to liturgy, festival observance, dietary laws, family and purity laws, and laws of sacrifice (Teferi 2005: 188). For example, the festivals of Purim and Chanukah, which are central celebrations on the Jewish calendar today, probably did not exist in Beta Israel custom until the twentieth century (Shelemay 1986: 56). On the other hand, they observed the laws of ritual purity especially carefully, continuing to separate menstruating women from the family home until their immigration to Israel.

Ritual difference may emanate from Beta Israel origins: ethnomusicologist Kay Kaufman Shelemay's flagship study on Beta Israel liturgy analyzes Christian liturgy to demonstrate that they may have emerged as a discrete religious group in the fifteenth century (1986). And regardless of their origins, Beta Israel—most commonly known to world Jewry as Ethiopian Jews—were totally cut off from rabbinic, i.e., Ashkenazi (European) and Sephardi/Mizrahi (of Spanish origin/ from Muslim lands) Jews for most of their history. Following extended trips to Ethiopia by Faitlovitch throughout the twentieth century (Trevisan Semi 2004) and advocacy from diaspora groups, they were accepted in 1973 as the "lost tribe of Dan" by then-Sephardi Chief Rabbi Ovadia Yosef. The reconnection with world Jewry was welcomed by the community in Ethiopia, but they were not universally accepted by religious authorities in Israel. Although Ovadia Yosef's ruling entitled Beta Israel to immigrate to Israel as Jews (which they saw as a renewal of the biblical covenant), once they arrived the rabbinate grew suspicious of their legitimacy and requested symbolic conversion (Seeman 2009). The conditions of immigration were already traumatizing, and this request was widely denounced by Beta Israel.

I will discuss the dramatic immigration process in chapter 4. The first major wave took place in 1984–1985, when Beta Israel villagers left their homes in Gondar and descended the Ethiopian highlands at great personal risk (several thousand are estimated to have died en route), settling temporarily over the Sudanese border in refugee camps such as Gedaref (Parfitt 1985). The Israeli government airlifted eight thousand Beta Israel clandestinely in January 1985 in what came to be known as Operation Moses (Mivtsa Moshe). Some of the villagers who were left behind moved to Addis Ababa to await later transport to Israel, and a second airlift called Operation Solomon (Mivtsa Shlomo) brought fourteen thousand Beta Israel to Israel in May 1991 during the last days of the Ethiopian Derg regime.

The Beta Israel were thrilled to arrive in Israel but found it difficult to adjust to life there. They did not yet speak the language (and some never learned it), their skills as smiths and potters were unsuited to the Israeli economy, and their extended family networks were broken up by a housing policy that favored the nuclear family (*mishpaḥa garinit*). The extended families that lived together in households of up to thirty people are scattered today across Israel, with major populations as far apart as Netanya, Rehovot, Kiryat Malakhi, Haifa, and Be'er Sheva. The uprooting of the extended family unit in Israel has caused substantial damage to Ethiopian-Israeli family life (Davids 1999: 139, Elias and Kemp 2010, Weil 2004, Westheimer and Kaplan 1992: 59), fostering ongoing problems of crime, domestic violence, and suicide.

In Israel, Beta Israel are referred to simply as *Etyopim*, the Hebrew word for Ethiopians, or *yotsei Etyopia* (those who left Ethiopia). This is a descriptive reference to ethnic origins (*edah*), consistent with the labeling of other Jewish groups ("Iraqis," "Yemenites"). It is perhaps not insignificant, though, that the Hebrew term contains no acknowledgment of Jewishness: there has been extensive debate in the rabbinic courts and in the government over whether or not Beta Israel are "really" Jewish (Salomon 1995: 127, 1999: 5). The academic subdiscipline called Beta Israel studies addresses this debate in detail, and the work of scholars is often used to support or deny the credibility of a new group of immigrants. There is no doubt a racialized angle to the rabbinic suspicion, but it is framed in terms of roots and validity of religious practice.

In the past fifteen years the debate over Jewishness has become more complex, since the majority of Ethiopians who have immigrated to Israel since 1992 have been members of a small group known as Falash Mura, or people who converted from Judaism to Christianity in the late nineteenth and early twentieth centuries (Seeman 2009 explains the paths to and from Judaism in detail).[10] They began to immigrate to Israel in the 1990s under family reunification laws, and since then many thousands have converted back to Judaism (Seeman 2009: 91). Today they make up approximately a third of the total Ethiopian-Israeli population, or 45,000 out of an estimated population of 135,000. In the same vein as a Beta Israel-Falash Mura schism (which existed in Ethiopia and remains today in Israel), some Ethiopians in Israel prefer to identify through religious practice, calling themselves *Oritawi* (Torah-true) or *Maryam Wodet* (lovers of Mary, or Christians). To avoid wading into debates over religious authenticity, I refer throughout this book to all Ethiopians in Israel as Ethiopian-Israelis. Also, I find that the metaphorical hyphen that separates the two sides of contemporary Beta Israel status—the Ethiopian from the Israeli— succinctly articulates much of the intersectionality and disjunction of the experience of being black in Israel.

GREATER TEL AVIV

This book deals with national imaginaries of citizenship, but most of the action takes place in and around Tel Aviv, a city that is at once distinct (politically, religiously) from the rest of the country and representative of it demographically. Initially I spent a year in south Tel Aviv (July 2008 to July 2009), conducting ethnographic research through participant observation there and in many venues around Israel. I spent little time in Rehovot, the suburb that for two decades had the largest Ethiopian-Israeli population, or Tiberias in the Galilee, which has an enormous absorption center (*merkaz klita*). I spent no time in Kiryat Malakhi, the "development town" (that is, a town created after the establishment of the state in peripheral regions such as the Galilee and the Negev—see Yiftachel and Meir 1998) with a disproportionately large Ethiopian population relative to its size and remoteness. Instead I carried out most of my research in the major urban centers of Tel Aviv, Haifa, and Jerusalem, as well as smaller cities like Ashkelon that are home to significant Ethiopian-Israeli populations. This multisited work, conducted in Hebrew but with use of Amharic words and phrases, highlights the emergence of new immigrant population cores in urban areas. I cover many of the institutions enumerated by Alex Perullo in his conception of a "music economy" (2011) comprising live music venues (nightclubs and Azmari houses, where I attended live music performances several times per week), music vendors (record stores, where I chatted with patrons and employees and increased my knowledge of contemporary music from Addis Ababa), state-run support bodies (absorption and community centers, where I interviewed musicians and social workers and took lessons in the massenqo, the Azmari's one-stringed fiddle), and musicians themselves (approximately a dozen of whom I cite by name from interviews in this book, and many more of whom I anonymize).

Tel Aviv's city center is home to only a small Ethiopian population,[11] most Ethiopian-Israelis being dispersed across more remote towns, but as the cultural core of the State of Israel it hosts an avant-garde arts scene and a multicultural atmosphere. Like other urban cultural centers worldwide, it attracts tens of thousands of migrant workers who do the more thankless jobs rejected by Israelis, from cleaning office buildings to picking fruit to caring for the elderly (or, in the case of Eritreans, washing dishes in Tel Aviv's restaurants). Many of these guest workers depart after a few years, but some stay on as long-term residents, a small but visible number marrying Israelis and raising children who eventually serve in the Israeli military (military service being the ultimate symbol of integration in Zionist tropes). This urban environment full of international culture and migrant workers influenced my research immensely. Conducting fieldwork about marginalized minorities in and around Tel Aviv reveals multiple points of disparity, since the city's assets (a vibrant arts scene and an abundance of sushi restaurants) and its downsides (the abject poverty of its many immigrants and the exploitation of labor migrants) go hand in hand. Indeed, Ethiopian-Israelis are not the only population that has troubles in Tel Aviv, but they constitute a group that encapsulates the inherent paradoxes and hypocrisies of the cosmopolitan city.

Finally, although I refer throughout this book to Tel Aviv, the city is officially called Tel Aviv-Jaffa, and the relationship of Israeli Jews to their Arab neighbors, on both sides of the Green Line (1949 armistice lines), affects everyday life profoundly. I will touch only briefly in this book on issues pertaining to the Israeli-Palestinian conflict, but it looms in the background of any discussion of race, ethnicity, class, religion, culture, language, and national identity in modern

Israel. It is relevant to this book insofar as the conflict is the source of many Israeli cultural and political anxieties, but I also submit this book as a case study of a minority trying to come to terms with Israeli citizenship through cultural output.

OVERVIEW

In the first three chapters, I unpack the narratives of Ethiopianist, Afrodiasporic, and Zionist imagery. Chapter 1 examines Afrodiasporic myths of citizenship through the work of Ester Rada, perhaps the most prominent Ethiopian-Israeli entertainer today. Through her convention of singing in English, while constructing a composite Afrodiasporic style comprising soul, reggae, jazz, gospel, and Ethio-jazz, she suggests that Ethiopian-Israelis look to the African diaspora as a mechanism for upward mobility and acceptance in Israeli society.

In chapter 2, I outline the Ethiopianist myths that glorify a certain version of Ethiopian history and frame Ethiopian-Israelis as central to it. I describe a weekly performance at Habesh, an Ethiopian restaurant in Tel Aviv, as a prism through which to understand Ethiopian musical principles. For decades scholars have relied on Michael Powne's *Ethiopian Music* (1968), a descriptive work based chiefly on secondary sources, to understand the Ethiopian modal system (*qignit*) that descends from church modes and forms the basis for popular mid-century Ethio-jazz. The typology is contested but taught today in conservatories in Ethiopia (Weiser and Falceto 2013: 2). The first mode is called *tezeta*, translated as "nostalgia"; it is a feeling, a style of song, and a musical mode based on the song of the same name (the major variant is the common pentatonic C D E G A C). Tezeta is a major focus of chapter 2. The second mode, *anchihoy*, is the most common in Ethio-jazz, built on the tritone and played C D♭ F G♭ A C. The third, *batti*, is named after a city of the same name, and widely used in Azmari music (C E F G B C). The fourth mode is *ambassel* (C D♭ F G A♭ C). All four modes were on display at Habesh, which served as a central meeting point for the geographically scattered Ethiopian-Israeli population. Ethiopian imagery (instrumentation, tonality, ornamentation, choreography) is invoked there as a mechanism of nostalgia (tezeta) and critique of Ethiopian marginality. Ethiopianist imagery offers a foil to a dominant Israeli perception that Ethiopians "came without culture."

Chapter 3 focuses on the work of one band: the internationally renowned group the Idan Raichel Project. This chapter offers a close reading of three of Raichel's songs, arguing that the heavy emphasis on Israeli musical conventions renders the inclusion of Ethiopian musicians and source material an appeal to the Israeli public to accept them in Israeli society, writing them into dominant Zionist national narratives of home and return.

After exploring the three divergent narratives of citizenship, I devote the next two chapters to their reconfiguration for performance for the wider Israeli public. Chapter 4 explores public and national performances of Eskesta, the Ethiopian shoulder dance, arguing that public displays of physical virtuosity reveal and subvert the often-explicit prejudice against Ethiopian-Israelis as lesser citizens. I argue that the public display of bodily otherness borrows from Afrodiasporic conceptions of blackness, and from Ethiopianist imagery of rural life as a mechanism for framing Ethiopians as valuable citizens.

Chapter 5 further considers the reconfigurations of Afrodiasporic, Ethiopianist, and Zionist myths through Ethiopian-Israeli hip-hop. Hebrew lyrics and consistent invocation of the repressive state apparatus render Ethiopian-Israeli hip-hop more concerned with integration into Israeli society than with political subversion. Through a close examination of the best-known Ethiopian-Israeli hip-hop/reggae song to date, Axum's "Ma Im Hakesef" (What About the Money), I demonstrate that Afrodiasporic narratives of exclusion and Ethiopianist iconography of exceptionalism ultimately serve a narrative of Israeli multiculturalism. I deal in this chapter exclusively with music created by Ethiopian-Israelis, and not with the primarily imported hip-hop that Ethiopian-Israeli teenagers listen to. That material is treated thoroughly and sensitively by David Ratner in his Hebrew-language book about (usually African American) rap shaping the lives of young Ethiopian-Israelis (2015). In effect, Ratner engages in reception theory while this book's chapter engages in close reading of a locally produced song.

Throughout my examination of Ethiopian music as framing the rights of struggling citizens, I acknowledge that the city of Tel Aviv has been thoroughly transformed over the past decade by a wave of immigration from Eritrea, consisting primarily of asylum seekers who live in the poor southern districts of town. Chapter 6 describes Levinski Street, the nerve center of Tel Aviv's Ethiopian life, and I map the city's Ethiopian music scene around it. The encounter along Levinski between Ethiopian citizens and Eritrean asylum seekers sets the tone for the frameworks and challenges of citizenship for Ethiopian-Israelis. By mapping the emerging local Horn of Africa mediascape, I establish the limitations of Ethiopian-Israeli citizenship in tension with other black cohabitants and with other citizen minorities.

Finally, in the conclusion, I frame Tel Aviv as an emerging node in the Ethiopian transnational migration network—a stop on the tour circuit for Ethiopian musicians like Rome, London, or Washington, DC (the latter already written about by Shelemay 2006a and 2009). By facilitating the establishment of discrete citizenship narratives, Ethiopian-Israeli musicians have opened a dialogue with Ethiopia that the rupture of emigration curtailed. Therefore, Ethiopian-Israeli musical influence is beginning to feed back into Ethiopia and across the network, establishing new peripheries and dialogues across Ethiopian cultural life.

As a mechanism for the Azmari, wax and gold facilitates the negotiation of ostensibly fixed boundaries of speech. Ethiopian-Israeli musicians challenge the seemingly inflexible boundaries of Israeli citizenship through the same mechanism; they occasionally do so through lyrics, but more commonly by invoking schizophonic, often decontextualized sounds as challenges to accepted ideologies. Across musical styles, rappers, dancers, and instrumentalists mobilize nonverbal mythologies of cultural history to reposition and reimagine their status in Israeli society, proposing an alternative to the state's unfinished attempts at immigrant absorption. Considering the tension in Israel-Palestine over citizenship and belonging, evidence that musicians bypass the policymakers' top-down frameworks effectively might offer some alternatives to the nationalist narratives dominating the headlines today.

ONE

Afrodiasporic Myths

Ester Rada and the Atlantic Connection

Levinski Street, the congested hub of migrant south Tel Aviv, came to be one of my regular haunts during fieldwork. But when I first stepped off the train from the airport in July 2008, I had the same initial impression as most Tel Aviv residents—that it was run-down and looked unsafe. It hardly resembled the "White City," the secular, left-wing, and gay-friendly Bauhaus capital on the beach that is notoriously isolated from the rest of the country. I walked the length of Levinski en route to my friend Sam's apartment, passing a number of Ethiopian businesses on the way, the bus station (see Hankins 2013), and the Nahum Records Ethiopian music emporium, plus the abandoned spots that would some years later become the Red Sea Internet Café and the Ethiopian restaurant Tenät. As I turned onto Ha'aliyah Street, the neighborhood began to change, and by the time I reached Florentin Street I was in a different world. This was the neighborhood of Florentin, the capital of hipster Tel Aviv, and its aforementioned main street is lined with renovated Bauhaus buildings, mixed with bars like the nearby Hudna ("truce" in Arabic, a mixed Jewish-Arab project, where deejays spin records outdoors until 4 a.m.). This former working-class Mizrahi neighborhood (inhabited by Jews of Muslim lands who have immigrated to Israel, known in Israel as Mizrahim, the plural term) has slanted younger in the past decade, with the soundscape of Greek folk songs on Friday afternoons replaced with psy-trance, and Bukharian pastries traded in for quinoa. Florentin is still grungy, but it's privileged, and today it's the epicenter of creative energy in the controversial capital, a gathering-point for left-leaning middle-class young people postmilitary. There aren't many Ethiopians on this side of Ha'aliyah, though, and the imaginary border between Levinski and Florentin delineates Israel's insiders (middle-class citizens) from its others (visible minorities, '48 Palestinians, African refugees). Yet thanks to the profusion of hipsters who listen to reggae and sport dreadlocks, iconographies of blackness adorn the bodies of Tel Aviv's tastemakers. These young people have a patron saint: her name is Ester Rada, she is Ethiopian-Israeli, and her music navigates marginality through the musical vernaculars of the Middle Passage.

Rada wasn't known yet to the residents of Florentin in 2008, and given the stark contrast between rich Bauhaus Tel Aviv and poor migrant Tel Aviv, perhaps separated by Ha'aliyah, I couldn't have predicted upon my arrival that an Ethiopian-Israeli soul singer would be Israel's next ambassador to Glastonbury and WOMAD. Ethiopian-Israelis are not just economically marginalized in Israel; the admittedly complicated basis of their citizenship is still sometimes called into question by the religious mainstream (Anteby-Yemini 2004, Seeman 2009). Yet in just a few years, Rada became Israel's most popular export in Europe, and she did so by negotiating a complex relationship with Israeli society. Rada's musical style connects her to Ethiopia and to the African diaspora, and in this chapter I examine the musical vernaculars that she references in her repertoire, arguing that she exemplifies a key Ethiopian-Israeli strategy of citizenship by mobilizing Harlem, Kingston, and Ethiopia—i.e., the "New Zion" of Rastafarian imagery (see Raboteau 2014 or Ratner 2015 for comparison)—as an alternative narrative of embodied otherness. This strategy is a paradox. In order to negotiate the contested citizenship of Ethiopian-Israelis, musicians connect to alternative narratives of belonging, and in the case of Ester Rada, the compelling insertion of Ethiopian-Israelis into the imagined community of the black Atlantic has earned the acceptance of Ethiopians in Israel. Making it as a performer across the African diaspora has facilitated belonging in Israel.

Rada's rise to international prominence happened quickly. In 2011 she was performing for Ethiopian-Israelis on the Tel Aviv club scene with her ex-husband Gili Yalo of reggae band Zvuloon Dub System, and by 2013 she played the Glastonbury festival in the UK. She released her first EP, *Life Happens*, in 2013, followed by the album *Ester Rada* in 2014. Her second album, *Different Eyes* (2017), came out to great critical success just as this book was going to press.[1] The transitions from local popularity (among Ethiopian-Israelis) to national popularity (among Tel Aviv elites) and international attention were swift. Yet the social processes through which she rose to the vanguard of the Israeli music scene reveal the complexity of the Ethiopian-Israeli experience. Considering the socioeconomic obstacles facing Ethiopians in Israel (Parfitt and Trevisan Semi 2005), and the isolation of many Beta Israel from Ethiopian society since emigration (Karadawi 1991), the reception of Rada is a surprise—not least to Rada herself; when I interviewed her in 2015, she described her rapid ascent as unexpected. Because of the aforementioned paradox of belonging, Francis Falceto, the producer of the influential *Éthiopiques* CD series, further remarked to me when I interviewed him that it seemed ironic that she was the first Ethiopian musician to "cross over," or achieve mainstream success in the all-important European and North American markets.[2] However, by examining Rada's musical style in detail, this chapter will reveal a narrative that borrows from the iconographies and musical vernaculars of the African diaspora as an avenue to accruing cultural capital among Israelis and using "black music" (*musiqa sheḥorah*) as a main strategy toward integration. A close examination of songs that incorporate influences from soul music, funk, reggae, and Ethio-jazz reveals the common theme of the repertoire: a triangulated narrative of Afrodiasporic origins (see Chivallon 2011).

By exploring the musical influences on Rada's performance style—the deep, throaty vocal timbre that references Nina Simone (who, as I learned when I interviewed Rada, is her favorite singer), the funky bass lines from Parliament, the hemitonic pentatonic modes on brass from Ethio-jazz icon Mahmoud Ahmed, and the offbeat rhythm incorporated from reggae and dub, I will unpack one alternative paradigm of Ethiopian-Israeli citizenship. In the context of the wider Ethiopian-Israeli experience, it is truly unexpected (particularly to the leftist-oriented Rada, but also to producers and promoters) that the biggest Israeli star abroad in 2017 is Ethiopian. Ethiopian-Israelis remain religiously suspect to many Israelis (Seeman 2009), their youth presumed to be criminals by community workers and in the press. I present Ester Rada first in this book as a counternarrative of that experience, beginning with a successful example of integration through music, and of making a success by drawing on alternative paradigms of citizenship.

It is equally bewildering that Europe's first Ethiopian crossover artist is Israeli, that she trained in Hebrew, and that she sings almost exclusively in English. Finally, it is ironic that given these factors, and the religious baggage that the Ethiopian-Israeli population carries, the first Ethiopian-Israeli solo star performs not Israeli pop music but Afrodiasporic music, acknowledging that the integration efforts of the Israeli state failed to mainstream Ethiopian citizens.[3] Despite these ironies, the narrative that Rada promotes stylistically, a grassroots story of black otherness in a white society, has established a valuable model of citizenship for Ethiopian-Israelis, whereby they demonstrate their contribution to Israeli society through a reconfiguration of the paradigm of exile, shifting their experience from the Jewish exile to the African one.[4] For the Ethiopian-Israelis who supported Rada's rise but who do not turn up at her concerts in increasingly elite venues, this musical style points them to a paradigm of belonging, and they increasingly look to the experiences of African Americans to relate to the prejudice in their own society (see Ratner 2015). The citizenship strategy of embodied otherness—of distancing themselves from Israeli society[5]—transpires at the level of musical style and performance, and this chapter examines how a commercially successful Ethiopian-Israeli musician uses music to position herself as political subject in Israeli society.

ESTER RADA

Ester Rada performs a combination of original songs and soul and Ethio-jazz standards, resulting in what music critics call Ethio-soul. She was not yet a gigging musician when I lived in Tel Aviv in 2008–2009, and I first heard of her as she was about to perform at Glastonbury. Since she sings in English, it didn't occur to me that she came from Tel Aviv, nor did it occur to me to pay attention to her increasingly busy touring schedule. Between her skin and her lyrics, she doesn't resemble most international audiences' idea of an Israeli, and she can travel the festival scene in France with little drama. She tends to be quiet about her origins in concert, and her reticence can lend itself to farce, such as the anecdote she relayed to me about arriving onstage and finding herself faced with protesters waving Palestinian flags, who were temporarily rendered mute when they saw that she was black. I myself wouldn't have noticed that she was Israeli, because she has established a musical style (Afrodiasporic) and a performative self that are culturally ambiguous enough to render her nationally ambiguous. By the time she released a series of hit songs toward the end of 2013 such as "Life Happens" and "Bad Guy," I had nearly missed a permanent, almost imperceptible shift back into Israeli society because of her success. For the first time, a black solo Israeli musician was touring internationally, yet she was doing so without her audience necessarily knowing that she was Israeli. And whether these are aesthetic decisions made to astutely navigate an antioccupation cultural boycott of Israeli musicians, or subtle political statements rejecting racism, she does all of this exclusively through her musical style.

While in some ways she is placeless, Rada's music does bear a strong influence from her upbringing in Netanya. Considering the coastal stopover city halfway between Tel Aviv and Haifa, which claims the highest absolute number of Ethiopian citizens in Israel, allows several elements of her music to fall into place. When I interviewed her in 2015, she explained that African American culture influenced her early in life. At that time black role models at the margins of Israeli society were scarce, and the soundscape of her childhood was, in her own words, a combination of anonymous Ethiopian and popular African American songs: "A lot of music that—I don't even know the names of the performers. Music that my mother played at home . . . When I was in Netanya, I listened to Afro-American music—MTV—hip-hop—total hip-hop—Tupac"[6] (interview, Jaffa, March 5, 2015).

Given a climate of prejudice that Ethiopians encountered in the 1990s—beginning with the rabbinate's request for symbolic conversion and culminating in the "blood affair" (Seeman 2009: 163)—Rada would have been aware of racism from a young age. In a migration context, where Ethiopian culture did not yet have cultural capital, and where African American music was popular across Israel, "black music" would have been an effective outlet for catharsis and prestige. Other young Ethiopian-Israelis in Netanya, such as the future rap group Axum (see chapter 5), were, like Rada, likely to emulate African American musicians instead of Ethiopian ones. Rada's throaty, low, raspy vocal style symbolizes this debt to the music of the African diaspora (see Ratner 2015 for examples from hip-hop) rather than to Ethiopian musicians like Aster Aweke, whose high-pitched voice and melismatic songs punctuated by ululation mark her as Ethiopian. I have written elsewhere about Washington, DC, Ethiopian soul singer Wayna (Webster-Kogen 2013),[7] whose vocal style is a melismatic and ornamented R&B sound. However, her high-pitched tone still bears the traces of Ethiopian vocal style and tonality. In contrast, Rada sings nearly an octave lower than Wayna, erasing all trace of Ethiopian accent or tone color from her performance.

Her repertoire similarly draws from African American musical form. Her cover of Nina Simone's song "Four Women," for example, implores Ethiopian-Israelis to look beyond local, failed forms of integration and to find black voices that speak to them from among the cultural resources of the black Atlantic. In a splintered community that lacks political leadership or patronage in the corridors of power (Kaplan 2010, Weil 2004), musicians like Rada intervene in political discourse about the Ethiopian place in Israeli society, even when they avoid explicitly political associations. Rada's music, which is the least Israeli-influenced of the source material in this book, constitutes an understatedly powerful critique of Israeli prejudice. My analysis centers on close reading rather than ethnographic description; I interviewed Rada, have met her on several additional occasions, and have attended many of her concerts, where I have spoken with her fans. But as is the case throughout this book, I look to music for evidence of that which goes unsaid because of social taboos against explicit critique. Through her musical critique, on the other hand, Rada offers an alternative narrative for Ethiopian-Israelis that transforms the attribute of blackness into a source of cultural capital.

In this chapter I offer a close reading of five songs from Rada's concert repertoire, considering her body of work as a unified whole as I disentangle the Afrodiasporic myths that influence Ethiopian-Israeli performers today. I borrow from Dick Hebdige's explanation of cut 'n' mix from the book of the same name (1987) to define Rada's compositional and arrangement style, arguing that the iconic sounds of Ethiopia and the African diaspora insert Ethiopian-Israelis into a black Atlantic narrative.[8] Each song described in this chapter combines African American, Caribbean, and Ethiopian sounds in different combinations to connect Rada to a lineage of black musicians in white-majority societies,[9] linking Ethiopian-Israelis to the historical narrative of the African diaspora instead of the Israeli narrative of rejecting the Jewish diasporic state of exile (*shelilat hagalut*). When considering these songs and their multidirectional musical influences together as a single style—Ethio-soul—I discern a reconfiguration of an otherwise unstable narrative of marginal citizenship characterized by limited participation in national culture. First, I examine "Four Women," the Nina Simone song that features centrally in Rada's live performance; second, three original songs: "Sorries," "Life Happens," and "Bazi," all of which combine Ethiopian and Afrodiasporic styles in different ways; and third, her rendition of "Nanu Ney," an Ethio-jazz standard from the 1970s, the performance of which connects musicians directly to their African roots and cuts them off from their Israeli ones.

AFRODIASPORIC MYTHS

I previously defined myths as a set of narratives of origin, election, and ethnohistory (Smith 2008: 40–43). I arrive at a working definition of myth from the disciplines of folklore and religious studies (see Segal 1999; also Campbell 1978, Ellwood 1999), cultural or area studies (see Herskovits 1961; Mintz and Price

1992 for African diaspora; Levine 1965, 1974, for Ethiopia; Gertz 2000, Morris 1988, Sternhell 2002 for Israel), and nationalism (Smith 2008). From these disciplines' divergent approaches, I arrive at a definition of myth as a narrative that symbolically constructs or binds a group. This is not a judgment about the truth of a narrative but an analysis of the way the narrative becomes emotionally charged and powerful for a group. In the first half of this book, I spend a chapter on each of the three sets of myths, interpreting Zionist/Jewish, Ethiopianist, and Afrodiasporic myths through the lens of musical performance, and examining the social mechanism through which musicians actively create new myths of origin, election, and ethnohistory. In the Ethiopian-Israeli context, these creations and collections of myths can be read as political positionings that navigate citizenship, ultimately making space for Ethiopians in the Israeli public sphere.

Among the Zionist, Ethiopianist, and Afrodiasporic myths that mobilize musical style to construct citizenship narratives for Ethiopian-Israelis, the three sets of narratives converge around the Ethiopian-Israeli experience in their collective sense of ethnohistory. These narratives are modern reconfigurations of older tropes based initially on the paradigm of Jewish exile, the dispersal of the Jews by the Babylonians in 586 BCE (and later, and lastingly, by the Roman Empire in 70 CE). The nineteenth-century Zionist myths that propelled the founding of the State of Israel are based on medieval narratives of Jewish return to the biblical homeland—called *shivat Tziyon* (return to Zion) or *ahavat Tziyon* (love of Zion) —that were incorporated into Jewish liturgy, theology, and thought, and into the modern nation-state.[10] But the metaphor of Jewish exile was also mobilized across the African diaspora, with African American slaves forcibly converted to Christianity in particular identifying symbolically with the people of Israel via the biblical myth of slavery in Egypt ("Let my people go"). The initial paradigm of Jewish exile has been refashioned repeatedly, and Ethiopian-Israelis draw inspiration from many of those refashionings.

First, the Jewish longing for return transformed into a set of political movements for Jewish self-determination during the nation-building nineteenth century (see Gertz 2000, Morris 1988, Sternhell 2002, and chapter 3). Second, the Solomonic narrative in Ethiopia claimed that Ethiopia supplanted Israel as Zion (Levine 1965, 1974). Third, African American appropriation of biblical metaphor (see Gilroy 1993, Mintz and Price 1992) transformed African American vernacular English. Most students of black music will be familiar with the "spirituals" song style of Southern slavery, in which "Let my people go" borrows from biblical myth and reimagines slavemasters as Pharaoh. Fourth, the Rastafari return to Ethiopianism through Marcus Garvey's prophecy, and subsequent worship of Haile Selassie (Ewing 2014, Grant 2010, Lemelle and Kelley 1994) confirmed Ethiopia's importance in the African diaspora. And fifth, the pan-African awakening in the era of postcolonial struggle and negritude looked to ancient Egypt and Ethiopia as African seats of power (Fredrickson 1995, Wilder 2015).

These themes fit together heterophonically in Rada's musical style. In the United States as in Israel, "black music" stands in for a history of violence that is expressed through and mitigated by a musical tradition. Much of the African diaspora can relate to this experience through a shared history of chattel slavery, and for many people around the African diaspora, Ethiopia symbolizes black independence. The long-established connections between Haile Selassie, Jamaica, reggae, the black Atlantic, and African American music create a network of identity resources. The links between the black Atlantic and Ethiopia are slowly developing, with Ethiopia's best-known musician Teddy Afro placing on international charts for the first time in 2017 with his album *Ethiopia*. Likewise, Ester Rada creates a musical connection between Ethiopian-Israelis and the black Atlantic through Ethio-soul by adapting the lexicon of Ethio-jazz to a disparate array of Afrodiasporic popular music, linking the musical style to shared narratives of suffering and longing. However, in the absence of socially conscious lyrics, this dynamic plays out entirely at the level of musical structure, especially through Rada's call-and-response with the band. Rada's phrasing and flow, legato but syllabic (sharply articulated at the level of individual words), in contrast to the horn section's staccato stabs and dull articulation, connect African American popular music to Ethio-jazz, heterophonically demonstrating the spiritual links between the United States, the Caribbean, and Ethiopia.

Afrodiasporic Myths and Style

I describe the collections and reconfigurations of recognizable myths that Ethiopian-Israelis mobilize to define the terms of citizenship as resting on their positioning as black, Jewish, and having arrived directly from Africa. I call the myth clusters mobilized in this chapter the Afrodiasporic myths, because they draw from a set of narratives originating in the African diaspora, with which Ethiopian-Israelis had little direct contact before immigration to Israel. When these narratives reference Jewish or Ethiopian experience, they draw Ethiopian-Israelis in as active participants in the cultural history of the Middle Passage. Rada's music symbolically mobilizes the circuit (see Ratner 2015)—New York–

Kingston–Addis Ababa—in her musical style, and by doing so she frames the Ethiopian-Israeli experience in the context of Afrodiasporic oppression.

In different combinations, the aforementioned five-point list of narratives works in tandem to create a circuit of black ethnohistory, in which a dignified African history coexists with a brutal present in exile. The imagery of the narratives can be mobilized to imagine an equally glorious future. This chapter focuses on the latter three points from that list (the African American, Rastafarian, and pan-African narratives), which Rada builds into the genre of Ethio-soul as a mechanism that connects Ethiopian-Israelis to the black Atlantic experience. She does so at the level of musical style exclusively, since she neither makes political statements onstage nor writes political lyrics. The song texts that Rada writes herself usually address personal growth or romantic relationships, and the absence of political material is noteworthy. Coming from a tradition of Israeli popular music (which is tremendously politicized) and adopting African American music, her tendency to skirt controversy in her songs is conspicuous. In the Ethiopian lyrical/poetic tradition of wax and gold (*sem-enna-werq*), or hiding deep layers of meaning or critique in material deemed light or safe, her lyrics are the wax and her musical style is the gold, a collagelike style that attaches the Ethiopian-Israeli experience to the myths of the African diaspora.

An Afrodiasporic narrative is bolstered by the Israeli media, which implies that skin color defines Rada's experience, drawing indirectly from the hardship narratives of great female African American singers like Billie Holiday or Aretha Franklin. Profiles like her interview in the left-leaning Israeli newspaper *Haaretz* in 2013[11] describe her rise to fame as a victory for all Ethiopian-Israelis, sometimes portrayed in the profiles as helpless and desperate. She makes this connection implicitly, too, since her repertoire includes multiple covers of songs by Nina Simone. The articles about Rada frequently mention that she was born in Kiryat Arba, perhaps the most controversial settlement in the West Bank,[12] raised by a single mother in Netanya, and that her childhood was religious; she was a member of B'nei Akiva, the religious-Zionist youth group that is especially popular among settlers, before spending her military service in a musical troupe (*lehaqa*). In those media profiles, music is described as a personal journey, her outlet to rebel against religious life,[13] which she left in pursuit of creative freedom.

In Rada's personal story, we find a conflicted relationship with the State of Israel, which marginalized her community, and the institutions that have cultivated an outstanding musical talent. Her musical training came by way of performing in a military troupe during her compulsory service, where she developed high-level performance skills. In our interview she talked about learning the standards of the Israeli repertoire, sung entirely in Hebrew, and about the level of professionalism she developed working in a troupe. Motti Regev and Edwin Seroussi explain in their chapter on Israeli musical institutions (2004) that the military fed directly into the recording industry in the 1960s and 1970s, with members of military bands becoming some of the most beloved rock musicians of the 1970s. In that respect, Rada's early life and her pathway into the music industry tell opposing stories of marginality and patronage.

The transition from Hebrew-language national repertoire to English-language soul music has also been enabled by a patronage network of state-supported arts education and European influence. As Regev and Seroussi go on to explain, the flocking of elite musicians to Tel Aviv, first from Germany in the 1930s and later from the Former Soviet Union in the early 1990s, has offered the State of Israel a constant stream of classically trained musicians and conservatory teachers. Despite the other ways that Israel has become culturally marginalized, it has kept its status as a destination for musical (and artistic) study. Rada and the seven members of her band—Michael Guy on bass, Ben Jose on guitar, Lior Romano on keyboard, Dan Mayo on drums, Inon Peretz on trumpet, Gal Dahan on saxophone, and Maayan Mylo on trombone—all gained their music education in the military or in an excellent European-influenced conservatory system. These musicians credibly perform Ethio-jazz, a genre that relies on dissonant tones like augmented fourths and minor seconds, and that regularly flummoxes European studio musicians.[14] The conservatory system in Israel that produces top-notch studio musicians is part of the infrastructural machinery that benefits any Israeli musician looking to expand into different genres.

A competent backing band is a major asset for Rada: Kevin Le Gendre argues that the affective power of soul music comes from the call-and-response between the solo singer and the band, a dynamic that he associates with the heterophony of the cotton field (2012: 26). With the accompaniment of her band, Rada constructs an Afrodiasporic connection as a musical lexicon of black alterity—what Le Gendre calls "not just a musical form but a sociological and emotional lexicon" (2012: 27)—built on the offbeats of reggae, the fuzzy guitar riffs of funk, the affective intensity of gospel, and the heterophonic movement of voice, horns, and strings that create a polyrhythmic effect in soul (Maultsby 2006: 274). In place of expounding ethnohistory or political ideologies directly, Rada invokes the painful lineage that bore black music. I will unpack the symbolic meaning of these musical vernaculars across the five songs analyzed in this chapter. In brief, though, their combination of Afrodiasporic influences is summarized in table 1.1. As it suggests, Rada and her band borrow a variety of elements from African American popular music and its Caribbean counterparts. They do so through melody and instrumentation, but also through the establishment of a style in a certain song or section of a song. As we can see, there is much brass and much modality in her music, and these elements are shared by Ethio-jazz and soul music.

Rada's musical style is evidence of Afrodiasporic solidarity, but a critical element of her appeal beyond the Ethiopian community resides in the narratives built around her musical style. Instead of appealing to the well-known Zionist myths of return from exile and attachment to the land (on full display in chapter 3), Rada (as well as some Ethiopian-Israeli reggae musicians whom I introduce later) draws from the Afrodiasporic myths of going into exile invoked in the music of the black Atlantic. She plays black music (*musiqa sheḥorah*) and sings in English, connecting herself to black musicians outside of Israel more than to progressive musicians inside Israel. In the process, she leapfrogs the genre of "world music," a quasi-market for cosmopolitan Europeans that Israeli musicians usually appeal to, and connects to a network of Afrodiasporic musicians in North America and Europe.

The narrative conventions and embodied iconographies that I highlight in this chapter are:

- Journey not as return "home" to Israel but as exile, analogous to the Middle Passage;
- African American memories of suffering and poverty, and the personal narrative of redemption through music;
- Rastafari orientation toward Ethiopia, sometimes presented through dreadlocks;
- Invocation of the *Kebra Negast*, the medieval epic in Ge'ez that establishes Ethiopian/African civilization as a religious center;
- Triangulation of influence, or the combining of several different Afrodiasporic styles within one song, and collaboration with African musicians.

A casual listener might find Rada's music indiscernible from popular music emanating from North America because it is a collage style comprising a variety of Afrodiasporic musical elements. Once unpacked, however, this combination makes sense as the output of an Ethiopian musician in Israel. Although she

TABLE 1.1 Funk, soul, jazz, Ethio-jazz, and gospel characteristics in Ester Rada's songs

	"FOUR WOMEN"	"LIFE HAPPENS"	"SORRIES"	"BAZI"	"NANU NANU NEY"
Single style throughout				x	x
Sections in 6/8	x	x			x
Sections in 12/8	x (verse 4)	x			
Brass: stop-time		x		x	
Brass: unison	x	x		x	x
Melodic emphasis on minor seconds	x		x		x
Pentatonic modes	x	x	x		x
Heterophonic texture/multiple melodic lines		x	x (flute)	x	x (brass during bridge)
Drum introduction	x (brief, with guitar)	x (leading into brass)	x (gospel, including a cappella melismatic vocal and clapping)		x (counting instruments in only)
Brass/keyboard/strings emulating rhythm instruments	x	x (offbeat)	x (keyboard)	x (guitar bass)	x
Funk section	x (verse 4)			x	
Reggae section		x			
Gospel section			x (coda)		
Raspy vocal timbre	x		x (verses only)		
Melismatic vocals		x		x	
Wide vocal range	x (verse 4)	x		x	
Backup vocals		x (bridge)	x	x (chorus)	x
Guitar/bass emphasizing offbeat	x	x			
Wah-wah effect and fuzziness	x (verse 4)			x	x

downplays any obvious elements of Israeli music, such as the minor melodic lines of Shirei Eretz Yisrael (Songs of the Land of Israel; see Regev and Seroussi 2004), sentimental biblical references, and the Hebrew language itself, as well as the specific political narratives of national vulnerability and anxiety over military service, her music is a projection of the lived experience of dislocation. Even without any Israeli source material, Rada's music bears the imprint of the Ethiopian experience in Israel, and by assembling the African iconographies and Afrodiasporic vernaculars into a myth-narrative, she establishes Ethiopian-Israelis as Israel's racial other.

Arrangement Style: "Four Women"

Rada told me in our interview that Nina Simone is her favorite singer, but if she hadn't, her preference would be apparent from the dominance of Simone's repertoire on Rada's 2015 EP *I Wish*.[15] On each of the EP's four tracks — three Simone originals ("Four Women," "Sinnerman," and "Feeling Good") and one Simone cover (Bill Taylor's "I Wish") — Rada pays homage to Simone's vocal style, and in concert, Rada's non-Ethiopian audience responds the most enthusiastically to her Nina Simone covers. From a 2014 performance in New York's Madison Square Park that I attended, to the Montreal jazz festival the same year,[16] to Hulugeb (the annual Ethiopian-Israeli cultural festival in Jerusalem, where she introduced the song "Four Women" in Hebrew), her Nina Simone covers draw as much attention as her original compositions. As an audience member in New York, London, and Jerusalem, I have found that "Four Women" is the Nina Simone cover that consistently sparks the most dramatic audience reaction, performed in a style alternating between soul-jazz and Ethio-soul. She introduces the song to her audience as representing the African American female experience, and her arrangement of the song implies that Afrodiasporic narratives of violence inscribed on the body inform the way that Ethiopian-Israelis can relate to their host society.

Nina Simone first recorded "Four Women" in 1966, performing it widely in France shortly after she composed it (Audio file 1). The lyrics introduce a set of first-person African American narratives through the gendered language of sexual violence, establishing a fictive kinship with black women everywhere. In each verse Simone sings from the perspective of a different woman, describing in few words a set of obstacles for African Americans from the era of slavery to the civil rights struggle of the 1960s (for analysis of the song's lyrics, see Feldstein 2013: 108–109). Like much of Simone's repertoire, the song has come under scrutiny from critics, torn between interpreting it as allegory or as stereotype. African American studies scholar Ruth Feldstein interprets the song as a set of paradigms of black women's experience in America (ibid.: 111). First, Aunt Sarah is dark-skinned and her "back is strong," indicating that she is a slave (and, presumably, forcibly converted to Christianity). As the first of the story's matriarchs (like the biblical Sarah), her gentle voice represents her as a mammy figure, the maternal and comforting housemaid of the plantation. Next, Saffronia is biracial or "yellow," the result of the rape of a black woman by a "rich and white" man. Her clearly enunciated diction, along with the violence implied by her skin color, evokes the pressures on black women in a Jim Crow postemancipation America that was still explicitly racist. Then comes the "tan" Sweet Thing, available to "anyone who has money to buy." In a lineage of black women exploited by men, her life in the sex trade was typical of many African American singers before the civil rights era (see Feldstein 2013, Maultsby 2006). Finally, the "brown" Peaches is "awfully bitter." In both versions, Nina Simone and Ester Rada sing this part in a raspy voice punctuated by crescendo and emotion. The characters' personal obstacles are indexed by their phenotype, skin color, and hair texture, revealing a history of violence against black female bodies, from slavery to rape to forced prostitution (see Burnim and Maultsby 2006).

Analysis of the song often focuses on the narrative structure and the biographical paradigms of the four women, but less attention is devoted to the musical structure, in which Simone articulates the tension in the lives of black women in America equally poignantly. It is worth spending a moment on Simone's aesthetic choices, because Rada's version is substantially different. Both communicate tension through syncopation, and examination of Simone's musical structure—especially her blurring of duple and triple meter—illuminates Rada's arrangement of the song (Audio file 2). By comparing the two versions, we see that Rada creates musical tension through a hemiola effect (the pitting of duple pulse against triple pulse), while Simone uses additive meter, with a tresillolike 3+3+2 pulse, but that one might prefer to follow as a syncopated 4/4. Simone's voice and lyrics communicate the tension, too, but the song's subtle metrical structure expresses struggle and opposition through an ongoing conflict between duple and triple meter within and across the bar lines.

The bass instrument (in some versions a double bass, in others a keyboard) enhances the syncopated feel in Simone's version, playing on one, four, and seven in the cycle of eight. This syncopation implies triple meter, which her voice enhances: she usually begins a line on the seven, pausing halfway through the line and eventually ending at the end of the next measure. Likewise, her piano solos subvert 4/4 counting: they usually begin on an upbeat, just after the bass begins the 3+3+2 pattern. The syncopated metrical structure within each measure therefore creates a polyrhythmic effect between voice, piano, and bass. This syncopation of the supple structure creates the effect of triplets when following the bass notes on one, four, and seven; of triple meter when combined with other instruments; or of polyrhythm when the bass is subdued by a flute or cello. The effect of Simone's syncopation of her voice, the piano, and the accompanying instruments is tension and delay, matching the lyrical themes of internal struggle, political vindication, and life narrative as national allegory (see Jackson 2013).

Bolstering the dramatic tension created in the lyrics and through the syncopated meter, Simone's voice works with the melodic instruments to gradually thicken the song's texture and navigate the melodic contour. The first verse includes only voice, drums (playing just the second half of each measure), and a keyboard (or a double bass) playing the bass notes. Each verse adds another instrument to build counterpoint: guitar in verse 2, flute in verse 3, and a low-register string (viola, cello) in verse 4, with Simone playing a piano solo between verses 3 and 4, and finishing the song on a dramatic staccato ascent. In concert, a hand drum often comes in during verse 3 to exoticize Sweet Thing. But most of the drama is contained in Simone's voice, which draws from different timbres to emphasize the characteristics of each woman. In addition to increasing her ornamentation in each verse—from the minimal decoration of Aunt Sarah to a melismatic Peaches punctuated by vibrato—Simone increases her vocal range as the song progresses. Maintaining a virtually identical skeletal melody throughout, Simone sings almost in monotone for Aunt Sarah, and jumps across an octave for Peaches.

The vocal tension created by Simone's voice is a key element of her style, and she creates that tension in "Four Women" through timbre and dynamics. From her near-whisper of Saffronia's name in verse 2 to an abrupt transition to raspiness for Peaches in verse 4, she punctuates the song's rhythmic structure with her own commentary on the characters. Most recognizable for Simone's fans, though, is the song's cadenza (see Maultsby 2006: 280), the rapid ascent at the end of verse 4 complemented by an ascending and then rapidly descending piano, an ending that she popularized with her hit song "Sinnerman." In "Four Women" she commences this cadenza between the lines "What do they call me" and "My name is Peaches," the piano delaying the climactic announcement of her sarcastic and decidedly anticlimactic name. The ascent with her voice, in contrast to the piano's crescendo and cascading, descending contour, concludes the song with a contrapuntal tension that mirrors the narrative structure. Indeed, quite apart from the lyrics, the song's melody and rhythmic structure emphasize the diversity of life stories that the lyrics express explicitly.

Ester Rada imprints her own style on "Four Women" through an Ethio-soul arrangement, reimagining the song entirely at the level of song structure and instrumental arrangement (Rada follows Simone's melodic contour, her lyrics, and her vocal timbre). The black otherness that Rada expresses through musical vernaculars of soul and Ethio-jazz is represented in the song's lyrics about abuse of black women, but she also plays it out in the juxtaposition of African American musical vernaculars (jazz, funk) in the verses and Ethio-jazz in the bridge. The shift from minor scales to hemitonic modes, and from syncopation to triple meter are small but significant adjustments to the instrumental accompaniment, forming the basis of Rada's reimagining, in which Ethiopian-Israelis share the experience of blackness with African Americans.

Rada's voice is strongly influenced by Nina Simone's raspy timbre, low vocal register, and minimal ornamentation, but for all the similarities of vocal delivery, Rada's version adapts the structure of "Four Women" substantially. In contrast to Simone's syncopated 3+3+2 structure, Rada and her band delineate the verses by creating a chorus from the "My name is Aunt Sarah/ Saffronia/ Sweet Thing /Peaches" section. After an introduction with Rada singing "My skin is" on the pickup, the first measure of the verse begins on the word "black," as it does on each subsequent verse on "yellow," "tan," or "brown," the skin color of each character, with skin color explicitly forming the rhythmic and narrative delineation of the verse. Each verse lasts twelve measures, with drums and keyboard accompanying Rada's voice, followed by a two-measure transition that brings in a swelling brass section. At the end of the two-verse transition (fourteen measures in total), the band changes meter, moving into a 12/8, including the three brass instruments (saxophone, trombone, and trumpet) plus the guitar and bass (see Le Gendre 2012 or Maultsby 2006: 297 for an explanation of the soul convention of transition from 4/4 to 12/8 to heighten syncopation). While Rada sings "My name is Aunt Sarah/ Saffronia/ Sweet Thing /Peaches," the strings outline the skeletal melody in eighth and sixteenth notes, and the brass play ascending minor seconds. Between the triple pulse and the minor second notes, this bridge evokes the hemitonic pentatonic modes of Ethio-jazz, played in 6/8. Therefore, the melodic effect is jazz verse and Ethiopian chorus. The brass section, prominent in soul arrangements (Maultsby 2006: 274), forms a sonic barrier between the two styles.

The alternation between soul-jazz and Ethio-jazz continues for three verses, and the fourth verse (Peaches) comes in as funk. Portia Maultsby defines the transition from soul to funk as "the interlocking of the drum pattern and a two-bar bass line, counter or contrasting guitar, keyboard and horn riffs, and a vocalist singing in a gospel style" (2006: 297). The brass instrumentalists continue to play for this verse, but they switch to 4/4, with the saxophone accenting the pickup of each phrase. As Rada reaches a crescendo and incorporates rougher timbre, the combination of textural density and dynamic climax brings the song to a frenzied, affectively powerful end, similar to Simone's version in the feeling of climax, but perhaps with her non-Ethiopian band relying too much on instrumental dynamics to bring about that climax.

Rada first recorded a Simone song in 2015, but she has been paying homage to Simone frequently in concert, the most widely circulated example online being her performance at Hulugeb in December 2013.[17] In this rare instance, Rada stepped off-script briefly to explain the song to her audience in Hebrew. An audience member who has heard Rada introduce Simone's "Feeling Good" in English, complete with demanding that the audience answer the question "How do you feel?" in English even in Israel, might be surprised to hear Rada taking such a pedagogical approach to a song. But for the audience at Hulugeb, many of whom were Ethiopian-Israelis not conversant in English, Rada's careful explanation of the premise of "Four Women" and its multiple interpretations gave the audience a sense of the gravity of the subject matter. Whether in the dramatic case of Hulugeb or anywhere else on the festival circuit, it comes across that Rada takes this repertoire seriously and that it illuminates the Ethiopian-Israeli experience.

Rada does not offer onstage the full-throated repudiations of racism and occupation that left-wing Israelis espouse in protest songs, but her musical style itself borders on a political agenda, since the linking of soul and funk to Ethio-jazz transpires in "Four Women" through the narrative of violence against black women. She keeps her positioning subtle: she sings in English, does not usually mention Israel onstage as that might alienate her left-leaning audience,[18] and connects Ethiopia to the United States via modal brass and triple meter. Yet Rada's method works as a maneuvering through the Afrodiasporic myths of citizenship because it is understated. In "Four Women," she forgoes a discourse of identity politics that has left the Israeli electoral system crippled. Instead she draws from Afrodiasporic influences that young Ethiopian-Israelis recognize in their own lives.

CUT 'N' MIX COMPOSITION: "SORRIES," "LIFE HAPPENS," AND "BAZI"

In the video to "Sorries," Rada walks around the Old City of Jerusalem with four members of her band.[19] One immediately notices irony in the performance of reggae in the Old City, since reggae reconfigures "Zion" as none other than Ethiopia (see Raboteau 2014). Not that the song is explicitly political; the lyrics in English are about a romantic relationship, and the symbolic power of the song's performance unfold entirely at the level of musical style. To understand Rada's original material, and particularly three original songs from Rada's album—"Sorries," "Life Happens," and "Bazi"—I describe some key musical vocabularies of blackness that, for Ethiopian-Israelis, offer alternative narratives of belonging.

Ethiopian-Israeli musicians frequently deploy reggae (and dub) references to Rastafarian imagery as a way of accruing cultural capital with Caribbean subcultures and among Israeli audiences. In Rada's case, the negotiation of diasporic identity transpires entirely at the level of musical style, her repertoire constituting her public voice; her referencing of reggae is an effective framing device. At the same time, a number of songs from her album borrow from elements of Ethiopian traditional music and from funk to position Rada and Ethio-soul within a continuum of Afrodiasporic musical styles. Her compositional style might be best understood as a variant of the methodology of cut 'n' mix, a style that Hebdige characterized in the 1980s as a musical dialogue between African American and Caribbean cultures. Hebdige identifies the roots, musical bloodlines, and influences in reggae as coming from a mixture of African American popular music, African "revivals" (see Herskovits 1961), and Rastafarian ritual, propelled by the sociopolitical milieu of recently independent Jamaica (1987). In this spirit, Rada's syncretic style connects varied Afrodiasporic cultures to her own personal narrative; she draws elements from the musical cultures to which she actively connects herself, which carry a lineage of experience that parallel the Ethiopian-Israeli experience.

Looking at three of Rada's original songs, I will demonstrate that her cut 'n' mix compositional style is part of an exercise in what Gilroy calls "anti-anti-essentialism" (1993: 99), or flexible movement between essentializing and de-essentializing the features of black culture. Gilroy contends that in black music, a set of vernaculars takes the place of widespread literacy to which slaves were barred access. Those vernaculars can be mobilized to signify blackness, and they can also constitute pastiche, and Rada uses the formalizing of those vernaculars as the basis for her own Atlantic blackness. Her compositional style presents a sort of canonized vocabulary, or textuality of blackness. Reggae, Azmari, and funk all serve as building blocks, and when performed under a singular umbrella they render her conversant in black Atlantic performance.

Here I look at three songs from the album that characterize Rada's style in unique ways. First, "Sorries," which bears the strongest reggae influence on the album, with the verses emphasizing the offbeat rhythmically and brass playing in unison (Audio file 3). Second, "Life Happens," which incorporates a massenqo (Ethiopian spike fiddle) and Ethiopian modality (Audio file 4). Third, "Bazi," which has the strongest funk influence on the album, funk forming the primary structural foundation of the song (Audio file 5). This combination of funk, reggae, and Azmari music, in addition to soul and Ethio-jazz in Rada's other work, contributes to an overall sound—Ethio-soul—that articulates an image of blackness frequently associated with otherness.

The essence of the cut 'n' mix style, what Hebdige calls an absolute reliance on "versioning" for creativity, is on full display in "Sorries," a song that traverses four musical genres in as many minutes. Following a brief drum solo, it begins with a pentatonic brass passage in 6/8 reminiscent of Ethio-jazz. The brass then transitions into a four-measure section in stop-time, the instruments playing in rhythmic unison. Next is a transition into 4/4 reggae rhythm, with the guitars playing on the offbeat for the duration of the verses and the brass playing in unison on the pickup between measures. Each verse lasts four measures, followed by two measures of brass, with the cycle repeating. After twelve measures, Rada sings a soul-style bridge with vocals overlaid for eight measures. The rapid transition every four measures or so from Ethio-jazz to R&B to reggae to jazz to soul defines Rada's syncretic style.

Alongside this musical montage of styles, the "Sorries" video demonstrates the degree to which Rada's potentially intense political statements emerge entirely at the nonverbal level (and sometimes at the visual level). The song lyrics contain no hints of subversion or protest typical of the genres she references (see Le Gendre 2012), but the video makes a statement anyway. Part of her commentary comes from choosing this song in the first place for a video staged in the Old City, the ownership of which is contested by Israelis and Palestinians. As Rada walks around the Old City—the closest analogue to the biblical Zion—playing reggae, she implies a Zion-Zion connection that reads as a multilayered commentary on exclusion and public space. This reading might only be readily apparent to someone who is aware of the problematic existence of black bodies in Israeli public life. By choosing the only song on her album that invokes the other Zion—the Zion that means Ethiopia—she inserts blackness into one of the world's most controversial sacred spaces.

The methodology of making a statement exclusively through sonic cues and visual signifiers—making musical style her public voice—continues across Rada's album. "Life Happens" is a polished music video, and her most viewed song on YouTube by a factor of ten.[20] The musical style and visual imagery illustrate a complex set of multidirectional influences, particularly through instrumentation and harmonic modulation. The song can be broken down again into a collage style: first, a two-measure Ethio-jazz exposition that repeats (with the four-measure section opening each new verse, a massenqo featured in the second verse). Next, she sings a four-line verse in minor key. Finally, the chorus modulates to major for four measures, eventually cycling back to the Ethio-jazz section, with a brief gospel-style vocal passage at the song's end. The collage effect repeats itself in virtually all of her original songs, and indeed lends itself to the music-video genre.

The imagery mirrors Rada's songwriting style, displaying multidirectional Afrodiasporic sensibility. As the video opens in a warehouse, the camera pans in to Rada playing a drum kit and dressed in the style of 1970s Swinging Addis (see Falceto 2002). Next, at 0.06, she is wearing a disco-style silver dress and playing a saxophone, and at 0.10 she is wearing glasses and playing the keyboard with one hand. At 0.13 she wears purple and plays the flute, which sounds like an Ethiopian *washint*. We appear to be moving through decades chronologically; at 0.16 she is wearing a jumpsuit, and at 0.18 she is holding a massenqo and wearing West African prints and headdress. At 0.20 she is wearing an '80s-style fedora, playing the bass. The images of Rada from different eras, playing different instruments, in different styles of ethnic dress, offer a collage of multidirectional influence coming from Ethiopia and the United States. The video expresses her combination of eras, regions, tone colors, and melodic structures through an easy-to-grasp visual medium.

In contrast to the collage form of the other songs, "Bazi" sticks faithfully to funk. It begins with a fuzzy guitar and a bass muted by a wah-wah effect (see Le Gendre 2012: 137 for a clear explanation of the effect of the pedal on guitar timbre), moving quickly into a brass section playing in unison, to be followed by a bass line reminiscent of funk trailblazing group Parliament. Formally, "Bazi" establishes a funk groove through the bass, via a low-pitched, rhythmic melody that responds heterophonically to the other melodic instruments throughout (see Le Gendre 2012: 106 for the role of the bass in establishing groove in funk songs). The lyrics are about love and heartbreak, but the language does not convey the double meaning that in many funk songs substitutes sexual relations for unfulfilled political desire. Rada has, in a context removed from the black Atlantic, used iconic funk vernacular—fuzzy guitar, bassline as parallel melody, brass in unison, and contrapuntal melodies—to sound African American. Table 1.2 suggests that Rada and her band employ the lexicon of African American musical style to create substantially different effects from one song to another. Individual effects may not be especially meaningful, but the composite demonstrates fluency with a variety of Afrodiasporic approaches to composition and melody, instrumentation and ornamentation, and flow and timbre.

In each song, Rada uses the main signposts of African American popular style—call-and-response, flow, articulated attack, and embellished coda—to create divergent effects or to signify a variety of styles. Not included in table 1.2 but apparent to any listener is the subject matter of song texts, namely personal relationships. Among the Afrodiasporic musical styles that contributed to the civil rights movement in the United States (jazz, soul, funk) that Rada references, lyrics constitute an explicit part of musicians' political message (and the part that scholars focus on disproportionately). Soul and funk, and later, reggae, emphasized themes of freedom and dignity for black activists, and song titles like "Say It Loud (I'm Black and I'm Proud)" and "(To Be) Young Gifted and Black" complemented songs about personal relationships that stand in for political struggle like "I Will Survive" or "What's Become of the Brokenhearted." The absence of explicitly political themes in her lyrics not only distinguishes Rada from the politically conscious black music that she references directly but also protects her from having to engage directly in Israeli politics. By avoiding any topics of national interest, and indeed even the language of those debates (Hebrew), she frames Ethiopian-Israelis beyond those debates.

Rada's international prominence and rapid ascent demonstrate that diverse audiences respond to her cut 'n' mix approach to songwriting, made up of apolitical English song texts and a collage of Afrodiasporic melodic and rhythmic styles. These compositional techniques rely on mastery of a variety of techniques—syncopation, pentatonic modes, melodic lines emphasizing the offbeat, muting for

TABLE 1.2 Comparison of African American musical elements

	"FOUR WOMEN"	"LIFE HAPPENS"	"SORRIES"	"BAZI"	"NANU NANU NEY"
Flow (vocals)	Legato, sharp diction, syllabic pronunciation	Legato with some staccato articulation in response to brass	Breathy articulation	Pronounced ornamentation, bends in notes	Legato, dull articulation within vocal lines; articulation on individual syllables
Brass attack	Stabs clustered around minor seconds	Stabs emphasize notes 1 and 4 in measure	Brass replaced by massenqo in second verse	Combination of short stabs and lingering notes later in measure	Focus on notes 1 and 3, trumpet stabs highly punctuated
Call and response	Vocals in verses, brass in chorus	Vocals in verse, brass in bridge, backup vocals in bridge	Backup vocals, backup brass in bridge	Brass and flute alternation—between phrases and within phrases (flute plays brass rests); bass plays alternate melody in verses	Vocals in verses, brass in chorus and on pickup
Coda	Instrumental: drums and guitar	Brass pattern: unison, highly syncopated	Gospel: a capella vocals, hand clapping	Scatting, saxophone solo	Instrumental: brass and guitar

amplified strings—that amount to a musical lexicon of Afrodiasporic popular music. These techniques are part of an oral tradition that has accrued cultural capital because, in Gilroy's (1993) estimation, that music's affective and symbolic power exists as an alternative to textual traditions that were strictly curbed by racial slavery. Rada's compositional approach engages and masters those musical styles as de facto texts, transforming them into a canon to be rehearsed and referenced. In her original songs, Rada inserts Tel Aviv into a circuit of blackness that includes New York, Kingston, and Ethiopia by becoming an insider through mastery of this vocabulary.

ETHIOPIAN SOURCE MATERIAL: "NANU NEY"

"Now THAT was a good version of the song."
"Amazing! Ester's version is great!"
"Much closer to the original."

It was the evening of March 6, 2015, and text messages were coming in. I was in Tel Aviv for a few days, and my friend Moshe Morad had invited me to join him on his radio show *Misaviv La'olam beShmonim uShmoneh* (Around the World in Eighty-Eight) on 88 FM, a Kol Yisrael national radio station. I joined the live broadcast for an hour, discussing Ethiopian music in Tel Aviv and playing songs by musicians performing around town that spring. To represent Rada's music, Moshe chose the Amharic track from her album, "Nanu Ney" (Audio file 6), and as my acquaintances listened to the broadcast they sent me a barrage of messages, soon followed by comments on the show's Facebook page indicating their preference for Rada's version over the one they had heard before (see chapter 3). Some of the commenters could have been referring to the Ethio-jazz standard by Muluken Melesse, but most of them were comparing Rada's cover to the sample of the song that most young Israelis have heard, "Mima'amakim" by the Idan Raichel Project (2005). I had myself discussed all three songs with Rada only the day before, when I interviewed her, since her engagement with source material from Ethiopia constitutes an important dimension of her positioning as an Afriodiasporic musician.

The original, "Nanu Nanu Ney" (Audio file 7), is a staple from Swinging Addis (see Shelemay 1991 for a description of the repressed music scene in the Derg years of the later 1970s). Like most of the Ethio-jazz repertoire, it is brassy, modal, and fast-paced, and fans of the important *Éthiopiques* CD series know it. Yet unlike the Ethio-jazz stars who tour widely like Mahmoud Ahmed and Alemayehu Eshete, or who remain beloved at home like Tilahoun Gessesse, Melesse has retired from the music industry and does not have a presence on the touring circuit. His version has taken on a life of its own outside of Ethiopia, since it has been covered and sampled without interventions of its original performer.

In contrast to the arrangement of African American covers, and to original compositions, "Nanu Ney" is Rada's only recorded rendition of Ethiopian source material, in this case Ethio-jazz. Ethio-jazz developed within a framework of exchange between African and African American musicians in the 1960s and 1970s (Le Gendre 2012: 242), spanning South Africa (Ballantine 1991, Muller

2006), Ghana (Collins 1987, Feld 2012), and Swahili East Africa (Sanga 2010, White 2002). As African musicians adopted rock 'n roll, blues, and jazz, African American musicians visiting Africa for the first time in the 1960s and 1970s looked to ancient Egypt and Ethiopia for iconographies of black power in service of a pan-African ideology. Therefore, "Nanu Ney" is part of a lineage of Afrodiasporic music returning to Africa, Rada's cover of the song engaging a set of pan-African ideologies that connect her to African American musical vernaculars through their mutual exchange.

The Ethiopian state began to incorporate foreign musical influence from 1924, when Haile Selassie (then regent rather than emperor) brought the Arba Lijotch, a brass band of forty Armenian orphans from Jerusalem, to Addis Ababa. Once brass instruments were introduced, the musical climate of the capital changed quickly, with military bands presenting new repertoire to the public (see Falceto 2002). Within a few decades, Ethio-jazz emerged as a local example of a trend sweeping Sub-Saharan Africa: incorporation of African American musical styles framed as a "return to Africa" inspired by blue notes and political solidarity. According to Francis Falceto, the period of 1960–1974 (when Haile Selassie was overthrown) was a "golden era" for Ethiopian cosmopolitanism and cultural production, with the music scene in Addis Ababa one of the liveliest on the continent thanks to the emperor's patronage.

The proponents of African fusion forms, like Fela Kuti in the case of Afro-beat (see Waterman 1998), crisscrossed the routes of the black Atlantic — London, New York, and Lagos, eventually transmitting across Africa. In the process they produced syncretic styles that in turn influenced music in the United States in the repertoire of jazz and funk musicians, reaching Addis Ababa in the 1960s. Ethio-jazz is distinctly local, borrowing from the modal system of Azmaris (*qignit*) and from folk repertoire, but its style stems from cultural processes whereby Ethiopia connected itself to the African diaspora through music. The vernacular of jazz, which incorporated the same instrumentation as the marching band, propelled hybridity based on Western instrumentation and song structure along with Ethiopian melodic lines and Amharic lyrics.

During the Derg period of military rule (1974–1991) following the overthrow of the emperor, the Ethiopian music industry virtually closed down because of (among other factors) a curfew in Addis Ababa and strict border controls (Shelemay 1991). In that period Francis Falceto, working with Buda Musique, rereleased albums by beloved Ethiopian musicians from the regional traditions of the Gurage, Amhara, and Tigray people. The result, now known as *Éthiopiques*, continues to produce traditional and paraliturgical musical, but the modal, brassy sound of Swinging Addis is still the main Ethiopian musical export today.

At the Madison Square Park concert in New York (June 2014) as at the Rich Mix in London (July 2015), Rada closed the show with "Nanu Ney." The version adhered closely to her version on the album, which, at under four minutes, is shorter than both her Nina Simone covers and the original by Muluken Melesse. But rather than include it in a medley as she often does in-concert for other covers, she sang the entire song, dancing a makeshift Ethiopian shoulder dance (Eskesta) between the verses, to which the audience responded ecstatically. After presenting a repertoire in New York with a heavy American influence, she concluded by reminding the audience of her African origins.

Rada's rendition of "Nanu Ney" hews closer to Melesse's version than her other covers do to their sources. Rather than incorporate her band's syncretic style, her version follows Melesse's song structure, including nearly identical instrumentation (rock band plus brass section), meter (6/8 that can be counted or transcribed equally as 4/4), and tonality (modal, heavy on tritones and minor seconds). The band has transposed the song upward by a major second, cut the synthesizers, and reduced the ensemble size, but these modifications still leave the song close to the 1970s version. The band's adaptations mostly incorporate Afrodiasporic techniques: the string section makes use of funk elements including the wah-wah effect, while the brass section plays slightly after the downbeat (creating subtle syncopation), and handclaps punctuate the introduction.

Meanwhile, singing Melesse's lyrics about "unfinished business" between estranged lovers in the verses, Rada incorporates minimal ornamentation, retaining the low-pitched and smooth timbre from her other repertoire. The scale provides most of the vocal contrast: each line of verse begins with Rada ascending by a perfect fourth, and then singing the rest of the line on the fourth. In an extended verse of twelve lines, she does this eight times followed by a bridge, where she sings the guitar's opening motive. Instead of imitating the melismatic Ethiopian vocal style, she does not add improvisation, vibrato or grace notes to her performance. Indeed, her most explicit punctuation is her pronunciation of the explosive letters ጨ (ch'ä) and ጰ (p'ä) in Amharic, the trilled ረ (rä), and the vowel እ (ë). The emphasis on Amharic pronunciation over vocal ornamentation makes sense, since one of Rada's main achievements in this song (as she told me) is to introduce the Israeli public to an Amharic song.

The Israeli public had heard this song before, in a heavily mediated format. In 2005, the multiethnic Israeli mega-band the Idan Raichel Project—Israel's closest analogue to Paul Simon's *Graceland*—used "Nanu Ney" as the opening to the title song from the album *Mima'amakim*. I examine the song of the same name in detail in chapter 3, arguing that it conveys a nationalist (Israeli) agenda by drawing on the musical conventions of Israeli popular song. A Zionist interpretation of the song partly hinges on the fact that Raichel, the bandleader, samples the opening, without incorporating Ethio-jazz tonality into the full song. For Raichel's fans, a mix of Israeli progressives and world-music fans in the United States and Europe, the Ethiopian section offers a bit of ethnic flavor to a pop song, such that in-depth treatment of tonality (modal), instrumentation (brassy), or lyrics (Amharic, dealing with heartbreak) need only be glossed schizophonically (Feld 1996).

That Rada chose this among Ethio-jazz standards to cover can perhaps be read as a commentary on "Mima'amakim" (Audio file 8) and its selective sampling of particular Ethiopian sounds. As the only Amharic song on her album, one that she renders faithfully with minimal arrangement, the song feels like a corrective to the Idan Raichel Project's more cannibalistic approach to the classic song.

Rada's perspective is different, though. When I interviewed her, she explained the choice in some detail:

> ER: I think it happened when I heard an Amharic song for the first time on Israeli radio. To hear an Amharic song on Israeli radio . . . here, Idan Raichel did something really nice, because there was never anything like this in Israel. And I got quite emotional, and went to hear the original song. And I loved it. And I thought that someone had to do the original. Because it's an amazing song. Not to do, like *that* to Idan Raichel [makes a stabbing motion] . . .
>
> IWK: You do the whole song, and you dance, and the audience loves it.
>
> ER: That's what I wanted. It's something that the audience knows, and a lot of people think that Idan Raichel wrote the song, so I wanted people to know that it's an Ethiopian song, that it has an origin, that it's a complete song, even that's a good [outcome] in my opinion. And people have really liked it. It's been on the radio a lot in Israel. It's the first time a full Ethiopian song has been on the air in Israel. (interview, Jaffa, March 5, 2015)

Rada explains that she did indeed intend to correct misperceptions, but her concern was for Israelis to recognize and acknowledge Ethiopian culture. She notes that a listener might (as I did) interpret the song as a dig against Raichel, but she rejects that interpretation. The primary outcome in covering this song is to reconfigure its symbolic meaning for an Israeli public and, for Ethiopian-Israelis, to connect their source material to her Afrodiasporic source material.

This version of "Nanu Ney" can claim several accomplishments. Rada delivers an iconic African sound to an Israeli audience, turning a schizophonic product ("Mima'amakim") into a part of Israel's tapestry of ethnic origins (*edot*).[21] The source material itself, though, carries the history of the African diaspora, of blackness, and of pan-Africanism in the postcolonial moment. Whether or not the song fits neatly into the black Atlantic discourses of musical exchange, the amount of cultural negotiation that went into producing it—from the proto-Rastafarian political speeches of Marcus Garvey to the syncretic jazz-funk of Miles Davis—has turned "Nanu Ney," and a good deal of Ethio-jazz, into a part of the reawakening of black pride. For this song to be the choice of Israel's first black star works in tandem with the American-influenced source material to create a lineage that connects blackness from New York to Addis Ababa, via Tel Aviv.

———

"How long will you be here?"
"Four days."
"And what have you come for?"
"An interview."

Wrong answer. I should have just said that I was here for the beach. I had done this a dozen times before, and knew better. Waiting in the immigration queue at Ben-Gurion Airport, I had a feeling that I might well experience the bureaucracy that my students and Palestinian friends knew well, but that I had always been protected from as a Hebrew speaker with an Israeli-sounding name. Every time I entered the country, I worried that this time would be difficult. I should have given my usual answer, that I was here to visit my cousins . . . .

"What kind of interview? Do you have an invitation?"
"No, it's not formal. I arranged it over email."
"Where is it?"
Deep breath. Tell the truth. Don't look guilty. Be prepared for a long wait.

"In Jaffa. I teach music in London, and I'm here to interview Ester Rada."
"Wow, what fun [*Eizeh keif lakh!*]. Enjoy [*Teheni!*]!" Passport handed back, visa issued. The security apparatus identified me as a desirable.

The Palestinian rappers I've worked with who have Israeli passports, as well as my students and colleagues (and husband), have all been in the interrogation rooms. I am fortunate to have avoided any unpleasantness from the Israeli security apparatus in my many visits, but the privilege comes at a price, and this visit clarified for me what that price is.

Ester Rada is currently Israel's biggest star on the international music circuit, and the Israeli recording industry is excited to claim her. She overcame systemic prejudice growing up, earned professional credentials in a music troupe during her military service, and made a success of herself abroad. As a leftist who veers away from Israeli politics in her repertoire, Rada is the product of a system that she often disagrees with politically, and she navigates the international festival scene carefully. Non-Jews buy tickets to her concerts in France and the United States, and across Europe, where the international Boycott, Divestment, and Sanctions (BDS) movement increases in strength with every Israeli diplomatic misstep. This leaves her with some decisions to make about her career, such as whether to move abroad, or whether to collaborate with African diaspora musicians. With these complex entanglements, explicitly political lyrics would be limiting. I understand why she performs in English.

Yet the self that Rada portrays in recordings and onstage is the result of a complex set of cultural processes and multidirectional musical influences. Rada's collation of Ethio-jazz, neo-soul, jazz, funk, and reggae represents sonically a gradual reorientation of Ethiopian-Israelis in their host society. By backing away from political or subversive lyrics, and working entirely at the level of source material, musical structure, visuals, and ornamentation, Rada works through a set of identities—Ethiopian, Israeli, black—that read differently in front of diverse audiences. As long as "black music" is the language of her performance, Rada's political ideology can be discerned by an engaged listener. She proposes a route to belonging that circumvents the nationalist narratives that have until recently excluded Ethiopians from one paradigmatic story of exile (Jewish) by inserting them into the alternative paradigm of exile (Afrodiasporic).

For Ethiopian-Israelis, Rada's cut 'n' mix compositional style, her Ethio-soul arrangements of jazz standards, and her contemporary interpretations of Ethio-jazz standards represent a dramatic reconfiguration of the Ethiopian position in Israeli society via Afrodiasporic narratives of citizenship. For the immigrants who struggled to integrate through the 1980s and '90s (Parfitt and Trevisan Semi 1999), and their children who are disappointed that proud military service (Shabtay 1999: 174) has not yielded upward mobility, the narrative of Jews returning to the homeland (BenEzer 2002) no longer seems an apt metaphor. Instead, young people I know like Shoshana from Haifa, who wears dreadlocks and thinks about moving to New York, are identifying with the opposite global flow, of leaving Africa and encountering blackness as a disadvantage. For these Ethiopian-Israelis, Rada's music establishes their experience within a lineage of black otherness, blackness serving for her as a route to cultural capital. In her cover of "Four Women" as in her cover of "Nanu Ney" and her original compositions, Rada draws from Afrodiasporic narratives, connecting the United States to Jamaica, Jamaica to Ethiopia, and the Ethiopian-Israeli to the African American experience. Afrodiasporic solidarity suggests a route to prestige and acceptance in Israeli society, demonstrating ironically that a performer is better accepted as a representative of Israeliness the further she moves away from Israeli musical style.

TWO

Ethiopianist Myths of Dissonance and Nostalgia

June 29, 2009, Jerusalem

"Don't worry, the food here is kosher." Little did Fantahun know that that was the least of my worries. In fact, the meat's religious credentials made things worse. As a vegetarian, I decline meat regardless of its ritual status. I don't even know how to say "vegetarian" in Amharic, and thanks to a communication mishap in Addis Ababa, where I had to make do with a lunch of "fasting macchiato,"[1] I'm loath to just ask for fasting food, roughly the Ethiopian equivalent of vegetarian. To decline expressly prepared kosher meat will certainly offend my hosts, who would presume that I don't trust their precautions. Virtually every Ethiopian restaurant in Israel (apart from one that has cleverly gone vegan) displays its certificate of religious supervision (*te'udat kashrut*) flamboyantly. A refusal would be tantamount to a repudiation of the hard-fought battle for Beta Israel's religious acceptance by the Ashkenazi elite. *I have to eat this plate of meat*, I realize.

When Fantahun, my massenqo (one-stringed spike fiddle) teacher, invited me to lunch, I assumed that he meant the rather upscale Ethiopian restaurant in south Jerusalem, popular among intellectual types. Instead we veered onto a side street in the Russian Compound and into a private residence. I didn't really know where I was, but Fantahun said that it was one of his regular haunts. At the threshold stood an Ethiopian woman dressed in street clothes, rather than the white robes I had grown accustomed to at every Ethiopian restaurant from Washington, DC, to Abu Dhabi. After taking an order from Fantahun she disappeared into the back of the house, a platter of beef materializing fifteen minutes later. We talked as we ate but the informal setup made me nervous. I had no official status (Israel doesn't issue research visas—I was there on a tourist visa), and there was certainly some kind of zoning restriction against a restaurant in a private home. Getting busted wouldn't do me any favors at passport control. *Relax*, I thought, *as long as nobody's chewing* chat *next door,*[2] *there's nothing to worry about.*

Alas. We finished lunch and moved to the next room, where a small group of men with bloodshot eyes were making their way through a giant pile of leaves. The *chat* plant is known in some of Ethiopia's neighboring countries as *khat*, and its legal status, as an amphetaminelike stimulant, varies from place to place. It is popular among men in Ethiopia, Eritrea, Somalia, and Yemen. When chewed, it produces a mild head-buzzing, euphoric effect (Anderson, Beckerleg, Hailu, and Klein 2007). Or it makes people violent; female travelers in Addis Ababa have to be especially vigilant when traveling by taxi in the late afternoon. Originating in the Horn of Africa and Yemen, where men consume it socially, *chat* is prevalent wherever there are Ethiopian, Eritrean, or Somali populations. It has an in-between status in the UK, most Ethiopian-owned convenience stores advertising in the window in Ethiopic script (*fidal*) that they sell it. But whereas in the UK I would pass such notices without giving them a thought, the sight of a group of intoxicated men in a neighborhood I didn't know gave me pause. Still, not wanting to insult Fantahun, I clutched the mini-bushel he passed me, half-heartedly chewing a small piece and wondering what its legal status was in Israel.

Such is the level of formality and legality of most Ethiopian-Israeli establishments that provide food and entertainment. These semilegal restaurants are an important part of the social network of Horn migrants, the newer of whom are young, single men who might not have access to kitchen facilities where they live. But such restaurants remain marginal, hidden from main roads and never advertised. This place certainly didn't have a *te'udat kashrut*, even if it did serve kosher meat. Visiting with Fantahun was fascinating (since I've never been offered *chat* anywhere that I went alone), but it wasn't a place where proprietors would grant me an interview to quote (see Weil 1995). I'd consider this a background trip, having to restrict my officially collected data to material offered by citizens with passports whose names I could cite and whose locations I could name without anxiety. There's a lot to learn in the liminal zone, but most of it can't be repeated even discreetly. This scene is a stark contrast with my standing weekly visit to Habesh.

Virtually every city with a substantial Ethiopian population has a restaurant called Habesh (or Habesha), including obvious places like Addis Ababa and less likely diaspora enclaves like Seattle. The word "Habesh" means, roughly, Ethiopian; the word "Abyssinia" is an adaptation (Levine 2000: 118), and Eritreans and northern Ethiopians refer to themselves as the Habesha people. Like the restaurant in Tel Aviv that I visited weekly, many iterations worldwide provide live music, facilitated by beer or Ethiopian honey-wine (*tejj*) and Eskesta dancing. The one in Tel Aviv, which moved to a different location in 2010, had a kosher certification and was adorned with Israeli flags, but apart from that it much resembled comparable iterations around the world. It was adorned with a fair share of formulaic kitsch: the interior resembled a *tukul,* a tentlike structure from the Ethiopian highlands with wooden pillars and beams holding up a canvas; images of farmers handling coffee beans (*buna,* a major Ethiopian cash crop) adorned the walls (see Seeman 2015 for an innovative discussion of its moral properties), and waitresses wore white robes. Ethiopian pop spilled out of the speakers at all hours, while the smell of coffee beans wafted across the bar. Decommissioned musical instruments sat in an alcove as decoration. Apart from the Israeli flags, the only visual reminder of the Ethiopian-Israeli population's unique position in Ethiopia was that the walls were free of the panels that depict scenes from the *Kebra Negast,* the Ge'ez-language Ethiopian national epic that holds importance for Beta Israel but contains a polemic against the Jews (Levine 2000: 94).[3]

Today Habesh is located near the bus station, and still boasts its *te'udat kashrut*. During my fieldwork in 2009, though, it sat anonymously in a seedy commercial center at the corner of Allenby and Kaufman, steps away from the beach. Discernible only to someone who was looking for it, the entrance was obscured by a tangle of neon shop signs (figure 2.1). A burly Russian-speaking security guard and a sign emblazoned with a small Ethiopian flag and the word "Habesh" in Ethiopic script were all that announced it, though the security guard checking your bag might have asked (if you weren't Ethiopian) whether you were sure you wanted to go in. This was a part of Tel Aviv frequented by tourists, teenagers, and immigrants. Local residents consisted mostly of students, Russian speakers, and pensioners whose durable presence was a source of frustration to property developers. Middle-class professionals had abandoned this part of the center of town for the historic "White City," the Bauhaus-concentrated UNESCO World Heritage site (Cohen 2003: 11). In other words, the restaurant's location had about the same reputation as the Azmaris had back in Ethiopia (see Kebede 1975).

Musically, Habesh was similar to a regional folk night in London or Washing-

FIGURE 2.1 Site of Habesh restaurant, 2017 (author photo)

ton (see Shelemay 2006a about the Washington scene) in its ensemble, instrumentation, and melodies, and its controversial incorporation of a drum machine
for dancing.[4] On Thursdays, Menilek (on *krar*, the six-stringed plucked lyre)
and Avi (on massenqo) started playing at 9 p.m. and finished at 3 a.m., joined
for several hours by Almaz the dancer. Through the evening, they played for
forty-five minutes of each hour, spending their breaks chatting with patrons.
The sets often consisted of one extended piece that lasted for the duration, especially later in the night. At the beginning of a song, Menilek started the drum
machine and after counting in, played the krar to a 6/8 beat, and then Avi joined
him on the massenqo. The melody often began with the same five-note phrase
in a minor pentatonic mode like *ambassel*.[5] The krar melody often repeated for
long periods while Avi improvised. Between Avi's reserved personality and the
scratchy timbre of the massenqo, it likely suited them that Avi sat farther away,
behind the extroverted Menilek. Occasionally Menilek and Avi played a folk
standard from Gondar, and just as often they played material from Addis Ababa
that could accompany dancing. They often played the same piece with multiple
variations, Avi's part making the difference in discerning modes and repertoire.

In this chapter I introduce some of the fundamental concepts of Ethiopian musical aesthetics through description of my weekly visits to Habesh. Habesh was a hybrid of an *Azmari-bet*, a music house where an Azmari performs, and a "cultural restaurant," a tourist-oriented restaurant that offers folk entertainment. The format was a self-conscious pastiche of Ethiopian culture, offering a snapshot of life in Ethiopia via the music of Addis Ababa, a place most of the patrons hadn't visited. In the course of this discussion, I examine the ways that Ethiopian-Israeli musicians look to Ethiopian culture to define the terms of their citizenship in Israel, drawing from a set of myths of Abyssinian (Habesha) glory to reframe their contemporary social problems in Israel, from which the home country is seen as an "iconic, almost monolithic Ethiopian entity" (Salamon 1999: 12).

Those myths are well rehearsed across the literature about Ethiopian culture, and well represented in the preeminent work of Donald Levine (1965, 1974) and Edward Ullendorff (1968). They center on the characteristics that render Ethiopia exceptional in Africa in terms of history, religion, and culture, and focus particularly on Amhara culture. Although Ethiopia is a very splintered society with no one dominant culture, most discussions of Ethiopia in a national framework take the Amhara as a starting point. Therefore, scholarship focuses on the Orthodox Church (the world's second oldest), the Ethiopic writing system (*fidal*—the only indigenous writing system in Africa), and the independent past (Italy occupied briefly, but Ethiopia was never colonized). This tripartite formula puts the Christian Amhara at the center of Ethiopian culture, distinguishes Ethiopia from its African neighbors, and emerges as something of a scholarly counternarrative for a country that is famous for its heterogeneity.

Applying the myths of a glorious Ethiopian past to musical analysis, I first examine the unique role played by the massenqo in representing Ethiopian music's tonality, interpreted as dissonant by Israeli and non-Ethiopian ears (Powne 1968: 47). Second, I analyze the abiding popularity of the staple song "Tezeta" in Israel (based on the feeling and musical mode that means "nostalgia" in Amharic— Shelemay 1991, Woubshet 2009).[6] Third, I explore the influence of the literary method of wax and gold (*sem-enna-werq*), the style in which words hold different meanings according to context, on the way that Habesh's musicians engaged the discussion of life in Israel. By incorporating all three of these key mechanisms of Ethiopian musical aesthetics, performers and audience enlist a narrative of Ethiopian glory as a foil for their unstable status in Tel Aviv.

———

I first visited Habesh in mid-August (vacation season), so it was sparsely attended. Compounding the calendar issue, I arrived at 9:30 p.m., prompting my Ethiopian acquaintances to later chuckle that I was irredeemably *Yekke* (a German Jew, obsessed with timekeeping). I went by myself and couldn't work up the nerve to speak to the musicians. I tried to order food in Amharic, but my accent being thick and the music loud, the waitress, Hadas, failed to understand me (my accent didn't improve over the year, so I never tried again; as with virtually all of my research, I conducted conversations at Habesh in Hebrew). My attempt at ordering *tejj* was equally ineffective; it was listed on the menu, but I was told that they didn't have any and that most customers were drinking beer. I ordered lentil *wät*, a stew served with *injera*, a spongy flat bread. I stayed for two hours, the number of guests never exceeding fifteen. Had I known to stay past midnight, I would have left with an altogether different impression.

On most nights subsequently, the crowd would grow as the evening progressed, with the restaurant reaching its capacity of eighty people around midnight. When the restaurant was full, people would dance, tipping the musicians by placing banknotes on their forehead. Almaz wore a headband for this purpose, and on especially busy nights it would flutter with twenty-shekel (then worth about five dollars) bills. The audience's generosity was partly a function of its relative affluence: Habesh's clientele was upscale by the standards of the state's poorest Jewish minority.[7] Most audience members I met would travel in from cities around the coast. People from towns like Rehovot and Hadera would come in to meet friends as a special occasion, while the musicians Menilek and Avi lived in Jerusalem. I didn't meet anyone who lived in affluent Tel Aviv, but neither did many guests come from an absorption center. Zelelew, a young self-taught Azmari and bandleader who figures prominently in chapter 4, was a notable exception, and he not only visited Habesh but occasionally got up onstage, too. I also never saw a customer in white robes or bearing a tattoo on their forehead (see Seeman 2009: 36), visible everyday signs of being a new arrival or a Falash Mura.

Indeed, it emerged in our discussions that Menilek and Avi presented a musical picture of life in Ethiopia that was far removed from the experience of most of their audience members, and a distant memory for them.[8] Both musicians had come to Israel from the Gondar region, via a stay in the refugee camps in Sudan (see BenEzer 2002, Parfitt 1985), and had never lived in Addis Ababa. Lacking a lineage of hereditary training (see Kebede 1975), they modestly called themselves musicians (*muziqa'im*) instead of Azmaris in our conversations, the tradition in Israel being left in the hands of the mostly self-taught.[9] They explained that their recollections of Gondar thus consisted mostly of childhood memories of village life (see Salamon 1999 or 2010), their musical taste shaped by the capital city they hadn't visited. So the music performed on Thursdays at Habesh signaled nostalgia for a memory of Ethiopia, but of a constructed memory that was removed from the reality of rural Beta Israel life. By invoking key concepts from Ethiopian musical aesthetics—dissonance, nostalgia, layers of meaning—Ethiopian Israeli musicians reinsert themselves into Ethiopian history, not as marginalized villagers but as active shapers of Ethiopianist narratives of Abyssinian (Habesha) glory. In the process, they frame themselves as actualized citizens.

THE MASSENQO AND REINSERTION INTO ETHIOPIAN CULTURE

When I arrived in Tel Aviv, I thought I might study the krar, which sounds beautiful and has some literature available. After listening to a lot of Azmari music, though, I realized that I probably had to learn the massenqo if I wanted to understand *qignit*, the Ethiopian modal system. During my second week of fieldwork I went to a multicultural concert at a prestigious Jerusalem venue and saw a massenqo player onstage, so I approached him and, with the help of a bemused Qes (Ethiopian clergy) translating from Hebrew to Amharic over the noise, we set up some lessons. Because of my background in violin, many performance elements transferred neatly for me. My teacher Fantahun never focused on my bowing technique, for example, though it felt strange at first to play the instrument in an upright position. Fortunately, that position made other elements easier, such as stretching the fingers wider than one usually does on a violin. I became acclimated quickly to stretching my fingers.

The biggest challenge in learning to play was the unresolved sound of many of the intervals. Scales were difficult: one learns a mode by ascending the five notes, doubling the octave, and descending directly to the root note (Kebede 1977: 389). When descending and ending on the open string, I often felt that I was playing out of tune, but listened constantly to a rare example of a locally produced Azmari CD by Dejen Manchlot (2007, bought at Ethiopian music hub Nahum Records). I soon started to recognize the different ways that notes resolve, or at least to recognize my discomfort with the prevalence of minor seconds. As I discovered, Azmari music becomes great fun for the listener who can appreciate the massenqo's sound, but that goes together with training ears and participating in live performance. My most frequent encounters with live massenqo performance, at Habesh, illuminated some of the tonality issues in Ethiopian musical aesthetics, and the importance of instruments in the development of genres and narratives.

Learning to play in sequence was my first important hurdle; it enables a student to recognize the mode's tonal features. It doesn't take long to be able to play the five notes, but it takes a great deal of practice and listening to get used to a mode.[10] One does so next by learning to ornament the skeleton of the sequence. Ornamentation includes harmonics, trills, and faster sequences, advanced techniques to be sure, but a method that any violin student working through variations will recognize. In contrast to the way young Anglophone students learn the violin, though, Azmari training from the outset encourages improvisation, building it into the earliest stages of learning.

The initial repertoire on the massenqo forms the basis for *qignit*, the modal system: tezeta, *anchihoy*, *ambassel*, and *batti* (Abate 2007: 1215–1217, Herman 2012: 204, Kebede 1967: 154–61). On the krar this can be demonstrated by playing open strings (Kebede 1977: 387), but no such shortcuts exist for the massenqo. Since the massenqo has only one string, control over hand position is paramount. Learning how to comport the hand for each mode, and then how to rest the hand on the instrument, are the basic steps (apart from ear training) to understanding how to play each song and mode (ibid.). Once this task is achieved, one can play the sequence in a 6/8 tempo. This sequence forms the basis for both song and mode, and one can then learn lyrics, a process that in itself requires early adoption of improvisation. The voice of the Azmari usually follows the melodic progression of the massenqo homophonically, so the vocal melody emerges somewhat intuitively.

My flatmates in the early days of fieldwork were pleased to have Fantahun around the house to chat about music, but they were not especially impressed by my playing, and this was only partly attributable to my inexperience with the instrument. The massenqo produces a rough timbre due to the string's coarseness, and as the voice imitates the instrument, many Azmaris' voices have a scratchy quality too. As far as I can deduce from the reactions of non-Ethiopian friends who hear Azmari music for the first time, the massenqo's rough timbre bears responsibility for the underreception of Ethiopian music in global music markets.[11] New visitors, like Israeli or American friends who joined me at Habesh, are taken with the mythical, melodic krar, and the melodically limited massenqo seems sometimes to be relegated to backup instrument. The massenqo exposes the mode and patterns of a song, though, and in addition to its dominance for musical analysis, it serves as a visual symbol and a sonic signifier of a quintessentially "Ethiopian" sound.

The quintessentially Ethiopian sound is the unresolved tonality that fans of the *Éthiopiques* series recognize from the music of Mahmoud Ahmed. Yet on Ethiopian instruments, the sound is more challenging: I've heard live Ethiopian music across four continents, and I have grown accustomed to hearing non-Ethiopian audience members complaining that the music sounds the same from one song to the next. Non-Ethiopian audiences, not having had the opportunity to train their ears to the sound of unresolved semitones and scratchy timbre, have a hard time recognizing the nuances in a whole set performed within a single mode. To them the effect is repetitive because they aren't listening for the virtuosity on display through improvisation, ornamentation, and verbal dexterity. I first came to recognize this dynamic at Habesh, with non-Ethiopian visitors initially excited but, until the dancing began, underwhelmed by what they heard as repetitive repertoire.

Within a song's structure, Menilek and Avi sometimes played six-measure phrases in a 6/8 rhythm, and thus a pattern became easy to discern quickly. Variety from phrase to phrase came primarily from ornamentation and improvisation. That is why the massenqo is so important: in contrast to Avi's varied melodies on the massenqo, Menilek's part sounded much the same from set to set and from song to song. One could not always hear Avi playing above Menilek—or the drum machine that, like in Ethiopia today, often accompanied them—but his part was the most important in identifying the song's tonal center. Even so, whether or not the audience could discern the massenqo's melody, its presence was necessary onstage because it connected the scene visually to the Azmari tradition of northwest Ethiopia. In so doing, Menilek and Avi connected Ethiopian-Israelis to a past that was quite distant from their lives, both as lived in Ethiopia and in the contemporary context.[12] They—perhaps inadvertently—connected Ethiopian-Israelis to core narratives of Ethiopianness, making them central participants in a musical practice that had historically excluded them.[13]

Despite their remoteness from Addis Ababa, the musicians connected to mainstream popular Ethiopian music through repertoire. In their playlists they heavily favored the songs of Aklilu Seyoum, a major musical figure from the 1970s who grew up in Gondar, played in several national orchestras, and moved to Israel in the 1990s. He lived in the small port city of Ashdod, and since he was terminally ill during my fieldwork, I never met him before his death in December 2010.[14] He himself traveled back to Ethiopia to perform and record (giving interviews in Amharic),[15] and remains one of Israel's most popular musicians in Ethiopia. Menilek and Avi played some of his music every week, often devoting entire sets to his repertoire (Audio file 9), in the process identifying with and paying homage to his musical lineage.

For Avi, that someone like him (of Beta Israel lineage) should make a living from playing the massenqo was unlikely. The absence of a tradition of secular music distinct to the Beta Israel (in contrast to the liturgy, meticulously documented by Shelemay 1986, or the traditional music of Ethiopia's many ethnic minorities as documented in Tourny 2007), and the difficulty in Ethiopia for a Jew to become an Azmari, colored Avi's perception of his professionalism. One could detect unease in Avi about even thinking of himself as a professional:

AVI: So, here's how I got started. In my village, among my father's cousins, everyone plays . . . .

IWK: Ah, it's an Azmari family?

AVI: No, not Azmari. In Ethiopia, it was sort of prohibited, to be an Azmari, for Beta Israel, for the Jews in Ethiopia, to be part of the tradition, to be an "Azmari." It's just not permitted for us. But we sort of learned to play among ourselves, and it was fine. So that way, when my father's cousins were playing, I listened, I heard, and I loved the music, and I said, I have to learn. And my cousin was playing massenqo. So, of course, I didn't know the modes, and one of my father's cousins who plays massenqo, who knows how to tune the krar, because it's the same principle as the massenqo, he didn't know how to play it, but he knew how to tune it. (interview, Tel Aviv, June 25, 2009)

The connection between Avi and the Azmari tradition was a modern one that owed more to his circumstances in Israel than to long-established patterns of social interaction between musicians in Ethiopia. Prior to Operation Moses (1984–1985) and Operation Solomon (1991), the informal segregation that often limited contact with non-Jews to the sphere of commerce (Quirin 1992, Weil 2004: 76–77) precluded the sort of immersion or penetration into familial and friendly circles that is a prerequisite for the perpetuation and transformation of an artistic tradition. In other words, Ethiopian-Israeli musicians lack a genealogy of musical transmission: as in many oral musical traditions, Azmari music in Ethiopia was premised on a special relationship between its bearers, the bond between master and pupil that often overlaps with kinship ties (Fantahun studied with his father until he was ready to set off to Addis Ababa to study).

In contrast, Avi was effectively self-taught, but one area where his pedigree was less important than the knowledge he possessed was the tuning of the krar, and by extension, the basics of the modal system. Despite the morphological limitations of the massenqo that dictate the five-note system, there is room for variation in tonality. As Fantahun explained to me, the important differences between the modes can be discerned through the positioning of the hand. At our second lesson, I made a tracing of his hand positioning in each of the four modes that I kept and studied. Without knowing what Fantahun called any of the notes—he never gave them specific names, though Kebede explains that the root and octave are called *melash* and *memelesha* on the krar (1977: 387)—I deduced early that one might think of the modes not as notes per se, but as a cluster of sounds related to one another in a way that could be easily represented visually. In her book about traditional Ethiopian music in Israel, Marilyn Herman confirms that *qignit* is highly relative, with intervals being more important than pitches in establishing mode (2012: 204).

The massenqo and the krar are tuned today to the Western scale, but all musicians say that modes can be transposed or given major or minor variants. On the other hand, if the distance between two fingers were the only measure of a mode, then tonality would be extremely relative and the massenqo would never need to be tuned. Scholars know little about the history of the tuning of the massenqo, nor how long it has been tuned to the Western scale. Much more is known about the krar since it developed based on the ten-stringed religious instrument beganna, the so-called "Harp of King David." The krar's notes thus descend from church modes originally (Powne 1968: 88–89). The massenqo has no such affiliation with religious music, and the combination of its reputation as a rustic, rural instrument with its scratchy sound has left it out of the organological research in Ethiopian music, though an understanding of its roots is central to understanding the Azmari tradition.

While the massenqo is tuned to the Western scale, its intervals are conceptualized in relative terms and its modes cover the full Western range of tonality. Some modes are major and others are minor. But the massenqo does not always match up well with another instrument. The first time I met Dejen Manchlot, probably the best-known Azmari in Israel today (whose CD I used as a reference point), at Beit AviChai in Jerusalem in August 2008, he performed alongside a Yemenite singer and an Iraqi flutist. Or rather, they played one at a time. At the end, when they all played a psalm together, Dejen initially joined them but quickly dropped out until his solo because the massenqo sounded discordant with the other instruments. Marilyn Herman conveys this discord especially aptly in a comment from a musician that he only plays the black keys on the accordion because that specific kind of pentatonicism is the only way to match with Ethiopian music (2012: 9).

This distinctive tonality of the massenqo and its semitone-oriented modes, in addition to the cultural contradictions from which Azmari music has developed, makes Azmari music in Israel a tradition of its own today. Musicians are beginning to discover that preservation and transmission are imperatives to which any tradition is eventually subordinated. Avi was aware of this:

> IWK: What do you think about what's happening with traditional music here in Israel?
>
> AVI: Traditional music in Israel? Okay, so, here in Israel, they don't go according to—well, they sing a song—not necessarily to start at the beginning and end at the end, and not according to the order. Most people are interested, as long as there is a tune, some drums, people are happy whether or not [it's done properly]. At ceremonies and celebrations, they don't follow the order or protocol; they just want to have some music. And I don't really like that, I prefer for it to be done in a specific manner. But you can't argue with what people want. (interview, Tel Aviv, June 25, 2009)

Avi lamented the decline of an Azmari performance practice, while establishing a raison-d'être for his own work as the custodian of a tradition that might otherwise be eclipsed in the urban Israeli context. Yet because there was no Azmari tradition among the Beta Israel in Ethiopia—that is, lacking a canon and a master-pupil bond—the acquisition and transmission of musical knowledge central to the success of the new tradition is less certain, and the pool of potential recruits less clearly bounded; there are few, if any musical "dynasties" among Ethiopian-Israelis since there is no established Beta Israel Azmari tradition (yet). It is precisely this uncertainty and haphazardness of transmission that, on top of a need to stave off the threat of assimilation and the tribulations of a new quasi-diasporic identity (see Kaplan 2005), accounts for why Avi, and other self-taught massenqo players (like Zelelew in chapter 4), frame Azmari music as cultural heritage and themselves as amateur cultural custodians.

Menilek spoke particularly eloquently about the obstacles facing young aspiring musicians. Articulated together in our discussions were the ideas that culture needs to be respected within the community and by the majority group (Israelis); and that educating and nurturing young people is the best way to ensure continuity. For example, he proposed to institute a state-sponsored platform for talented young people to develop their skills (interview, Tel Aviv, June 18, 2009). Coupled with this passion for cultural preservation was a reverence for the "real" Azmaris, i.e., those who had filial ties to the tradition (such as Dejen Manchlot, whom he mentioned with admiration), which stemmed from an assertive pride in Ethiopian culture viewed as homogeneous, all-embracing, and egalitarian, in stark contrast to the patriarchal, authoritarian, and hierarchical Ethiopian society.

Yet, in order to preserve Ethiopian heritage, musicians have to gain access to the tradition so as to play it competently. As Avi stressed in his account of learning to play the krar and the massenqo, instrumental technique is the top priority:

AVI: I thought at first about the krar. So I bought myself a krar, and I started playing a little bit. Once I got the tuning ["way" literally], then I started to play. That's how I learned. And after I learned the krar, I said to myself, "Fine, now I'll try with the massenqo." So I started learning the massenqo, too. Now, the difference between the krar and the massenqo, it didn't take me a long time to get it, because it's the same principle, though the krar has several strings while the massenqo has just one. On the krar, each string is tuned according to the tone you need, and on the massenqo, it's according to the fingers. And they're the same modes. So that's how I went. And within a month, a month and a half, I was already on the way [figuratively "in the mode"], so I started playing a bit on the massenqo. And from there, bit by bit, I improved . . .

IWK: So, how did you learn the material?

AVI: Well, that depends on whether you mean national songs or modern songs. For national songs, it's what we listen to. All of the melodies, it's just by ear [that we learn]. There's no sheet music for it. I didn't know what sheet music was, and I learned about it first here in Israel. So we learn by ear, in principle. The modern songs, I'd hear on the radio. They play it on the radio, so I guess that's [learned] by ear, too. And I started to play everything. And after that, I came by way of Sudan, and I brought the massenqo. (interview, Tel Aviv, June 25, 2009)

At Habesh, the visual image of the instruments, the tonality of *qignit*, and the collective participation in dancing are weighted above improvisation of subversive or multilayered lyrics. To a purist, this might be an unusual configuration for recreating a rural tradition: the Habesh musicians do not improvise lyrics; they use a drum machine; and the massenqo is often too quiet to hear. And yet this arrangement works, the audience responding ebulliently.

In Addis Ababa—a place that, notwithstanding increased Ethiopian-Israeli tourism and investment in Ethiopia, many of my informants have never visited—no such fanfare surrounds attending an Azmari-bet, where the Azmari systematically insults each of the patrons. The patrons, in turn, would hardly see their attendance as solidarity, subversion, or resistance, their attitude toward the Azmari being casual and taken for granted.[16] For Ethiopian-Israeli patrons and performers, though, the social function of the Azmari is the discursive anchor of live traditional musical performance, particularly since an extensive musical vocabulary did not survive the journey. The importance of the massenqo in live performance, for performers and audience alike, lies in the instrument's symbolic power to build Ethiopian-Israelis into a distinctive but idealized Ethiopian history, rendering them active participants in the society that they left, and building a cultural heritage that can frame one boundary of citizenship.

"TEZETA" AND DIASPORIC NOSTALGIA

The first time I visited the CD store Nahum Records on Levinski Street in August 2008, I was confident that I would demonstrate that I knew a lot about Ethiopian music, rather than passively buying whatever was recommended. Dor, working behind the counter, asked me what I liked, and I told him proudly that I had seen Alemayehu Eshete perform live a few weeks earlier. Dor cracked up at the reference to the "Ethiopian James Brown," a star from the '70s—"Is he still performing?! I can't believe it"—and shook his head as though non-Ethiopian (*faranji*) consumers would buy anything. Deflated and sheepish, I asked, "What's popular this week?" and was handed a synthed-up solo album that I probably never listened to a second time. In that first week of fieldwork, I learned that "classic" doesn't necessarily translate to contemporary popularity, and I realized that I would have to update my repertoire pretty quickly.

Yet as I started going to Habesh on Thursdays, I met young Ethiopian-Israelis like Shahar from Rehovot whose listening practices were complex. Shahar would start his evening at Habesh with two or three friends, and transition around 11 p.m. to meeting a group of Ethiopian-Israeli friends on the beach, who all downloaded Ethiopian music on their phones and listened to hip-hop that sampled Ethio-jazz. I noticed a contradiction in their collective musical taste. It was true that young people no longer necessarily sought out the greats of Swinging Addis, but at the same time, I heard the classic song "Tezeta" constantly. Piped in at record stores, or during set breaks at concerts, or as tinny ringtones, this singularly iconic song, performed in innumerable styles, was everywhere. Mahmoud Ahmed remains a perennial favorite across generations, too, visiting Israel in 2012 (photographic evidence provided on Ester Rada's Instagram feed). But "Tezeta" in particular, whether in a slow and syrupy rendition from global Ethio-pop star Aster Aweke or a stripped-down minimalist version from Ethio-jazz musician Mulatu Astatke (see Shelemay 2006a or 2009: 186, or Woubshet 2009: 630), was recorded and remixed and repeated constantly. It was the canon.

"Tezeta" is a song to which an entire *Éthiopiques* disc is dedicated; it has been covered as an Azmari standard and an Ethio-jazz one; it has been sampled by Afrodiasporic rappers; and it is appreciated equally at home and abroad. But the song is also the name for a mode, and thus, for a style of sorts, of song that signals the quality of tezeta, nostalgia for a lost person or time, who is acknowledged as difficult but is nonetheless idealized (see Shelemay 1991 for an explanation of tezeta as a worldview, or Herman 2012: 253 as song form). For Ethiopian emigrants around the world, many of whom left under not-dissimilarly ambivalent and desperate circumstances as the Beta Israel, the object of longing is not an alienated lover, but the homeland. This might make music a source of pain, such as for Malkeh, who told me that he didn't like music because it made him think of what he'd lost (his family, who remained in Ethiopia). For Ethiopian-Israelis in particular, the nostalgia implied in the song is especially bittersweet since they know that the object of longing is not real, and that life in Ethiopia was more difficult materially than life in Israel (Salamon 1999 or Weil 2004: 80 for rates of divorce and domestic abuse). Nonetheless, "Tezeta," the song and the quality, remains a key feature of Ethiopian musical aesthetics in Israel, and the embrace of Ethiopia's chief canonic song creates a place for Beta Israel in Ethiopian history.

The song "Tezeta" is immediately recognizable across musical styles for its melodic line regardless of instrumentation (massenqo, brass, or guitars) or tonality (mode, contour, register), and, secondarily, for the lyrics' use of double meaning (lyrics that change from version to version). The melody is built on a five-note line that lays the foundation for improvisation. The tuning of the five notes can vary, but it usually clusters around a similar, anhemitonic set of intervals and follows the same contour from one version to the next. In the case of the mode tezeta, published musical analysis does name the notes in each of *qignit*'s modes (Abate 2007, Kebede 1977, Powne 1968), but scholars generally agree that the modes are built on contour and intervals instead of tonal absolutes.

"Tezeta," and a narrow range of nostalgic standards like it, were played with such frequency at Habesh—punctuating upbeat sets as well as set breaks via CD—that I came to associate the experience of going to Habesh with the mournfulness and regret of the restaurant's consciously cultivated musical mood. Tezeta songs tap into perennial feelings of loss, pain, and hardship, which they express lyrically in the form of the lovesick lament. And yet, consistent with the Azmari hallmark of the technique of wax and gold (Levine 1965), tezeta songs contain several layers of meaning, one explicit and literal, another allusive and figurative. In the recordings of Seyfou Yohannes and Getatchew Kassa on disc 10 of *Éthiopiques*, the feeling that is tezeta is personified as a woman for whom a man—the singer—is tormented by love. In both songs, like in the "traditional" version, there is a strong sense that the relationship is precarious or one-sided: "Tizïtaye anïtäwï nähï, tizïtamï yäläbïñï / Ämät'alïhu äyalïkï, äyäkärähïbïñï" (My tezeta is you, I don't have tezeta / You say you're coming, yet you never do).

In Mahmoud Ahmed's and Menelik Wesnatchew's renditions of "Tezeta" (both on disc 10 of *Éthiopiques*), tezeta is a quality belonging to a woman whose very character is chimerical. In each of these versions, tezeta is unstable: both source and object of passion; thing and quality; tangible and elusive; malignant but enthralling. The seamless shifting of tezeta from one status to another is evident in Wesnatchew's lyrics, where it denotes a person, a quality, and an emotion all at once: "Where can I find you? How your 'tezeta' obsesses me. . . . I see you, hands on your face, smiling. And you call out to me, saying 'Come, my tezeta'" ("Tezeta," Menelik Wesnatchew, *Éthiopiques*, disc 10). The elusiveness of tezeta and the ambivalence of both singer and audience toward it make for a versatile style capable of holding multiple, contradictory interpretations at the same time. In that respect, the concept of tezeta exemplifies wax and gold.

By listening to a sequence of versions of "Tezeta," one can discern some general trends in Ethiopian traditional and popular music between 1960 and the present. In Ethiopia, a gradual shift transpired during the reign of Haile Selassie, beginning with his 1924 invitation of brass bands from Jerusalem (Falceto 2002). The incorporation of Western instruments paved the way for the arrival of guitars, keyboards, and drum sets, and Ethio-jazz resulted in the 1960s from experimentation with Ethiopian tonality on Western instruments. Upon Haile Selassie's ouster in 1974 and the installation of the Derg, Mengistu's Stalinist military regime, "Tezeta" took on strong political undertones about censorship for those residing in Addis Ababa and for emigrants. In the course of half a century, Ethiopia experienced so many dramatic upheavals—regime change, separatist battles, economic development—that a narrative of nostalgia

FIGURE 2.2 Skeletal melody for *tezeta*

for a Christian, literate, self-reigning past (Levine 2000, Ullendorff 1968) seems almost an understatement.

Listening to a progression of the song's recordings, even within the *Éthiopiques* series, reveals this dramatic cultural change. Azmari versions on discs 16, 18, and 23 give way to electrified vocal versions on disc 10. In Azmari versions the song is played on massenqo or krar, with the vocal line mimicking the massenqo in contour and timbre. Finally, Mulatu Astatke's instrumental and Getatchew Mekurya's almost Afro-pop versions indicate a vague melodic remnant of the song that has been deconstructed and modernized. The Azmari influence is still recognizable, but the song bears no trace of the massenqo timbre, nor does the vocal line emulate it. All of this technological adjustment is to say nothing of Aster Aweke's synthesized version or rapper Common's sample, each of which render the song appealing to younger and international audiences.

An Azmari version of "Tezeta" is most likely to be performed live, and was least likely to be projected over the sound system during the set breaks at Habesh. The "traditional" versions such that I have often heard live would most commonly be performed on the massenqo. A male voice usually sings the lyrics while playing a major pentatonic melody on the krar. Its notes can follow the tezeta mode of C D E G A, or it can be transposed in any direction, provided that it follows the intervallic structure of major seconds and minor thirds (Abate 2007: 1216). Some versions will even follow the tezeta contour while borrowing the notes from an *anchihoy* mode of C E ♭ F A ♭ B ♭, as in figure 2.2. The scale can be transposed easily to krar tuning, and the melody is immediately recognizable through its contour.

Perhaps the closest Ethio-jazz rendition to an Azmari version comes from Tesfa-Maryam Kidane, the two differing primarily in instrumentation (Audio file 10). The melody's skeleton of G B ♭ C E ♭ (with a high G implied) is much the same, neither emphasizing semitones. A saxophone plays the melody as the voice or *washint* would in an Azmari recording. Indeed, we can note from recordings like this one that some instruments substitute well for others, like the bass for krar or saxophone for *washint*.

A third version is offered by Mahmoud Ahmed, perhaps the most beloved figure in Ethio-jazz (Audio file 11). He is best known for the song "Ere Mela Mela," and two discs from *Éthiopiques* are devoted to his work. This rendition of "Tezeta" is an important historical document, having been recorded just as the emperor was overthrown. In the political upheaval and ambivalence that eventually led to political disillusionment, what he means by nostalgia is hardly mysterious. With Western instrumentation, Mahmoud Ahmed's version is distinct from an Azmari version, with a minor scale of B D E ♭ G A ♭, which notably contains two minor seconds. The two versions share some important features. First, in Mahmoud Ahmed's rendition, the bass plays the scale and keeps time, as the krar does in the Azmari version. This is followed by a saxophone playing an ornamented melody, and finally the lyricist sings the scale while the bass keeps time. Despite the obvious differences in instrumentation and mode, these two recordings are structurally similar.

One can easily find fourth, fifth, and sixth versions of "Tezeta" that equally demonstrate Ethiopia's changing musical climate. A fourth recording, by Seyfou Yohannes, is the most iconic of the canonical Ethio-jazz versions of "Tezeta" (Audio file 12), widely publicized when it was sampled by American rapper Common in his 2007 song "The Game." Although Common's sample is beyond the scope of this discussion, he quite brilliantly imitates the descending contour of the piano in the also-sampled chorus from rapper O. C., "It's only right that I address this."[17] The tension in the Seyfou Yohannes version presents itself within the first ten seconds, the opening bracket referenced by Common. A piano plays the introduction, joined in the third measure by a brass section with a subdued vocal. This transformative rendition innovates instrumentally, experimenting with jazz influence, and applies the musical idioms of *qignit* to the piano.

A fifth version, from Mulatu Astatke, bears direct influence from jazz due to his time spent in the United States (Audio file 13). It is deconstructed and without lyrics, the main melody played on the vibraphone. Getatchew Kassa's version has the heaviest pop influence, intent to transform the melancholy melodic line into an upbeat one through major tonality, ascending contour, high register in the nonverbal chorus, and cut-time tempo (Audio file 14). It is a great distance from the Azmari recordings in its tonal center as well as its pace and mood.

All of these versions share some characteristics, and enough differences to argue that there is no single authoritative rendition of shape-shifting "Tezeta." Most versions employ an ascending triad in the melodic line and a peppering of semitones, and they all share roughly the same contour of ascending and ending on descent. On the other hand, only some of them bring in the tritone as a melodic interval; play a 6/8 rhythm consistently (some employ an apparent 4/4 pulse); or draw on the same five notes uniformly within the mode. None of these stylistic differences seem to hamper the song's popularity among Ethiopians anywhere. Yet since Ethiopian-Israelis are working hard to integrate into Israeli life, few ever considering a permanent return to Ethiopia, it is worth considering precisely what was the object of nostalgia for the audience at Habesh.

Admittedly, even though life in Israel is materially more comfortable, Ethiopian-Israelis have something to be nostalgic for: life in the lush Ethiopian highlands, and memories of a time when the family unit was intact (see Weil 2004: 77 for an explanation of the kinship concept of *zemed*) and assimilation was not a primary concern. An important component of Ethiopian-Israeli nostalgia for the highlands can be traced back to the *Kebra Negast*, the foundational epic of Ethiopian civilization. According to the epic, Ethiopia supersedes biblical Israel as the Holy Land on the grounds of ownership of the Ark of the Covenant. The story explains that when the Queen of Sheba visited Jerusalem (mentioned in the Bible), she had an encounter with King Solomon (not mentioned in the Bible), resulting in a son, Menilek. When a grown Menilek visits Jerusalem, his retinue steals the Ark of the Covenant and takes it back to Ethiopia, establishing Ethiopia as the new Zion (Levine 1974, Ullendorff 1968). In addition to a brief polemic against the Jews, the epic articulates an Ethiopian attitude that theirs, and not the biblical Holy Land, is the earthly Eden. In this extract from the *Kebra Negast*, Ethiopia is compared with Judea, to the disadvantage of the latter: "Our country is the better. The climate of our country is good, for it is without burning heat and fire, and the water of our country is good, and sweet, and floweth in rivers. . . . And we do not do as you [*sic*] do in your country, that is to say, dig very deep wells in search of water, and we do not die through the heat of the sun; but even at noonday we hunt wild animals, namely, the wild buffaloes, and gazelles, and birds, and small animals" (cited in Levine 1974: 102). Like the *Kebra Negast*, "Tezeta" draws what performers know is an incomplete picture of life in Ethiopia (or with the erstwhile lover). Yet it overshadows every other Amharic-language song in ubiquity by some margin, and the song's popularity at Habesh and across Ethiopian-Israeli musical subcultures in general emanates from its ability to draw marginalized migrants into a portrait of their homeland, where they can imagine a life of dignity.

For my Ethiopian-Israeli acquaintances, who are accustomed to hearing constantly that they should be grateful that life is better in Israel (see Parfitt and Trevisan Semi 2005), and who still fail to be considered Israeli by some

Israelis (Shapira 2012: 459), nostalgia for Ethiopia constitutes, partly, an attempt to insert themselves credibly into a national narrative. Whereas many Israelis have, after decades of immigration, failed to accept the religious legitimacy of Beta Israel immigrants (let alone Falash Mura converts and new arrivals), in the Israeli context, Ethiopian-Israelis have the space to frame their history as part of Ethiopia's story.[18] Israeli music places a great premium on attachment to the land (see Regev and Seroussi 2004), and as rural smiths and potters, Beta Israel also value groundedness in their surroundings. But equally importantly, nostalgia for the past enables Ethiopian-Israelis to shake off a frequent source of instability, that Israelis think "we came without culture" (*banu bli tarbut*). With Ethiopia's ascent in the world, from famine to development success story (see Levine 2000: 9–23), and the positive associations of Rastafari imagery (Raboteau 2007), embracing Ethiopian culture via a sonic representation of ambivalence allows Ethiopian-Israelis to acknowledge among themselves that life in Ethiopia was difficult, but that there is something worth remembering for the purposes of pride in cultural heritage and family history (see Goldblatt and Rosenblum 2011 for examples of second-generation nostalgia for life "there"). Among a people worried about forgetting their roots, or worse, about being perceived not to have roots—to have come without culture—the ambiguity of "Tezeta" (both the song and the concept) facilitates the repositioning of Ethiopian-Israelis, reinserting them into a narrative from which they themselves acknowledge their alienation.

Ethiopia's national narrative—a complex, multiethnic, and highly fragmented society described in the work of Donald Levine—repeatedly returns to its unique religious history, its literary tradition facilitated by the church, its empire and history of independence, and its writing system. As the country embarks on rapid economic development and addresses the separatist movements at each of its borders (Eritreans in the 1990s, the Oromo in the south today), the narrative has morphed into what Donald Levine calls "Greater Ethiopia," or the embrace of minorities into the same narrative (1974, 2000). The Oromo, who are not Christian, who periodically seek to break away, and who do not use the Ethiopic syllabary *fidal* as a writing system are, in a sense, as much a part of the narrative as the Afar or the Amhara. Donald Levine's books, like many others about Ethiopian culture, accord a disproportionate amount of space to Beta Israel (usually called Falasha in the Ethiopian context, even today) social structure as a mechanism for showcasing Ethiopia's vast ethnoreligious diversity, permitting Beta Israel to include themselves in Greater Ethiopia. But as we see from the touring patterns of Mahmoud Ahmed or Aster Aweke, today's more upwardly mobile Ethiopian-Israelis go one step further, bringing Ethiopian musicians to perform for them in Tel Aviv and Jerusalem, demanding acknowledgment from contemporary Ethiopians that they are a part of the Ethiopian diaspora (see Webster-Kogen 2016 or Shelemay 2006a for a broader survey of music in the Ethiopian diaspora).

As a flexible song that allows for seemingly infinite stylistic and lyrical variation, "Tezeta" can represent the Ethiopian-Israeli experience writ large. The song acknowledges the ambivalence about Ethiopia that many Ethiopian-Israelis feel, and it embraces Ethiopia anyway. Ethiopian-Israelis do likewise: they do not intend to move back, and indeed only a minority return to visit,[19] but they look back on life there with a certain nostalgia. That nostalgia comes not from a memory of superior quality of life, nor even from active participation in wider Ethiopian society, but from the perception that they can credibly take some ownership in a national narrative today, allowing them to claim a heritage that Israelis can acknowledge. This complex repositioning into Ethiopian history facilitates the exposition of an alternative to their marginal status in both places.

RECASTING WAX AND GOLD

August 1, 2008, Tel Aviv

IWK: How do you like living in Israel?

DANIEL: I have no other land [*Ein li eretz aheret*, quoting a pop song].

IWK: Are you an Ehud Manor fan?! [the author of the song]

DANIEL: Who?

IWK: Oh, an Israeli singer.

DANIEL: Oh. Why would I listen to Israeli music?

It was barely the end of my first week of fieldwork, and I'd made about the most amateur mistake possible: asking an Ethiopian-Israeli directly about life in Israel as an initial line of questioning. I had known Daniel for all of two minutes, and I was prepared to jump right into the subject of structural and everyday discrimination. It didn't occur to me until afterward that he might not want to talk about that with a stranger. This line of questioning failed, but I learned something important in the process that I would remind myself about frequently: that I might derive better information from people, and more frank opinions, asking about music instead of life in Israel. This observation is confirmed by David Ratner, who explains that "What do you listen to?" (*Ma ata shomeia?*)

was always his first interview question (Ratner 2015: 63). Maybe people simply don't like to open up immediately about sensitive subjects, but equally likely, for Ethiopians, it's a function of wax and gold: they have more sophisticated ways to frame their critique.

Being aware of wax and gold (*sem-enna-werq*) profoundly eased my transition into conversations with Ethiopian-Israelis who, apart from the occasional individual who has adopted the notorious Israeli forthrightness, are often reserved about sensitive subjects, especially with people they don't know well (and especially so among the less-integrated older generation). Researchers of Ethiopian culture find the same reserve across the diaspora and back in Addis Ababa, and it takes some time to understand that what appears to be reserve is actually a skilled subtlety based on the Amharic literary tradition. This technique of burying deep meaning in seemingly casual conversation descends from wax and gold, and Ethiopian-Israelis borrow it from Azmaris to express their perspective on structural problems and citizenship status using coded language that can best be parsed by people who recognize the dynamic (Seeman 2009: 75). For now, I will examine how wax and gold informs an Ethiopian-Israeli approach to citizenship.

The concept of wax and gold permeates Azmari lyrics, including the lyrics of "Tezeta." The crux of the concept comes from Amharic grammar, built on the root system common to all Semitic languages that allows words to contextually suggest multiple and equivocal meaning. The Azmari's chief skill is the cultivation of wax and gold, facilitating a quick tongue that can praise and taunt simultaneously. More than anything, wax and gold is a clever method of code-switching (see Wardhaugh 2009: 85–115 for an excellent overview from sociolinguistics, or Slobin 1992 for a musical analogue), in which the Azmari's ability to change meanings according to syntax or musical convention renders performances unique and engages the audience directly.

For centuries, wax and gold has been an effective means used by writers and musicians in Ethiopia to circumvent official censorship and defy taboos (see Levine 1965, who argues that it is effectively the basis for Ethiopian culture). In a continuing political climate of repression of speech, Ethiopians today can only express certain opinions with utmost discretion and subtlety.[20] Ethiopians have therefore grown accustomed to mobilizing wax and gold in everyday speech, to some degree learning to voice their opinions in ambiguous terms when appropriate. Familiarizing oneself with Ethiopian culture thus demands, above all, the development of a sensitive ear; whether listening to an Azmari sing or engaging in casual conversation with a new acquaintance, one should consider making the effort to listen carefully for what is implied as much as what is stated explicitly.[21]

In Israel there is a racial element to wax and gold, too, and with regard to how black minorities relate to society, I find in wax and gold some resonance of double consciousness. Articulated by W. E. B. Du Bois in *The Souls of Black Folk* (1904), the concept was borrowed from psychiatry to express metaphorical schizophrenia, the schizoid self-understanding of a racial minority considering oneself as a person and also as an Other. Positing that race would be the central problem of the twentieth century, Du Bois explains that being black is central to one's identity because it is imposed on African Americans by a white mainstream. Thus, a person's identity is demonstrably marked by "the color line." Ethiopian-Israelis, who often see themselves first as Jews, then as immigrants, and then finally as black (or some permutation of the three), can draw from the imagery of lost-wax casting, where a hollow wax model is built, fired, and filled with gold, a salutary metaphor for the construction of self. In the expression "First and foremost, I am a Jew" (*Kodem kol, ani yehudi*), which I heard at least a dozen times from Ethiopian-Israelis, outer layers of otherness or "wax" are replaced with a soul likened to gold.

Yet at Habesh the musicians did not use wordplay to taunt the audience like an Azmari would in Addis Ababa. In 2013, an Azmari in Addis Ababa asked my name, and, punning in English for the benefit of the audience, replied, "Ilana—like banana?" before making a disobliging remark in Amharic. In contrast, many of the sets at Habesh were strictly instrumental, and when Menilek did sing, it was repertoire the audience knew; he did not improvise lyrics. When they do use lyrics to insult someone or express a position explicitly, though, it is always in Amharic. As Zelelew, a young self-taught Azmari in Ashkelon (featured in chapter 4), said about whether he intended to write lyrics in Hebrew, "Yes, but not like a new immigrant [*oleh ḥadash*]" (interview, Ashkelon, June 23, 2009). Azmaris may feel self-conscious about their level of Hebrew, and they are more concerned with the quality of their lyrics than with the language in which they deliver their message.

Indeed, the performance style is often closer to what one would find at a "cultural restaurant," the kind of establishment in Ethiopia and abroad that serves Ethiopian food and offers entertainment often labeled kitschy, "inauthentic," or staged for tourists. Many characteristics of the much-grittier Azmari-bet on display at Habesh were similar to what a visitor would find in Addis Ababa: use of the massenqo or krar as principal/sole instrument; singing from the principal instrumentalist; entire sets based in a single mode; ornamentation by way of ululation (voice) or grace notes (usually on the massenqo); and Eskesta dancing. Yet the self-conscious verbal engagement with the audience was missing, and this is, at least in part, because the music at Habesh was oriented more toward invoking Ethiopian aesthetics than toward creating new repertoire.

In light of "Tezeta"'s consistent popularity in Israel, an observer might recognize that ostensible nostalgia for life in Ethiopia is as much a commentary on hardship in Israel as it is an expression of longing for familiarity. Through wax and gold, words can stand in for individual concepts within a song, or hold several meanings at once for purposes of signification. Specifically among Azmaris, Menilek in particular invoked tezeta, memory of and nostalgia for the past, as a way of critiquing marginal status in Israel. Although many Ethiopian-Israelis would readily acknowledge that there is little for which to feel nostalgic in their former life as a "despised semi-caste" in rural Ethiopia (Quirin 1992: 3), they are equally aware of the obstacles they face in Israel (Weil 2004: 80–82). In the absence of explicit critique of Israel, the mention of tezeta in song lyrics serves to undermine adeptly the "Ein li eretz aheret" trope invoked by Daniel. By reframing life in Ethiopia as worthy of nostalgia—juxtaposing "tezeta" with "Ein li eretz aheret" as songs or as concepts—Ethiopian-Israelis develop an unspoken consensus that need never be expressed explicitly. The reinsertion of Ethiopian-Israelis into Ethiopian culture frames them as inheritors of the Habesha tradition of Ethiopianist myths, thus reconfiguring a key narrative of Israeli citizenship.

Repositioning Ethiopian-Israelis through judicious use of wax and gold might be considered what historian Steven Kaplan describes as "resistance behavior" (1999b). Kaplan posits that Beta Israel immigrants express their dissatisfaction in Israel through what he terms "everyday resistance" (Kaplan 1999b: 114). Contrary to a perception today that resistance belongs to the public sphere and takes the form of mass demonstrations (such as the mass protests in spring 2015), Kaplan examines nonspectacular, mundane individual acts of protest and subversion such as obdurate refusal to learn Hebrew on the part of immigrant adults in the intensive Hebrew immersion system (*ulpan*) and refusal to take on Hebrew names, or conversion to Pentecostalism among the Falash Mura new arrivals in the 1990s.[22] We may add to this list of methods the inclination to identify with Afrodiasporic and Caribbean culture (ibid.: 121, Ratner 2015). Kaplan suggests that such actions should be viewed as strategies adopted by a peasant underclass to insulate the group from a system perceived as socially and culturally destructive.

Kaplan's paradigm of everyday resistance is especially useful in thinking about the rationale behind aesthetic choices in the development of musical styles, and the African diaspora is full of examples of musicians taking the lead in everyday resistance. For example, Capoeira developed as a song-dance form blending codified but physically intensive mock fighting with minimal instrumentation in preemancipation Brazil (Fryer 2000). The resulting self-discipline and healing of the psychic scars of menial work eluded the taskmasters, who thought of it as "mere" folk dance. Azmari music hardly derives from such violent adversity, but the power of music to intervene in troubled lives is comparable, considering the dramatically high suicide rate among Ethiopian-Israeli men (Westheimer and Kaplan 1992: 113). The perceived loss of honor, the fulcrum of the kinship system in Ethiopia, has battered individuals' self-esteem and hope, but since musicians are held in higher regard in Israel than in Ethiopia, their actions and statements are taken seriously, translated into sociopolitical terms, and interpreted as signs and promises of future ascendancy.

I devote chapter 4 to the centrality of dance in Ethiopian musical performance, but in parallel to mentioning Capoeira, one might mention briefly the general absence of in-depth dance analysis in scholarship about Ethiopia. Yet Eskesta is a crucial facilitator of audience participation in Azmari performance. At Habesh, the arrival of Almaz, the dancer, usually demarcated the sedate early part of the night from the rowdy later segment. Early in the night, Menilek and Avi played instrumental sets, and Almaz came out to dance as the crowd built after 10:30 p.m. or so (Ethiopian audiences prefer to go out late). Almaz sang occasionally, but mostly she wandered around the restaurant bringing the audience members to their feet. She usually began by the stage, moving from table to table and coaxing an audience member to dance with her, especially any non-Ethiopian audience members (both to make them feel comfortable and because Ethiopians often find a feeble first attempt at Eskesta hilarious). Sometimes she managed to get a whole table to dance, but more often one or two people at a time. Dance was often segregated by gender and generation, middle-aged women only rarely dancing, but middle-aged men were much more active (indeed, middle-aged male patrons were more common in the restaurant in general). Older men usually danced with their shoulders, cheered on by their companions and the audience. Young men, on the other hand, tended to use their knees more, and they often gathered in a circle and clapped while bending their knees with hands on hips. Like Almaz, the young women used their shoulders and jumped more than the men did. In the background of my recordings one occasionally hears an audience member ululating, and this is usually the person who was dancing with Almaz.

Despite the apparent impact of Almaz's dancing on the audience—I can tell from an audio recording whether she was there or not based on the audience's participation—her position in the group often left me puzzled (I never found a discreet way to ask about it). She danced for virtually half the night; she was largely responsible for the level of audience participation; and she was always enthusiastically received. But when traffic was heavy in the restaurant, she also served drinks. I never saw Menilek or Avi serve a drink, and I doubt they would have agreed to do so. But in a typical Ethiopian breakdown of labor responsibilities, in which men's work and women's work are divided strictly (Weil 2004: 77), playing an instrument would count as men's work, and dancing counts as women's work alongside food service and preparation. While the climate of traditional music actively questions certain dominant-subaltern relationships, other standard delineations of value seem to persist.[23] Wax and gold might apply on a collective level, but there is little impulse to overturn entrenched gender hierarchies.

For dancers being asked to serve drinks, or for immigrants engaging in resistance behavior, the value of wax and gold as a rhetorical device is self-evident. For immigrants who feel indebted to the government, or who rely entirely on governmental discretion to permit their family members to immigrate, drawing attention to communal problems or to political grievances can have as deleterious an effect in Israel as it did in Ethiopia. Music, and the coded language that musicians are uniquely positioned to use, balance delicately a widespread desire for intracommunal solidarity and extracommunal awareness of Ethiopian culture. Zelelew, a young self-taught Azmari I worked with in Ashkelon, put it this way:

> Israelis already know about our culture. It's important that *we* won't forget it, that we all know that we have a wonderful culture too, and not that we came without culture [*banu bli tarbut*], I don't want it to be that way, that they just give us money and don't get to know us. Now, Israelis already know us, and they want us to perform. Really, they want to know this great Ethiopian tradition, and they're trying to take my group to other places.[24] For example, this troupe that I'm working with, it is a really strong group, and they dance like in Ethiopia, but in Israel. (interview, Ashkelon, June 22, 2009)

In a climate of widespread unemployment, musicians like Menilek and Zelelew recognize Ethiopian cultural achievement as a key strategy for upward mobility. Ethiopian-Israeli mobility derives both from the development of support networks—of which Habesh was important affectively if not economically—and from the validation of the wider Israeli institutional power structure that generally excludes Ethiopian-Israelis. For the citizens who are concerned that their critique will be met with government retaliation via punitive immigration-policy initiatives, the Azmari approach to public debate is a safe way to explore those critiques.

At Habesh musicians created the atmosphere of an Azmari-bet, often absent the Azmari's key method of improvising lyrics to mock audience members and patrons. I contend that the lyrical practice of wax and gold is practically redundant in the Israeli context because individuals have broadened the practice of wax and gold beyond the Azmari-bet into many aspects of their everyday lives. The utility of layering the meaning of speech is evident well beyond song lyrics, and the practice has become a staple of all kinds of everyday interactions as an intervention in Ethiopian-Israeli social problems. Whether through musical codes signaling Ethiopianist or Afrodiasporic belonging, or speech that obscures as much as it reveals, Ethiopian-Israeli musicians and their audience accept the power of wax and gold to ensure that their opinions can only be readily deduced by sympathetic interlocutors.

ETHIOPIANIST MYTHS AND MIGRANT CITIZENSHIP

Habesh blended the nostalgic performance style of the cultural restaurant with the wry critique of the Azmari-bet, creating a hybrid institution that was adapted to the unique sociopolitical conditions of Ethiopian life in Israel. Menilek and Avi's renditions of themes without words or popular folk tunes retained stock Azmari features like instrumentation (massenqo and krar), 6/8 rhythm, Eskesta dancing, and the frequent reference to tezeta, both in concept and repertoire. They rarely departed from a rigid formula and downplayed the most virtuosic improvisational element of Azmari music, the lyrics animated by wax and gold. Yet they invoked wax and gold in a variety of nonlyrical ways, whether through guarded multilayered forms of everyday speech or through disembodied musical references to Ethiopian nostalgia. Through a style that seemed traditional to the point of conservative, the musicians at Habesh offered a commentary on Ethiopian-Israeli status.

That commentary was rooted in the historical baggage of Beta Israel life in rural Ethiopia, cut off socially from and disparaged as sorcerers by their neighbors (Salamon 1999). Yet the Ethiopianist narratives of Abyssinian glory often highlight Judaic or Semitic roots of Ethiopian civilization, the "Falasha" frequently featuring as a curious religious minority in ethnographic studies of the multiethnic society (Levine 2000: 60–63). The *Kebra Negast* imagines a direct lineage to Jerusalem, and the abidingly popular reggae trend worldwide frames Ethiopia as Zion. The Ethiopianist myths of a literate, Christian, and self-governing past accommodate Jews and Judaism far more than an Ethiopian government has in recent memory. By highlighting those narratives, Ethiopian-Israeli musicians reconnect to a country they do not intend to return to, and do not remember fondly, but that serves as a useful foil to the Israeli society that so far sees little place for them as full participants.

Thus, nostalgia, dissonance, and subversion via wax and gold manifested themselves in subtle and sometimes surprising ways at Habesh as across Azmari performance in and around Tel Aviv. It is not just that Azmaris incorporate tezeta and wax and gold into their performance style; rather, Ethiopian musical concepts inform a widespread method of circumventing pressure to integrate into Israeli society. Mobilizing the key aesthetic components of Ethiopianist myths, performers propose a kind of citizenship where Ethiopian-Israelis play a central role in constructing national narratives, to which they can relate more readily than to a potentially alienating reality. In the process, they overpower the shame and loss of honor that result from being unable to integrate into an adopted society that has not yet fully embraced them, and create a sense of belonging to a place that they left eagerly.

THREE

Zionist Myths and the Mainstreaming
of Ethiopian-Israeli Music

It was usually easy to talk to Menilek, the krar player. He was good-humored, and since he spoke fluent Hebrew I often turned to him for questions about how "the community" felt about an issue. So I was especially surprised when his brow furrowed and he paused thoughtfully to word his answer. "Idan Raichel? He's huge. He's a giant. And he's been successful. But that happened on the backs of Ethiopian musicians, anonymous musicians, people who don't get any of the credit. That's no good for us" (interview, Tel Aviv, June 25, 2009). I had heard other Ethiopian-Israelis speak this way about Israel's multicultural pop band (the Idan Raichel Project) and its bandleader Idan Raichel, but I was surprised that Menilek was so emphatic. Indeed, he articulated a paradoxical attitude toward the Idan Raichel Project (henceforth IRP) that I have encountered repeatedly, expressed by musicians and nonmusicians:[1] that this progressive Israeli pop star, one of very few who have promoted Ethiopian-Israelis and their music and brought them into mainstream Israeli culture, is also resented by many within the group he has empowered.[2]

The first time I heard the IRP, in 2007, they were already established on the international tour circuit. I might have written them off at the time as a *Graceland* replica (on which more later), and I had no real intention of working closely on their music. Yet after I had spent some time in Tel Aviv, this multiethnic band became central to my research because of the IRP's role in shaping wider Israeli perceptions of Ethiopian-Israelis. As I went about my daily business in Tel Aviv, and told non-Ethiopian-Israelis about my research, I faced the same two questions, repeatedly and alongside each other. First, "So, are they really Jewish?" and, second, "Have you heard of the Idan Raichel Project?" I was already familiar with this trope from reading the work of Don Seeman (2009: 8), and in time I learned that these two disparate questions go together for many Israelis: that the acceptance of Ethiopians into Israeli society is contingent on their being granted religious legitimacy (which is, in some cases, still pending) and on patronage from popular culture. As a result, I spent a lot of time discussing and considering this band, especially as it relates to the Israeli population's awareness of Ethiopian-Israelis and the ongoing debate over the group's Jewish lineage (see Kaplan 1992, Seeman 2009, Shelemay 1986).

Questions over Ethiopian-Israeli religious authenticity work as a sort of spiral of suspicion. At one end, some rabbinic authorities do not accept the documentation of Beta Israel practice dating back five centuries because a five-century lineage fails to establish an original Jewish bloodline (it is not long enough in the span of Jewish history). At the other end, the suspicion that the Falash Mura have only returned to Judaism because of the material benefits of immigrating to Israel renders all Ethiopians suspect. In between, some Israelis wonder aloud how it is possible that Judaism reached Ethiopia, while others reject nonrabbinic Judaism and presume that the Ethiopians must have been practicing incorrectly. Israelis frequently conflate the cases, imposing the suspicion of Falash Mura on all Ethiopian-Israelis, and in the most extreme cases of prejudice they explicitly doubt that remote black Jews could really be connected to their own tradition.

It surprised (and irritated) me whenever I noticed that the question of religious authenticity remained unsettled, but even more so, that it was brought up in the same breath as music. I thought, naively, that people should be talking about representation, and how problematic unidirectional power relations are when one musician is earning an enormous amount of money and his studio musicians make much less. That Ethiopians were the target of critique in the construction of these conversations made little sense to me, and I wished that my interlocutors would scrutinize the recording industry as meticulously as they followed the politics of religious lineage.

My attitude changed one evening in AM:PM (pronounced "Am-pam" by locals), Tel Aviv's main supermarket chain. On Fridays around sunset, the radio station piped through the store plays Shirei Eretz Yisrael, the nostalgic Israeli pop genre from the 1960s (explained at length later on, referred to as SLI after the English translation of Songs of the Land of Israel). As I was bagging tomatoes, I heard the radio station transition from "Lu Yehi" (Israel's version of "Let It Be") through "Shir Moledet" (Song of the Homeland) to "Mima'amakim" (Out of the Depths), the IRP's 2005 hit. I had been so tied to the description of the IRP as a cosmopolitan fusion project that it had not occurred to me that the IRP's musical style draws directly from the nostalgic early Israeli popular styles, and incorporates several iconic ethnosymbolic myths into its portrayal of Ethiopians and Ethiopian culture. The band's importance unfolded before me: Israelis who still suspect that Beta Israel are not really Jewish, and wonder openly whether they should be entitled to the rights of citizenship, can see them as legitimately Israeli when they are represented in songs about love and land.

In this chapter, then, I examine the compositional strategies deployed in the IRP's Ethiopian-influenced songs to reconcile, at a symbolic level, Ethiopian-Israelis with Israeli society. The main dynamic driving the IRP's Ethiopian-influenced songs is a dialectic of nationalism and cosmopolitanism (Stanislawski 2001), in which Raichel, the founder-bandleader of the IRP, presents a multicultural State of Israel to international audiences but works to incorporate Ethiopian voices into the Israeli polity. To do so he evokes Zionist mythologies that are unpopular among much of his left-wing audience abroad, while also engaging a cosmopolitanism that ignores the significant power differentials between the groups whose voices he includes.

I will first consider the connection between song structure and performance practice, on the one hand, and nationalist — Zionist — mythologies, before considering those ideological strands within three Ethiopian-influenced IRP songs. By discussing song structure and lyrics I elicit symbolic "logics" at play, and contend that these bear upon composition in ways reminiscent of their analogues in social policy. First, I explore a logic of cosmopolitan nationalism that juxtaposes autonomous "local" and "foreign" musical units; second, a logic of "discrepant cosmopolitanism" (Clifford 1997: 36, Feld 2012: 231) that potentially misrepresents the power differential between cosmopolitan groups; and third, a logic of "diasporic intimacy" (Boym 1998, Feld 2012), a variation on localized nationalism that marshals the minority's sounds with a view to incorporating it into a national narrative (Bohlman 2004, Herzfeld 1997).

Despite what I perceive to be an overtly nationalist (albeit left-wing) agenda in his music, Raichel makes his points implicitly through his song style rather than through explicit political statements, and I interpret the songs largely on the basis of Lila Abu-Lughod's argument that we must look beyond the text and explore the national ideologies that a popular art form promotes through its "relationship to historical processes" (2004: 242). As such, I will refer only infrequently back to musicians like Menilek, since I focus primarily in this chapter on the "unanticipated global entanglements in contemporary musical life-worlds" (Feld 2012: 7) that stem from the IRP's hypersyncretic style. I describe the IRP's style as "discrepant cosmopolitanism" (Clifford 1997: 36, Feld 2012: 231), meaning that multiple types of cosmopolitans—travelers, immigrants, elites—are blended together as a homogeneous entity (Clifford 1997). The IRP's musical style does indeed mix the music and life narratives of Ashkenazi (Western European) Jewish elites, Palestinian-Israeli/'48 Palestinian minorities, and Ethiopian-Israeli citizens who arrived as refugees as a single cosmopolitan style, creating a multiethnic "utopia" in place of resistance. But I will demonstrate that the IRP's method of mixing together the musical styles and life experiences of demographic groups that experience citizenship and the movement of culture in dramatically opposing ways is a political strategy, and that Raichel makes stylistic statements in lieu of overtly political ones that reveal a commitment to ubiquitous Zionist myths and symbols—particularly "land," "return," and "safe haven"—and to utopian cosmopolitanism. In the process, Ethiopian-Israelis are drawn into nationalist narratives not as Africans in exile, but as Jews returning home (Kaplan 2005: 381).

NATIONALISM, COSMOPOLITANISM, AND INCLUSION

> "If six or seven years after the song came out, Ethiopian kids are
> still being barred entrance to schools in Petach Tikvah,
> then that's a failure of the Project."
>
> *Idan Raichel, Oslo, December 2008*

Idan Raichel, the IRP's founder, producer, and bandleader, first encountered Ethiopian music while working as a counselor in an Ethiopian-Israeli boarding school (*pnimiyah*).[3] Before forming the IRP, he was a familiar face around Tel Aviv's Ethiopian clubs and record stores. From that early involvement with Ethiopian-Israelis, he developed a respectable knowledge of Ethiopian music and an appreciation of Ethiopian culture that is evident in the IRP's albums: *The Idan Raichel Project* (2002), *Mima'amakim* (Out of the Depths, 2005), *Within My Walls* (2008), *Traveling Home* (2011), and *Quarter to Six* (2013).[4] In addition to songs in Arabic, English, and Spanish, each album features several songs in Amharic, or the occasional passage in Ge'ez. Since Raichel's multiethnic band released its first album, its lineup has included a handful of Ethiopian-Israeli musicians, the most prominent of whom are singer Avi Wassa and Cabra Casay, the band's talented and charismatic central singer.

By including Ethiopian-Israeli singers, as well as Palestinian Israelis like Mira Awad or Yemenites like the beloved deceased singer Shoshana Damari, the IRP appeals to a broad-ranging audience and manages to frame its members and musical creations in terms of coexisting subjectivities. Its audiences can be conceptualized as a set of concentric circles—each of which roughly corresponds to the geographical coordinates of listeners I encountered during fieldwork—the innermost circle representing the local, Ethiopian-Israeli audience, and the outermost, a transnational, non-Jewish audience. Each audience's reception of the IRP is made distinct by its social and political circumstances and cultural proximity to each of the band's constituent musical genres. At the center of these concentric circles containing Israeli ethnic minorities, the Israeli mainstream, Diaspora Jews in North America and Europe, and world music audiences abroad, sits Cabra Casay, who provides a prism through which we can untangle and appreciate some of the complexity of nationalism and cosmopolitanism in the IRP's local context.

How the IRP bears upon its audiences' perceptions is often a matter of how Casay is deployed in concerts. She is nearly always center-stage, comprising a de facto contact zone (Pratt 1991, Feld 2000), and a disproportionate amount of the IRP's visual and promotional material is devoted to the story of her birth in Sudan during her parents' journey to Israel. This story, particularly with regard to the work of Gadi BenEzer (2002), bears the characteristics of a classic Exodus narrative and resonates with the Zionist/Jewish narrative of aliyah (return to the Holy Land) and assimilation into Israeli Jewish society.[5] This representation of Casay appeals directly to the Jewish narrative of home and exile, creating cultural intimacy (Herzfeld 1997, Stokes 2010) between her and Jewish/Zionist audiences through the mechanism of "diasporic intimacy" (Boym 1998: 499, Feld 2012: 204–205).[6] Indeed, Casay has told interviewers that the Israeli Jewish part of her identity is most salient.[7] In exploring the content of the IRP's Ethiopian-influenced songs together with an attempt to represent the Israeli population as cosmopolitan, we see the impulse to argue for the unity of the Jewish people, blurring the lines between nationalist and cosmopolitan agendas through the mechanism of Zionist mythologies of home and return.

Yet as Casay's role in the band expands to encompass singing in different languages, and indeed in her attempts to break out as a solo artist, she portrays multiple identities, including that of African icon. The same week that I ran into

Casay at an Ethiopian music festival in Paris in February 2011 (Webster-Kogen 2013: 156), she performed onstage with Abd al-Malik, a tremendously popular Muslim French rapper of Congolese (Brazzaville) descent.[8] As she makes new contacts as an Afrodiasporic musician and world music star, it is likely that the next stages in Casay's career will see her refashioning her artistic persona to appeal to diffuse transnational audiences in the outer circles of the IRP's fan base.[9]

Thanks to this expanding international profile, Casay is a potent symbol of achievement, a source of collective pride and prestige, and a cause for hope, even among the Azmaris like Menilek who are displeased with apparent power imbalances within the IRP. These achievements notwithstanding, Casay continues to answer to Raichel, and as with other "unilinear" (Stokes 2004: 57) world music projects, the discrepancies of power between majority-group leaders and subaltern members raise issues of curtailed agency. One might consider in particular the sometimes contradictory and oppositional implications in an endeavor like the IRP, in which diversity and elite status can be easily confused despite the fact that cosmopolitan hybridity often results from the merging of migrant or subaltern groups (Clifford 1997: 37, Feld 2012: 231).[10] As musicians from different national and ethnic backgrounds create new syncretic musical styles, it can be easy to forget the set of highly unequal power relations (globalization, colonialism, diaspora) that brings them together.

The appearance of equality is important in the band as long as Ethiopian-Israelis remain at the bottom of the Israeli social ladder, with problems of generational strife, crime, depression, and suicide (Elias and Kemp 2010, Seeman 2009) dominating most media coverage about them. Raichel provides a rare example of an ostensibly nonpolitical spotlight on Ethiopian-Israelis, in contrast with ongoing emotional public debate over Ethiopian immigration, lineage, and citizenship. Uri Ben-Eliezer refers to the commonplace denigration of Ethiopian-Israelis that stems from the accusation of religious illegitimacy as "everyday cultural racism" (2008), and I see in the IRP a modest attempt to present a more positive image of Ethiopian-Israelis and to "shape nationalist imaginaries" (Abu-Lughod 2004: 8). Considering that popular prejudice influences the political realm in Israel-Palestine (described vividly by Brinner 2009: 3–4), the image of Ethiopian-Israelis portrayed by the IRP's songs may even influence the outcome of the debate over whether prospective Falash Mura immigrants are granted the right to settle in Israel. Therefore, since the IRP potentially influences public opinion about Ethiopian immigration, the IRP's musical style—mediated by a non-Ethiopian—addresses subjectivities of citizenship explicitly.

So far, though, observers recognize that the disparity in power relations be-tween the IRP's participants is replicated in its reception among the majority of Israelis and its popularity among Ethiopian-Israelis, who have thoroughly internalized the logic of representation but are largely indifferent to the positive image of Israel the band projects. Young Ethiopian-Israelis generally listen to Afrodiasporic popular music like rap and reggae instead (see Shabtay 2001, 2003 for comprehensive work on the subject, or Ratner 2015: 74–79 for an analysis of why young people prefer rap over reggae or vice versa), or to Ethiopian music they download from the Internet. They tend to identify with the experience of other displaced young black people worldwide, and do not listen to Israeli music for the most part. As David Ratner explains, they often are not exposed to even the best-known national musicians (2015: 63). Instead, most Ethiopian-Israelis, irrespective of strictures of social identity, such as language, religion, date of immigration, age or national origins, participate at communal events in Eskesta (see chapter 4) accompanied by a massenqo, and listen to the wildly popular songs of Mahmoud Ahmed (classic) and Teddy Afro (contemporary). They ap-pear to be unaffected by the IRP's international acclaim, given the population's fragmentation, and one might note that the scholarly literature contributes to this fragmenting by engaging an identity politics that divides Jewish and Christian; Israeli-born and immigrant; Beta Israel-Falash Mura; or Hebrew-speaking/ Amharic-speaking Ethiopian-Israelis (BenEzer 2002).[11] In this local context of exclusion, disillusion, and fragmentation, virtually all public performance of music plays into a communal narrative of empowerment. Hence it may not be surprising that in addition to rap and reggae, the younger generation's taste veers toward material that sits astride the linguistic gap between Amharic, the language of their parents, and Hebrew.[12] It is perhaps not coincidental, then, that IRP lyrics are sung in Hebrew, while Ethiopian songs are sampled by the IRP in Amharic (or Ge'ez), framing language as an index in popular music of an immigrant group's class perception and/or collective identity (Ho 2003: 149, Hutchinson 2006).

Given the contradictions at work in representing Ethiopian-Israelis to the wider Israeli public, one could be forgiven for finding the overall dynamic in the IRP confusing, in part because the Project's appearance, public statements, and musical content demonstrate an "embrace of oxymoron and contradiction" (Feld 2012: 231) that epitomizes discrepant cosmopolitanism. However, while Clifford's and Feld's ideas are critical of obliviousness to power differentials, Raichel has made discrepant cosmopolitanism work for him as an effective strategy toward revealing an agenda while avoiding the quagmire of the Israeli-Palestinian conflict. He tours internationally, and generally is not subject to boycott. Circumspectly, Raichel has eschewed the role of political activist, or even propagandist, that left-wing musicians in Israel often occupy (Brinner 2009: 153, Swedenburg 1997).[13] By steering clear of the conflict, Raichel has distanced himself from the perception of Israeli culture that is tainted by the occupation, which partly explains his success in developing a fan base among North American and European world music fans. To listeners in the Jewish Diaspora, especially those involved to varying degrees with Israeli society and politics, the effect of seeing Arabs, Ethiopian-Israelis, and non-Ethiopian-Israelis onstage together has a poignant, bittersweet quality. Jewish listeners in the Diaspora, particularly those of a progressive bent, have embraced the band's multicultural and ostensibly nonsubversive style, interpreting the band's diverse makeup as a utopian vision of Middle Eastern cosmopolitanism.[14] On the transnational level, the presence of Ethiopian-Israelis in the band's seven-member core has afforded the IRP a gloss of diversity that supports the marketing of Israeli music to an audience that might otherwise be unsympathetic. Since band members and song style are translated directly into political terms, such as the descriptions of Raichel as a "one-man Middle East peace accord," one might reasonably interpret the IRP's performance practice as political strategy as well.[15] Therefore, a close reading of musical structure, style, and lyrics can help us unravel the connections between musical sound and political processes, or the way the IRP addresses immigrants and minorities like Ethiopian-Israelis in the process of political enfranchisement. Above all, I contend that through musical gestures toward nationalism and cosmopolitanism, Raichel frames Ethiopian-Israeli citizenship within a set of Zionist mythologies of home and return.

While this chapter's discussion focuses primarily on the aesthetic choices the IRP makes to fuse Ethiopian and Israeli popular music, the conventions of tonality, language, sampling, and instrumentation exhibited in these songs function as a barely perceptible yet unmistakable statement of nationalism and cosmopolitanism. I do not argue that Raichel is an activist like other left-wing musicians (see Brinner 2009), but his fusion techniques reveal an agenda through which he projects himself as progressive, inclusive, cosmopolitan, nationalistic, and communally oriented all at once. His efforts address the complex web of Ethiopian-Israeli social problems and identity issues connected to their idiosyncratic migration story and to attributions of racial difference. So while my predictions about the IRP's future impact are modest, one might keep in mind that Raichel could turn out to be an important agent for overcoming Ethiopian-Israeli disjunctions of citizenship. And although Ethiopian-Israelis might not pay his music much attention in their daily lives, the IRP's music is a dominant vehicle for touting Zionist myths in the construction and articulation of an Ethiopian-Israeli citizenship.

ETHNOSYMBOLISM OF LAND, RETURN, AND HAVEN

A dialectical engagement between Zionist, Ethiopianist, and Afrodiasporic mythologies is a key tension in Ethiopian-Israeli music and social life. This book makes the case that the interaction and conflict between the narrative strategies represents a battle among Ethiopian-Israelis for a definition of citizenship, namely the tension between returning "home" as Jews, joining an African diaspora, or reinserting themselves into a national narrative of the country they left. And indeed, rather than pitting the different strands against one another, these strategies often work in tandem. Ethiopian-Israeli musicians shape their performance style around the framing of citizenship narratives, and the story of their journey from Ethiopia to Israel advocates explicitly for inclusion of Ethiopians within the twentieth century's history of the return to the Holy Land from exile. The IRP's songs touch on this narrative in lyrics and promotional material, but the adaptation of Zionist myths by the IRP is varied and diverse, and the music of the IRP draws from the spectrum of nationalist myths so as to advocate for the inclusion of Ethiopians in Israeli society. In this part I will highlight a few of the main strands of Zionist history that revisionist historians call myths and that I contrast with Afrodiasporic mythologies as a narrative strategy.

Without defending the violence and occupation that comprise some of the political and religious manifestations of Zionism today, one might note that Zionism is a serious political ideology with an interesting history. In contrast to its public image today as a hegemonic regional force, Zionism's intellectual history in the prestate era—roughly 1860, with the publication of the first books about Jewish self-determination by Leon Pinsker and Moses Hess, to 1948—offers a fascinating window into the internal debates among Diaspora Jews over how to achieve self-determination (see Hertzberg 1960 for a compilation of primary sources, or Brenner 2003 for a much briefer overview). A main debate over the tenets of Zionism, at the most basic level, is a disagreement throughout the 1890s between Theodor Herzl and Asher Ginsberg, known as Ahad Ha'am (Shapira 1992: 6–7), over the condition of exile. The former, widely credited as the founder of "political Zionism," believed that the Jews would always be marked as different in Europe, and that a secular, possibly German-speaking state, inspired by the French Revolution, would serve as a safe haven for Jews escaping European antisemitism (Avineri 2013: 131). Ahad Ha'am, on the other hand, is credited as a founder of "cultural Zionism," and he advocated the promotion of the Hebrew language and a (secular) Jewish culture that would curtail Jewish vulnerability to assimilation. This fundamental disagreement, over whether antisemitism or assimilation posed the greater existential problem for the Jews of Europe, converged around the intention of cultivating the "empty" (see Eyal 2008: 81) land of the Bible collectively as a way of earning redemption from the indignities of exile (see Laqueur 1972: 589).

The values that came to be called myths by revisionist historians in the late 1980s are examined by Amnon Raz-Krakotzkin: "Images of return, of the ingathering of the Diaspora, and the construction of the Temple had always preoccupied the Jewish imagination. Nevertheless, the formulation of the elements in modern romantic terminology and their adaptation into modern Western discourse of progress gave them new meaning of the formulation of Jewish-messianic discourse as a modern political myth in modern political terminology" (2013: 54–55).

This formulation can be put more succinctly as the "return to history" (*hashiva lahistoria*), "return to the land" (*hashiva l'Eretz Yisrael*), and "negation of exile" (*shelilat hagalut*)" (2013: 38). The tripartite articulation of values formed the cornerstone of Zionist thinking, which only adapted moderately once the state was established. Today's offshoots of Zionism (religious, revisionist, and even post-Zionism) pivot around the reconfiguration of the main point of convergence between cultural and political Zionism forged from the 1890s.

By the late 1980s, a new generation of critical historians and social scientists making use of recently declassified documents were willing to question the core tenets of Zionism. Jaded by what the Israeli left generally perceived to be a false set of excuses for the continued occupation of the Palestinian territories, scholars identified a set of myths that comprise that main point of convergence from early Zionist intellectual history: land, text (Bible), return, and safe haven. Scholars from the many different schools of Israeli historiography basically agree on the main principles of Zionism that are now called myths. Mainstream Zionist scholars such as Anita Shapira, or the immediate predecessors of the New Historians such as Shlomo Avineri, set out the main ideas of the State of Israel as "Land; return; 'Jewish self-identity'" (Avineri 1981: 3–4). In the hands of the New Historians, these values are described as myths, and among post-Zionist and anti-Zionist waves of Israeli historians today, the myths are judged as misguided but are described in much the same language.

Each of the songs described in this chapter addresses at least one of those main themes that I might contrast with Afrodiasporic myths. As I describe the cosmopolitan musical style in each of the IRP's songs including Ethiopian textual content, I highlight the inclusion of each standard myth. In sum, I contend that the Ethiopian source material—the cosmopolitan element of Raichel's compositional style—is a gloss that ultimately serves a nationalist narrative.

STRATEGIES OF NATIONALISM AND COSMOPOLITANISM

The IRP's Ethiopian-influenced songs enact three broad sets of musical influences, each of which takes a turn as the dominant style in the three songs highlighted in this chapter. The first influence for examination is the Hebrew-language genre of Songs of the Land of Israel (SLI), an often mournful, communally sung Hebrew ballad style that focuses on natural imagery and homage to the land (Regev and Seroussi 2004). SLI dominated the Israeli recording industry through the late 1960s and roughly constitute the canon of early-state Ashkenazi popular material.[16] The second influence is Ethiopian folk, pop, and paraliturgical music, which in Raichel's hands is treated as a single unit of decontextualized signifiers of exoticism or "schizophonic mimesis" (Feld 1996). The third influence, a somewhat amorphous style occasionally known as "world beat," has been well documented in the literature (Feld 1996, 2000, Stokes 2004, Taylor 1997). The IRP combines these musical influences to create a multicultural "melting-pot aesthetic" (explained by Brinner 2009: 215 and Seroussi 1986) that has exceeded expectations in international record sales and in critical and national commercial success for an Israeli band.

The IRP's financial success and the unidirectional benefit to Raichel demonstrates the perils of world music collaborations as the convergence of migration, globalization, and power (Stokes 2004). Since the onset of the debate over collaboration via the seemingly universal scholarly panning of Paul Simon's *Graceland* (Keil and Feld 1994, Meintjes 1990), scholars have issued strongly worded critiques of hybridity and cosmopolitanism in popular music (Ballantine 2004, Greene 2001, Turino 2003), and one possible way of interpreting the

IRP is through Sydney Hutchinson's condemnation of these products as "post-modern pastiches" (2006: 37). Another reading might frame the IRP against a backdrop of national identity and nationalist ideology, insofar as Raichel draws Ethiopian-Israelis into Israeli narratives of cultural intimacy (Stokes 2010). A third interpretation of the IRP, which combines the postmodern pastiche with a recognizably nationalist style and with source material from migrant minorities, might be understood equally as a case of discrepant cosmopolitanism, a set of performance practices that serves a strategy.

Through a close reading of the Ethiopian samples, SLI influences, and Zionist rhetoric, an aesthetic of homogenization-heterogenization emerges that characterizes much of the world music market. I explore political agendas that are channeled through aesthetic choices, using three well-known songs from the IRP's repertoire: "Mima'amakim," "Bo'ee," and "Berakhot Leshanah Ḥadasha" as case studies. In "Mima'amakim" (Audio file 8), SLI influences point to a continuing progressive commitment to land and text; "Bo'ee" (Audio file 15) employs a discrepant cosmopolitanism that acknowledges power differentials among contributors to a hybrid product, and Israel's position as a haven for those diverse subjects; and "Berakhot Leshanah Ḥadasha" (Audio file 16) makes a case for acceptance of Ethiopian-Israelis into world Jewry, invoking familiar Zionist tropes of collective return or the "ingathering of exiles" (*kibbutz galuyot*) (Brinner 2009: 307; explained by Smith 2004: 88–89).

"MIMA'AMAKIM": LAND AND TEXT

"Mima'amakim" (2005) is the title song from the IRP's second album that catapulted the band onto the world music scene. The song is noteworthy because it combines nationalist and cosmopolitan elements, such as a biblical-style passage in Hebrew; an Amharic-language chant; and a seven-person band few of whose members share a mother tongue to produce a song that seems to have internalized a "vernacular cosmopolitanism" (Feld 2012: 229), or a method of blending that makes the Ethiopian and Israeli components blend seamlessly with one another. However, peeling back the Amharic-language sample that cuts in and out, the listener is left with a nostalgic song of love and land that might fit in the preimmigration heyday of SLI. Indeed, Raichel adeptly draws from a fount of musical symbols and literary allusions that Israeli listeners can identify as belonging unmistakably to the Zionist narrative of cultivating the land. Therefore, Raichel's deployment of a borrowed Ethiopian vocal passage presents an approach to the state that is, though potentially inclusive and progressive (Ben-Rafael 2007, Resnik 2006), in fact rather conventional, drawing from the most standard myths of nation-building.

Raichel employs new technology (like sampling) to blend musical styles, but the aesthetic he looks to for inspiration comes, in a sense, from the 1970s. One might describe the IRP's overall sound as the "melting-pot aesthetic," a multiculturalist impulse toward syncretism (Brinner 2009, Regev 1996, Regev and Seroussi 2004). Less a fixed musical style than a set of fusion strategies, the trend in the recording industry from the 1980s was to blend ostensibly contradictory styles of European and North African/Middle Eastern music (and, once the peace process commenced, local Arabic music) as a way of showing solidarity between different groups (Brinner 2009: 88). Although the notion of national solidarity remained largely veneer rather than reality in Israel (Shafir and Peled 2002: 2), the melting-pot aesthetic remains a key strategy in the representation of immigrant groups within the Israeli national narrative.

The song structure of "Mima'amakim" implies "vernacular cosmopolitanism" (Feld 2012: 229, Werbner 2006: 497): the song alternates between a passage in Amharic and an Israeli pop-song structure of verses and chorus sung in Hebrew. These two components share equal importance and, for analytical purposes, should be considered together since the Amharic sample and the Israeli song structure form the aesthetic statement that I interpret as a progressive strand of nationalism via vernacular cosmopolitanism. This narrative can be teased out through the signifiers dispersed through the song that signpost Zionist themes of land and text at key moments and "ethnic" quality at others. Raichel incorporates enough characteristics from SLI to render them recognizable to anyone familiar with the style.

As a broad genre, SLI contain three crucial characteristics as explained by Regev and Seroussi (2004: 60): first, the mournful lyrical quality that refers obliquely to the Bible and/or agriculture. Second is the "woman of the land" paradigm prevalent in early Israeli songs, represented in lyrics sung by a man to a woman, or more obviously in the figure of Cabra Casay standing silently at the microphone in the song's music video.[17] Third, "Mima'amakim" incorporates minor-mode musical conventions reminiscent of Eastern European folk song. These three influences emerge as the dominant components of the song's structure.

"Mima'amakim" begins with a forty-five-second recording of Amharic, accompanied by percussion. The song, "Nanu Nanu Ney" (Audio file 7), is the same covered by Ester Rada. A male voice chants the words "Nanu Nanu Ney," the opening from the original by Muluken Melesse. This introductory segment, the song's most important signpost, recurs between verses. Young Ethiopian-Israeli listeners may recognize "Nanu Nanu Ney" as a hit from the Swinging Addis of the 1970s, their parents' generation (though their parents were rural). For a young Ethiopian-Israeli hearing "Mima'amakim" for the first time (or for a musician like Menilek), Raichel's tribute is a welcome sign of cultural recognition in Israel—a sentiment expressed repeatedly to me by Ethiopian-Israeli teenagers who nevertheless would not buy an IRP CD or attend a concert.

Following the song's initial "Nanu Nanu Ney" section, Raichel switches into Hebrew for the main body of lyrics. The four-to-eight-measure sections cut in and out with a four-measure chorus while the "Nanu Nanu Ney" sample is recapitulated, and Raichel's treatment of the transition from Amharic sample to Hebrew verse reveals an attempt in "Mima'amakim" to work with the source material as it is. While the vast majority of Raichel's songs are written in 4/4 with a clear duple pulse, most Ethio-jazz written in 6/8 has a clear triple pulse, and we will see in later examples that Raichel addresses the challenges of triple meter or triplets through engineering. In this example he does no such thing, leaving the original sample more or less intact. That Raichel works around the original version rather than engineer the tempo to suit him may indicate a desire to incorporate the Ethiopian influences in more than a cosmetic manner.

In the verse that follows the Ethio-jazz-adapted chorus, the melody and lyrics produce the sentimental effect of SLI-style musical conventions. In the early days of the fledgling State of Israel, song style was suffused with nostalgia; most immigrants of the era arrived from Eastern and Central Europe, and national song style emulated Central and Eastern European melodies. Israeli demographics shifted with the influx of Middle Eastern and North African Jews in the 1950s and 1960s, and other musical styles (Israeli rock and *musiqa Mizrahit*, the Israeli-produced popular music of Mizrahim) rose to prominence (Horowitz 2010, Regev 1996). By the 1980s the national music scene came to accommodate the tastes of an increasingly diverse population through its production of Mizrahi music, but SLI left a lasting mark that is discernible in contemporary Israeli music (Regev and Seroussi 2004). Early Israeli music alluded frequently to the land and to the pioneering experience, and stressed the capacity of both to bring about collective emancipation. SLI helped construct a national narrative as an alternative to religion for the Israeli-born and made secular use of biblical imagery, which was used to develop the idea that nation-building brings redemption. SLI are still so widespread that everyday activities in Tel Aviv like riding the bus and sitting in a cafe guarantee some exposure to the standards.

An Israeli, Ethiopian, or European listener can detect the vernacular cosmopolitan blend between the entrenched SLI style and the conspicuously signposted "exotic" elements throughout "Mima'amakim." An initial reaction to the song may be that the Ethiopian influence sounds strongest, but even a minimal lyrical analysis will bring out the song's heavy SLI imprint. Following the Amharic-language introduction, the song switches to Hebrew language and accordingly, SLI images and themes:

Mima'amakim karati eilayikh,
Bo'ee eilai,
Beshuveikh yaḥzor shuv
ha'or be'einai
Lo gamur, lo ozev
h'amaga beyadayikh
Sheyavo veya'ir lemishma
kol ts'hokekh
Mima'amakim karati eilayikh,
Bo'ee elai, Mul yare'aḥ
meir et darkekh shuv eilai
Nifresu venamsu
mul maga shel yadayikh
Be'oznayikh loḥesh sho'el
Mi zeh koreh lakh halaila,
Hakshivi
Mi shar bekol eilayikh el ḥaloneikh
Mi yasim nafsho shet'hi me'usheret
Mi yasim yad veyivneh et beitekh
Mi yiten ḥayav,
yasimam mitaḥtayikh
Mi ke'afar leraglayikh yiḥyeh
Mi yohavekh od mikol ohavayikh
Mi mikol ruaḥ ra'ah yatsileikh
Mima'amakim

Out of the depths I called out to you,
come,
Your return shall rekindle
the spark in my eyes
Neither done nor forsaken
the touch of your hand
To the sound of your laughter
shall glow here again
Out of the depths I called unto you
come, 'neath a moon
that shines brightly your way back to me
Spread out and melted
to the touch of your hand
In your ear whisper, ask again
Who is it that calls out to you tonight,
Listen,
Who sings aloud under your window
Who stakes his soul just for you to be happy
Who'll lend his hand to build you a home
Who'll lay his life down
Who, like the earth at your feet, shall live on
under your footsteps
Who'll love you better than all your lovers
Who'll save you from the rage of the storm
Out of the depths.[18]

While the song expresses no overtly religious attitude, "Mima'amakim" exemplifies at once both the melting-pot aesthetic and the continuing influence of the canon of SLI songs. From the lyrics one may infer a debt to the Bible and an even stronger one to the modern state, a connection made naturally as nationalist discourse in Israeli poetry (Kartun-Blum 1999: 3).[19] The song's title and first line quotes Psalm 130 ("A song of ascent, as I call to you, Lord, from the depths"), and the imagery refers indirectly to Song of Songs 8:13: "O you who linger in the garden . . . Let me hear your voice" that is evoked in Raichel's words "Who sings aloud to you under your window." Meanwhile, the reference to building a house resembles Zionist metaphors of land and family, strongly reminiscent of the paeans to the land that abound in SLI lyrics such as the words to Shaike

Paikov's standard song performed by singer Ilanit, "Eretz Eretz Eretz" or "Land, Land, Land" (Audio file 17).

While these SLI characteristics are readily discernible, the nostalgic style on its own would not be commercially desirable because young Israeli listeners might associate it with political isolationism and militarism. In its updated, cosmopolitan, and above all, progressive form, "Mima'amakim" offers a bohemian, open-minded cover to a progressive yet ultimately mainstream worldview. The song's Ethiopian sample is deployed to counteract the potentially saccharine quality of biblical allusion. Therefore, the image of the State of Israel presented in "Mima'amakim" might be somewhat more diverse than the Zionism of SLI's infancy, which presumed Ashkenazi dominance within domestic power relations, but "Mima'amakim" integrates minorities into the Zionist vernacular.[20] This aesthetic and performative strategy safeguards the IRP against the conventional critiques of Zionism as insular and exclusive, but remains connected to mainstream nationalist ideologies. The incorporation of Ethiopian-Israelis into the national narrative therefore broadens the conception of who is an insider in a nation that defines itself in exclusive terms.

THE HAVEN MYTH: "BO'EE"

Ethiopian Christian musician Alemu Aga chants his paraliturgical "Tew Semagn Hagere" in a meditative vocal style with a buzzing, almost organlike accompaniment (Audio file 18). A female voice recites an Amharic passage solemnly. A melody riffs on Aga's Éthiopiques staple with a distant air. A drum turns the Ge'ez chant's swinging syncopation into an easy-to-follow 4/4. Then comes the chorus, with the singer's pleading voice, in Hebrew.

In 2003, the song "Bo'ee" (Come with Me) hit the Israeli airwaves and introduced to the mainstream a population overlooked by the Israeli world music market. Thanks to "Bo'ee," the wider Israeli population came to recognize a previously unconsidered fact: Ethiopian-Israelis had a culture of their own, worthy of recognition alongside the myriad musical styles in record stores.[21] The existence of this song made a case to the radio-listening public that Ethiopian immigrants might constitute a useful addition to a cosmopolitan nationalism (Turino 2000: 4–7). "Bo'ee" has remained the most widely recognized song in the IRP's repertoire since the initial broadcast and it was among the first Ethiopian-influenced songs offered up for popular consumption. The song's commercial success, however, masks the cultural contradictions of living as an Ethiopian-

Israeli, encapsulated in its awkward synthesis of Ethiopian and Israeli musical elements. The stylistic mixing represents an undermined myth of Israel as safe haven (commonly referred to by Israelis as *eretz miklat*) for Diaspora Jews.

At first glance "Bo'ee" seems to be thoroughly syncretic, since it incorporates multiple and sometimes opposing traits from liturgy (Aga's sample) and pop to create a sound that might be described as ethno-pop. Perhaps most important here are the iconic nonverbal sounds (e.g., groans, ululation) that can be separated from traditional source material and that a songwriter adds to render the "exotic" recognizable (Meintjes 1990: 46). These iconic nonverbal sounds delineate for all of the IRP's different audiences the "exotic" parts of the song.

At the same time, "Bo'ee" makes a strong statement in its song structure that evokes an Ethiopian-Israeli crisis of citizenship. A moment of transition in the song's third minute encapsulates the disjunction between the Ethiopian and the Israeli components of Raichel's song particularly poignantly. After the "Ethiopian" section chanted by Alemu Aga gives way to an unnamed/uncredited Ethiopian-Israeli female singer speaking in Amharic (see Raboteau 2007: 73–74 for the speaker's perspective), we experience a pregnant pause before transitioning to the "Israeli" section of the song marked by singing in Hebrew. The first section, with Aga's voice and the large ten-stringed beganna he plays (usually played in an unofficial/paraliturgical capacity during Lent), juxtaposes with the "Israeli" section comprising a Hebrew-language pop song played on Western instruments.[22] Raichel joins the two sections together through percussion and harmony, but the sections are too clearly delineated to suggest substantial contact between the segments. Indeed, the contact zone between the Ethiopian and the Israeli components of the song is the moment of transition, and this is a moment of sonic segregation. This tension works aesthetically for world music audiences but it rings terrifyingly true to the reality of life for Ethiopian-Israelis, whom Israelis classify as "Ethiopian" but whom Ethiopians classify as "Jewish" (Westheimer and Kaplan 1992) with the two subjectivities too often meeting only through a hyphen.

The Ethiopian section of the song from "Tew Semagn Hagere" possesses plenty of credibility as a stand-alone to world music audiences. The beganna looms large in Volume 11 of the Éthiopiques series (entitled *The Harp of King David*), thus bestowing on the instrument and the Ge'ez language some high-art panache. The beganna's warm, quiet, and buzzy sound, together with an anhemitonic pentatonic scale and cyclical meter, lend to the opening strains of "Bo'ee" the pulse of Ethiopian church music. However, the sample in "Bo'ee" offers a different

FIGURE 3.1 "Tew Semagn Hagere" melody, performed by Alemu Aga

FIGURE 3.2 "Tew Semagn Hagere" in "Bo'ee"

metrical effect to a listener who is accustomed to Raichel's compositional style. Raichel chose a sample from the fourth minute of the seven-minute "Tew Semagn Hagere" (at 3' 50") and he engineers the sample. Alemu Aga plays a swinging, syncopated six-note cycle, with the second and fifth notes shorter than the other tones (figure 3.1).[23] In "Bo'ee," however, the rhythm has obviously shifted. Upon first listening, one cannot discern whether Raichel lengthened the second and fifth notes to fit a more obvious duple meter or simply shifted the bar line by adding percussion instruments to drive the rhythm. The difference, however, is not insignificant (figure 3.2). Raichel has fit the "Tew Semagn Hagere" sample into a framework of eighth and quarter notes to work convincingly in duple meter. In both renditions the third note in the cycle holds longest, but the length of the first two notes equals the third. One notices the difference in speed when playing the two simultaneously.

So a structural reading of "Bo'ee" shows the song's sections to be disconnected, both linguistically—Ge'ez giving way to Amharic, which gives way to Hebrew, with neither mixed together—and stylistically, reflecting Raichel's decision to accommodate better the song's Ethiopian component into his 4/4 framework. In a sense, Raichel's structural delineation of Ethiopian sounds resembles symboli-

The Mainstreaming of Ethiopian Israeli Music **97**

cally the fraught sociopolitical context in which Ethiopian-Israelis are poorly integrated into society (again, see Abu-Lughod 2004: 242). The musical structure replicates the set of power relations in Ethiopian-Israeli daily life whereby incorporation into the broader culture happens through the beneficence of an established, progressive patron. The contact zone that is the transition from one musical style to the next encapsulates James Clifford's explanation of "discrepant cosmopolitanism," in which "such cultures of displacement and transplantation are inseparable from specific, often violent, histories of economic, political and cultural interaction" (1997: 36). The potentially emancipatory aesthetic hybridity of "Bo'ee" appeals strategically to international cosmopolitan audiences. In this regard, I might classify "Bo'ee" as part of what Vertovec calls a transnational "mobilizing structure" (2003: 654) since it produces cultural products that draw from multisited "social networks, social capital, embeddedness" (Vertovec 2003: 659).

The musical transition in this third minute of "Bo'ee" ends with the song's lyrical section, in which Raichel sings to a girlfriend about the need to depend on one another in the context of an interracial relationship. Imploring the girlfriend, "Tni li yad veneilekh / Al tishali oti le'an, al tishali oti al osher" (Give me your hand, and we'll go / Don't ask me where, don't ask me about happiness), Raichel promises a protection that cannot possibly be assured. The song's lyrics mimic the dynamic of the song structure, replicating the myth of safe haven—of people in society, of the ease with which cultures can integrate—and promising that the reliance of a subaltern on a more powerful Ashkenazi interlocutor is a safe gamble. However, Ethiopian-Israelis have learned in the past thirty years that this is not a secure gamble after all, and although Raichel assures his fictional partner or his real-life bandmates that everything will be fine, his Ethiopian interlocutors' lived experience demonstrates otherwise. The idiosyncratic song structure and the more explicit lyrics offer up the same nationalist myth, the myth of the safe haven, but the song's dramatic irony is that a critical listener can recognize with skepticism the myth that Raichel offers up eagerly.

The major intervention of "Bo'ee" in a discussion of minority citizenship is not its capacity to empower Ethiopian-Israelis, but the way it exemplifies the intractability of power differentials, whether on the level of a song or a society. Ethiopian-Israelis face this lack of integration in their everyday lives; they enjoy civil rights and serve in the military but often remain on the sidelines in Israeli culture. "Bo'ee" deploys discrepant cosmopolitanism as a means through which to navigate a seemingly unnegotiable politics of privilege and exclusion.

"BERAKHOT LESHANAH ḤADASHA":
JOURNEY AND RETURN

Although "Bo'ee" was the first IRP song to hit the domestic airwaves, Idan Raichel opened his first album (released in 2002) with a selection that pays equal homage to Ethiopian culture. "Berakhot Leshanah Ḥadasha" (Blessings for the New Year) never achieved the status of "Bo'ee," and has taken on a life of its own in performance, highlighting the political efficacy of the IRP's inclusion of Ethiopians in narratives of home and return. In analyzing "Berakhot Leshanah Ḥadasha" and its concert-circuit counterpart, "Back to Jerusalem" (Audio file 19), I suggest that Raichel frames Ethiopian culture in Israel through the key Zionist principle of *kibbutz galuyot*, the "ingathering of exiles." Articulated by Friesel (2006: 297) as the closely associated term *shivat Tziyon*, or "return to Zion" (a potentially controversial term because of its connection with Zion*ism*), *kibbutz galuyot* expresses the nationalist cornerstone that all Jews return home from exile when they arrive in Israel. The focus on the "ingathering of exiles" trope evokes a sense of "diasporic intimacy" (Feld 2012: 205) whereby Ethiopian-Israelis become more Israeli by connecting to longstanding Jewish narratives of escape from the uprootedness of diaspora.

Like Raichel's other Ethiopian-influenced songs, "Berakhot Leshanah Ḥadasha" begins with a short Ethiopian excerpt, in this case a five-second-long massenqo solo. This iconic nonverbal sound announces the non-Israeli timbre of the song. But this is where the similarities with the Project's repertoire end; the song is unique in Raichel's material as it contains a disparate set of auditory references alongside a rough melody that many Israeli listeners would not associate with mainstream pop music. Nevertheless, it represents a good-faith attempt at fusing different cultures.

After the opening snippet, the song sets into a speedy pace driven by a synthesizer playing a slow ostinato, creating a trancelike effect, while what sounds like a krar plays a fast 6/8. This rhythm remains steady throughout the song, while Raichel layers a series of lyrical samples above it. At three points in the song—approximately once per minute—the music is interspersed with a Moroccan rendition of the New Year's liturgy. These are blessings from the Musaf (additional) service on Rosh Hashanah (the Jewish New Year), some of which are specific to that service, such as Birkat Hazikhronot (the New Year's blessing), and others that are generic and used frequently during festivals and daily life, such as

Sheheḥeyanu. Two additional melodic elements add to the lyrical interest of the song. The song has no lyrics apart from the liturgical samples, and Raichel does not sing himself, but his keyboard backing plays the six-note ascending melody without harmony. On top of Raichel's keyboard, an opaque and trancelike male voice intones throughout the song in a nonlyrical Ethiopian vocal style. If one adds to this intonation Mizrahi liturgy and Western instrumentation masquerading as lyrics, the effect may be somewhat jarring for Raichel's international listening demographic, a speculation that is confirmed by the complete absence of the song in its current form on the concert circuit.

Compared to Raichel's other slick and polished songs, this song sounds like a demo tape (which it was originally), yet it also sounds, if anything, more like the sort of music one hears in an Azmari-bet precisely because the sound is unpolished. The aesthetic particularity explains why the song has not gone on to enjoy the commercial success that more exportable songs have. I have never heard the song mentioned by anyone, whether Ethiopian-Israeli, non-Ethiopian Israeli, or American, as a favorite, and it has been replaced on the concert circuit by an imagery-laden version called "Back to Jerusalem." The revamped song might be more easily marketable to international audiences since its lyrics are in English, but the change is disappointing because "Berakhot Leshanah Ḥadasha" demonstrates a unique attempt on Raichel's part to shape his song around the original source material, a process for which we might borrow the term "cosmopolitanism from below" (Feld 2012: 295). In "Berakhot Leshanah Ḥadasha," although the Ethiopian elements sound jarring alongside the non-Ethiopian constituents, their relationship to each other and to the overall structure is inventive and telling. The transformed song, on the other hand, has been hybridized for live performance to much success, and today the song is performed onstage to lyrics that tell a story in English of the journey "from the mountains of Gondar . . . to the refugee camps in Sudan . . . back to Jerusalem." This version sometimes includes a shofar onstage (the ram's horn that is used as a sacred instrument in the autumn festivals) and all of the backup singers, including Cabra Casay, sing Raichel's keyboard part as an ascending minor scale in unison.

Formally, some obvious characteristics make "Back to Jerusalem" more easily marketable to world music audiences. The English lyrics might be considered an overture to the liberal American audiences who, according to Tudor Parfitt (1985), were instrumental in lobbying for Ethiopian immigration in the 1980s. The second formal characteristic that differentiates the song's earlier and later (or recorded versus live) iterations is vocal, with the ensemble rather than the keyboard carrying the main melody. "Back to Jerusalem" is built upon verses with English lyrics and a chorus sung by the ensemble, whereas "Berakhot Leshanah Ḥadasha" offers no such easily identifiable song structure for a cosmopolitan listener. European and North American listeners who drive Raichel's international fame might be able to identify a melody more readily in the structured English version than in the amorphous Hebrew rendition.

In terms of the agenda they put forward, the two songs are actually very similar; both frame Ethiopian Jewish culture within a trope of home and return through lyrical structure and content. In the original version, it is up to the listener to draw conclusions through Raichel's placement of samples. In the revamped version, however, the discussion is overt and easy enough for any local, regional, or global audience to understand since the lyrics are written in basic English, with little attempt to follow the lyrical/poetic conventions that Raichel follows in other songs. Although I prefer not to presume Raichel's motives, it seems that "Berakhot Leshanah Ḥadasha" subtly intervenes in the controversial argument over Ethiopian Jewish religious legitimacy, i.e., "whether or not they are Jewish," that I encountered nonstop during fieldwork. Raichel gives equal weight to the Ethiopian and Mizrahi/Israeli segments of the song, alternating between the massenqo, the blessings, and the Ethiopian vocal without asserting dominance of any element. The sounds are jarring to me and to the audiences for whom I have played the song, but I would say that the Mizrahi/Israeli and the Ethiopian components contribute equally to the song's auditory confusion.

In the case of Ethiopian and Israeli cultures, this comparison is expressed in the progressive unfurling of the song. The three sections—the opening massenqo motive, the cacophonous Jewish Ethiopian middle sections, and the Hebrew blessings—place Ethiopianness and Jewishness on an equal level. Within this scheme, I deduce *kibbutz galuyot* (the return of Diaspora Jews to Israel) insofar as Raichel sets Ethiopianness alongside Jewishness instead of using the Ethiopian component as relief against the song's pop structure. Therefore, in this modest and undervalued song, Raichel begins his producing career with an attempt at "cosmopolitanism from below" (Feld 2012: 295) through a composition that follows his source material even if it leads to a song structure that his audience finds challenging and unappealing. There is much more to this song than samples and blessings, though; Raichel implicitly ascribes dignity and equality to an immigrant minority, thereby using those samples and blessings as a strategy whose results become political. The difference between the two versions of the song comprises aesthetic choices about instrumentation and lyrics, but these choices reveal a strategy by which Raichel argues to a global audience that Ethiopian-Israelis share with all Jews a common narrative, one of diasporic intimacy and return.

In all three examples, the characteristics that make Raichel's popular songs dialectical and often challenging are his Ethiopian samples, particularly the Azmari or Ethio-jazz source material that navigates the terms of Ethiopian-Israeli otherness. Through structure and lyrics, and the public portrayal of Cabra Casay, each song presents a cosmopolitan Israeli body politic, but the nationalist current of the IRP's music is equally important. Raichel lays out the tropes of the mainstream narrative—what Israeli historians call "Zionist myths," and which one can contrast with the schizophonic invocation of the African diaspora and Ethio-jazz across this book's source material. He does so by deploying a series of aesthetic strategies that reveal a progressive, cosmopolitan nationalist agenda valuing the return of the Jewish people to the biblical homeland, which they cultivate in exchange for safe haven.

The main fault line of Ethiopian-Israeli citizenship, whereby Ethiopians have little control over the nationwide acceptance of their legitimacy as Israelis, comes out frequently in this chapter's songs. On the surface, each song might appear to offer a "unilinear" view of appropriation (Stokes 2004) in which Raichel borrows an Ethiopian sample and splices it into his own Hebrew-language song. That dynamic suggests a parallel with the civic status wherein Israelis decide whether or not Ethiopians are legitimate citizens according to their own opinions and not by the strict criterion of owning an Israeli passport. Yet a wider view of the three songs together reveals the same impulse replicated: Raichel borrows Ethiopian source material, followed by a hybridized song sung in Hebrew and performed in a generic pop style by an Ethiopian-Israeli singer, sometimes with additional source material mixed in later. Ultimately, each song enacts a dynamic of interaction between an Ethiopian-Israeli person and an Ethiopian song text, making the stage quite literally a contact zone, where a cosmopolitan citizen confronts her own "diasporic intimacy" (Boym 1999: 499; Feld 2012: 204–205). Despite my unease that this top-down process limits agency for Ethiopian musicians, I interpret this method as a progressive political statement, advocating a utopian, integrated image of a conflicted nation.

In a sense, the interpretation of Raichel's Ethiopian-influenced songs presented in this chapter disputes the assumptions of both the popular press that ascribes real-world political powers to him, and of the academic debates that are so critical of homogenized world music products that might reasonably associate the IRP with projects like *Graceland*. Rather, these three Ethiopian-influenced songs are not so much the product of a worldview as they are a strategy that Raichel deploys on behalf of his utopian brand of cosmopolitan nationalism. Through samples and snippets, he channels his appreciation of Ethiopian culture as a mechanism for pushing a nationalist narrative of home and return. Ultimately, Raichel provides the backdrop before which Ethiopian-Israelis can experiment with Zionist mythologies as part of their own citizenship narrative, connecting them to the nation through the juxtaposition of Ethiopian samples and SLI musical structure.

FOUR

Embodying Blackness through
Eskesta Citizenship

From the train station: the train comes every forty minutes. Transfer to local bus 7, which should take about fifteen minutes. Getting off at Tchernikovsky, turn left and follow it around to Ben-Gurion. After three blocks, you should see the walls. Go through security and ask for the activity room (moadon). Must leave by 9:45 p.m.

Living in Tel Aviv and attending live Ethiopian musical performances wherever I could find them, I assembled an admirable collection of post-it notes with directions and reminders about how to reach a community center, which extra precautions I might have to take, and what time I would have to leave to make the last train home. The centrally located Levinski Street in south Tel Aviv is a welcome hub of Ethiopian soundscapes, but the vast majority of the Ethiopian-Israeli population lives in far-flung suburbs and small cities, and I would have had to spend substantial time commuting to them. Going for an interview during the day was easy enough, but an event in the evening (without a car) could have been an undertaking, requiring of me the inconvenience in reverse of what Ethiopian-Israelis experience when they commute to major cities. I worried about highlighting the community center's remoteness, and disliked making excuses for leaving early. "I have to catch the last train" might as well have meant "You live too far from the action," and I would dread the moment when an event was heating up and I had to depart. However, experiencing this inconvenience-in-reverse gave me a sense of what it meant to live at the geographical margins of

Israeli society, which affected my experience of the events themselves. After a period of attending event after event that, for reasons that eluded me, always seemed to involve a dance troupe, I realized, as if it had been obvious all along, that dancers were enacting that marginality with their bodies.

After attending a variety of events at community centers, I identified a familiar formula that took some time to parse. First, an Ethiopian-Israeli community leader—maybe a Qes (an Ethiopian cleric) or a school principal—would step up to the stage and make a short speech about communal achievement and incremental integration. Next, a young leader would be introduced, and he (usually he) would say a few words about his dance troupe. Then the dance troupe of about ten members would come out and dance Eskesta, the Ethiopian national shoulder dance, to prerecorded music, often consisting of popular standards from the Ethiopian repertoire.[1] One rarely heard a word about racism or exclusion, or even about Israel more broadly, but an invisible collection of Israeli interlocutors guided the structure of the event, and the subtext of the complete lineup constituted what Brenda Farnell terms the "agentive production of meaning" (1994: 931), or the establishment of consensual narratives by Ethiopian-Israelis. By unpacking three vivid examples of public events that mix celebration with Eskesta dancing, this chapter describes the mechanism through which Ethiopian-Israelis reconfigure the myths discussed in the preceding chapters as what Terence Turner terms an "embodied process of formation" of citizenship (2011: 103)—the negotiation of the terms of citizenship with their bodies. Eskesta's centrality at Ethiopian-Israeli communal events illustrates the daily embodiment of otherness that hints more at an attempt to construct alternative citizenship narratives than at an explicit lamentation of racism. Therefore, this chapter discusses the workings and dynamics of the Ethiopian-Israeli population much more than the previous chapters.

This chapter will leave a technical analysis of Eskesta's unique movements to dance scholars like Ruth Eshel, whom it will quote. But the movements are immediately recognizable because of the centrality of shoulder movement (together with neck and upper back/shoulder blades), often accompanied by jumping or twisting in place. I will describe different configurations of dancers (individual, paired, or in groups), audience participation (formally staged, fully collaborative), and level of virtuosity and athleticism, but they all practice variations of Eskesta since they are performing a shoulder dance set to Ethiopian music. The meaning of Eskesta's ubiquity at communal events is the main subject of concern.

PERFORMING MYTHS

In the previous three chapters, I identified a typology of myths that Ethiopian-Israelis mobilize creatively to build alternative citizenship narratives to the state's mainstreaming efforts. First, Afrodiasporic myths of kinship through blackness, and a reimagined Ethiopian-Israeli participation in the black Atlantic through African American music and reggae, portray idealized images of blackness among the Israeli public, ascribing cultural capital to certain black citizens through musical credibility. Second, Ethiopianist myths of a glorious if selective Ethiopian history, in which Beta Israel were actively involved rather than resolutely excluded, frame Ethiopian-Israelis as central characters in Afrocentric ideologies. Third, Zionist myths of home and return identify the Ethiopian migration story as part of the ingathering of exiles (*kibbutz galuyot*), a biblical exodus of fulfilling collective destiny. Ethiopian-Israeli musicians perform, repeat, and reconfigure these three myth clusters across a wide variety of musical styles, in each case adapting them through repertoire, language, instrumentation, and tonality. Certain genres inspire specific adaptations: reggae is Afrodiasporic, while Azmari music is Ethiopianist. However, Eskesta dancers do not speak or sing, their aesthetic and ideological positionings transpiring entirely through their bodies. Rather than offering a unified mythological message, dancers reconfigure the myths in multiple ways. Therefore, this chapter presents the myths as they are remixed for a national (Israeli) public, often combined in subtle ways to establish what Carol Kidron terms an "embodied-memory" of historical baggage (2011: 452).

This chapter examines Eskesta performance as a prism through which to interpret the entangled workings of the Afrodiasporic, Ethiopianist, and Zionist myths, which are refracted through the multiple uses of dance in communal and national public celebration. Eskesta dance in Israel constitutes what Tomie Hahn, in a different context, calls the "interface between body, self, and the world" (2007: 3), performers using their bodies to navigate their multiple, complex subject positions in Israeli society. Navigating the invisible presence of iconic Ethiopian musicians and of community workers who are well-meaning but often unsympathetic to Ethiopian-Israeli struggles, Eskesta dancers mobilize the bodies that are conspicuous on the Israeli street as a mechanism for negotiating a troubled and ruptured history of otherness in Ethiopian society and the Jewish world. In the process, some of them manage to propose positive alternatives to hyphenated citizenship.

My exploration of Eskesta involves a close reading of three events. First, I describe a book launch at the high-prestige Inbal Center for Ethnic Dance in Tel Aviv that features the Beta Dance Troupe, a Haifa-based group that tours internationally. Second, I examine the Eskesta stage at Sigd, the most important Beta Israel festival, which is celebrated today as a national holiday in Jerusalem. Third, I unpack a graduation ceremony at an absorption center in Ashkelon, a small coastal city near the border with Gaza. Each of the seemingly disparate events bears similar structural characteristics: the celebration of the success of a social project; Eskesta as the performative centerpiece of the evening; and the intervention of Ethiopian media (through prerecorded repertoire) and Israeli state apparatus (through top-down discourses of belonging). I argue that the three seemingly disparate events mobilize "the body as body politic and individual signature" (Dixon Gottschild 2003: 8), at once circumventing explicit engagement in identity politics but inhabiting the complexity of Ethiopian-Israeliness thoroughly.

REPERTOIRE: THE PROBLEM WITH PRERECORDED MUSIC

In this chapter's exploration of the sociopolitical agendas showcased in Ethiopian-Israeli dance, I identify some repertoire by name and refer to other songs generically as "Eskesta dance music" or, where applicable, Ethio-jazz. Indeed, in the limited case of public Eskesta performance, specific repertoire is often less important than the iconic sonic background of Ethiopian tonality (based on qignit) and instrumentation (including krar or massenqo, or drum machine or synthesizer). My evidence for this assertion is that despite the importance of traditional instruments in the public performance of Ethiopian music, virtually every dance troupe I encountered was accompanied by prerecorded music imported directly from Ethiopia. The complex dynamic of using prerecorded music as part of an embodied "agentive production of meaning" (Farnell 1994: 931) reveals an acknowledgment of creative debt and homage to Ethiopian culture for musicians often working to integrate into Israeli society.

Before examining the styles of prerecorded music favored by the dance troupes, I should briefly mention a paradox of Ethiopian musical performance that partly explains a relative absence of scholarly literature on Eskesta. On the one hand, urban Ethiopians consume live music eagerly, eschewing many of the styles that require extensive interaction with prerecorded music. Hip-hop, for example, is far less influential a domestic style in Ethiopia than in neighboring

East African countries (see Eisenberg 2012 or Perullo 2011). Because audiences place a premium on music performed live, sample-based music (see Katz 2012 or Schloss 2004) and sound systems are often dismissed in the vein of cassette culture (see Manuel 2003, or Horowitz 2010 for an Israeli case study) that is disposable and not very creative. Therefore, accompaniment to projected pre-recorded music is afforded little prestige.

At the same time, Ethiopian audiences in Israel display a preference in the way they talk about music for material that leaves a textual record, i.e., music that can be distributed digitally. Audiences enjoy live music, but they would not list Azmaris or Qessim (Hebrew plural for Qes, a Jewish cleric) as their "favor-ite" musicians. Inevitably, discussion about Ethiopian music steers quickly to contemporary Ethiopian pop, the music that has been most widely circulated internationally. Even my massenqo teacher Fantahun's list of favorite musicians was overwhelmingly focused on Ethio-jazz and contemporary pop: Tilahoun Gessesse, Tewodros Tandessa, Mahmoud Ahmed, Teddy Afro, Eshet Belaw, Hamra Mola, Malkamu Tacheche, Chachi Tedesse, Hirut Bakele, Fikri Addis, Hae Manut Grema, and Melesse Ashamaw (interview, Jerusalem, June 29, 2009). These were musicians we might know already from hearing their recordings. The focus on musicians who produce an album overlooks certain types of (usually self-taught) performers, and particularly dancers. Although the dancer at an Azmari-bet does not contribute to a transcribed document, she (often she) is directly responsible for eliciting enthusiasm from the audience. And scholarly emphasis on text further downplays the importance of dance, the one musical arena in which women are well represented.[2] When a distaste for prerecorded music is combined with the indifference displayed toward dance as text, we identify an atmosphere in which dance performed to prerecorded music gener-ates minimal cultural capital despite its ubiquity in public performance (not to mention its gestural iconicity).[3] The result is a scholarly presentation of Ethio-pian music that overwhelmingly ignores Eskesta while frequently mentioning its uniqueness.

Ethio-jazz, and its stylistic descendants like the contemporary Ethio-pop music of Teddy Afro (who has visited Israel for concerts multiple times) or Gigi, remains the dominant musical style projected during set breaks in the *Azmari-betotch* (plural for Azmari-bet) in and around Tel Aviv. Much of the music identified and described in this chapter comes from the Ethio-jazz-related song style from the Derg and post-Derg period, the era of Haile Selassie's ouster.[4] The prerecorded music in this chapter thus invokes affects of nostalgia and rupture.

In the case of the Beta Dance Troupe's performance, the particular Aster Aweke recording in question was recorded the same year as Operation Solomon (1991), and the recordings used by the troupe Inyalinya are more contemporary recordings that are popular in Addis Ababa now, and that use technology like drum machines. When I refer to the repertoire specifically, it will be to understand how musical choices engage the dance troupes' perspective on integration and citizenship.

ESKESTA AND THE "BLACK DANCING BODY"

Within the different cases of dancing Eskesta to prerecorded music, one finds a constant of enacting personhood through one's body and through the "iconic" sounds enumerated in the previous chapters. What gives Eskesta its urgency, though, is its physicality, through the emphasis on disciplining the body that the massenqo, use of tezeta as repertoire and concept, and wax and gold as a subversive lyrical-literary device do not give. Terence Turner's work on the Kayapo of Central Brazil interprets the subject-formation potential of embodiment metaphorically: "In sum, bodiliness includes the animal and cultural aspects of the body, and beyond the body as a singular object, its relations with other bodies, its processes of formation and disintegration, objectification, deobjectification, and the construction of subjectivity and of intersubjective relations" (2011: 117).

My interpretation supports Turner's: the fact that every Ethiopian-Israeli public event that I have attended includes a speech about communal progress, followed by group Eskesta dancing, indicates a cathartic, affective mobilization at play in this embodied musical practice. Indeed, dancing Eskesta—using one's body and drawing attention to "those same qualities that were repulsed [and] were also desired" (Dixon Gottschild 2003: 5) by "white" society—appears to be an effective tool for appealing to the Israeli public.

Meanwhile, Eskesta dancing serves as a de facto initiation ritual, as children learn the stance—shoulders bent forward slightly, hands on thighs, arms bent at the elbow while leaning forward and bending the knees—as soon as they can walk. This Eskesta stance can be applied to any kind of Ethiopian secular music, and one becomes conditioned to shake one's neck and shoulders when any kind of Ethiopian music is playing. Individually, these separate acts of playing prerecorded music and dancing Eskesta take place at virtually every Ethiopian-Israeli establishment or event. The combination of the two components, however, seems to be necessary at these special events where a troupe is brought out to complement a ceremony honoring communal progress. In this act, a troupe and its audience address the recognition of a "mimetic subaltern" self (see Taussig 1993), that is, a self who is conscious of all of the contradictions within Ethiopian-Israeli identity, and who actively draws attention to the bodily otherness that makes Ethiopians conspicuous in Israeli society.

While I mention scholarly literature on embodiment only briefly in this chapter, I will frame it within the affective turn in the humanities, to which scholars such as Matthew Rahaim (2012) and Ruth Hellier-Tinoco (2011) have made timely contributions from ethnomusicology. These scholars join a lineage in the discipline from Roman-Velazquez, who discusses how bodies are trained to move, determining that movement is an identity marker rather than biological impulse (1999: 117), to McDonald, who argues that for adolescent Palestinian boys, scars left by Israeli soldiers are a ticket to adulthood and a symbol that they are resisting occupation (2010: 197). While I would scarcely compare the treatment of Palestinians in the West Bank to that of Ethiopians in Israel, the public performance of national-ethnic consciousness delineates the "embodied process of formation" of subjectivity (Turner 2011: 103). Embodied performance demands the communal embrace of the physical markers that render a group other.

In the attempt to understand how the common practice of dancing Eskesta to prerecorded music propels the reconstruction of Ethiopian-Israeli citizenship narratives, I will describe these three performances in which the body serves as a sociopolitical battleground, and in which the complexity of Ethiopian-Israeli social status is demonstrated, performed, and challenged through the mimetic act of dancing to prerecorded music. As per Lisa Blackman, "The 'turn to affect' has become a factor for these debates to take form, particularly as they intersect with the question of how to understand the role of the body and embodiment within processes of subjectification" (2012: xi). This chapter addresses discussions of embodiment to illustrate a coded set of statements about skin color and alterity through Eskesta. While many Ethiopian-Israelis avoid charging Israelis explicitly with racism and prejudice in everyday conversations (or at least they did prior to the social protests in spring 2015), they have embraced Eskesta as the agentive process of displaying the body that others them. In Eskesta performance, the "black dancing body" (Dixon Gottschild 2003) takes up Blackman's process of subjectification.

INVISIBLE INTERLOCUTORS

The apparent musical influence on the Beta Dance Troupe, Sigd, and Inyalinya is Ethiopian culture writ large via Amharic-language popular music. By incorporating this repertoire, dance troupes demonstrate renewed solidarity with Ethiopian popular culture, however narrow an image of diverse Ethiopia that may constitute. Less obvious, though, is the influence of an invisible set of Israeli interlocutors, and I will briefly outline those figures from the Israeli power structure to whom the dance troupes are reacting. Some of those interlocutors are directly responsible for structural discrimination against Ethiopian-Israelis, while others are well-meaning community workers who engage in an ineffective strategy toward integration, and a few mediators are directly responsible for the dance troupes and the promotion of Ethiopian culture in Israel. Crucially, these interlocutors feature heavily in my encounters with this chapter's dance troupes, as gatekeepers and mediators about whom Ethiopian-Israelis often have mixed opinions.

First among outside influences is the State of Israel, whose wide reach affects most aspects of Ethiopian life. The rabbinate, administered by the state, determines who is Jewish, and sometimes who is permitted to immigrate (Seeman 2009, Shafir and Peled 2002, Shapira 2012: 459), and presides over life-cycle events (Ethiopian clergy will come up in this chapter's examination of Sigd). The military enjoys virtually universal participation among male Ethiopian youths, who serve in the highest proportion among population groups (ibid.) The school system, like the military, aims to mainstream Ethiopians into Israeli life (Herman 2012: 7, Shapira 2012: 459). And absorption centers house the new arrivals, often for years (Herman 2012, Shabtay 2001). Whereas Russian-speaking and ultra-Orthodox subcultures in Israel live as virtually parallel societies to an imagined, Hebrewist mainstream (Shafir and Peled 2002, Shapira 2012), Ethiopians interact with the state apparatus at virtually every level of daily life (to say nothing of the police force). In the eyes of that state apparatus, Ethiopian-Israelis are among Israel's most prominent others, and while they cannot change their skin color, the state often encourages changes of name, family structure, language, and religious affiliation (Seeman 2009). Whether an individual wishes to be considered a Jew, an Israeli, an immigrant, or an other largely depends on the positioning in these qualities.

A subset of interlocutors in communal affairs is the army of professionals employed, by the state or by nongovernmental organizations, to work with Ethiopians, whether as social workers or youth workers or advocates or, in some cases, as academic researchers who double as advocates. Now that a generation of immigrants has attended university, some of these community workers are themselves Ethiopian. A particularly effective example is Tebeka, a legal advocacy group in Rehovot that educates Ethiopians about their rights (see Weil 2004: 82 for further examples). Gadi BenEzer, a prominent psychologist in Beta Israel studies, is a board member, and it was at his book launch that the Beta Dance Troupe performed. In a small, vulnerable population, the overlap between state, advocacy, and cultural endeavors is substantial. Likewise, the dance troupe Inyalinya rehearses in Beit Gordon, the absorption center where the dancers live, and the Beta Dance Troupe rehearses at the Neve Yosef Community Center in Haifa. Arts organizations and advocacy groups feed into one another, and they are both often answerable to the state for funding, which is a problem insofar as their mingling tends to reinforce a top-down integration framework (Shapira 2012: 459–60).

The result of a seamless exchange of professionals between the military, the academy, and absorption centers is that the people who advocate for Ethiopian-Israelis overwhelmingly tend to do so through the discursive mechanism of framing them as Jews like any others who deserve equal treatment (see BenEzer 2002, Kaplan, Parfitt, and Trevisan Semi 1995). In order to confirm this narrative, scholars may present the Ethiopian migration story as a Zionist homecoming narrative of return from exile, thus comparing them to other "long-lost tribes" (Shapira 2012: 459). While I can hardly find fault with the advocates who use the resources at their disposal to combat discrimination, one cannot help but notice that the Israeli public is unconvinced, and the state apparatus remains skeptical of the Ethiopian contribution to a productive industrialized nation. Therefore, I interpret some aspects of Eskesta performance as a dynamic response to a stagnant integration policy, and in the descriptions that follow, dance troupes reframe Afrodiasporic and Ethiopianist myths in the context of home and return.

THE BETA DANCE TROUPE: PERFORMING THE JOURNEY

December 7, 2008, Tel Aviv

Book launch. Dance performance. Community event. The setup is familiar. First a community leader addresses the auditorium about how special and important the occasion is. Then a comedian jokes about his experience at boarding school, making an inside joke about acronyms at yeshiva that I was pleased to understand.[5] Next the author talks about the subject of the book, the journey narrative of Ethiopian migration to Israel. Finally, he introduces the entertainment. Four female dancers come out; they have their heads covered. The music starts and their set begins, and the concert hall is filled with the sound of Aster Aweke.

Gadi BenEzer's book *Hamasa* (The Journey, 2008) argues that "the journey" from Gondar to Israel defines the Ethiopian-Israeli experience predominantly, even more than skin color (2002, 2005). *Hamasa* is oriented toward an academic audience, but it is readable for any educated Hebrew speaker, and it posits that the trip to Israel through the Gedaref refugee camp (Sudan) is a marker of danger and bravery for a group often dismissively described as economic migrants. Implicit in this retelling is an Ethiopian contribution to the "ingathering of exiles" (*kibbutz galuyot*) that transpired in the decades after the State of Israel was established. The centrality of the journey narrative in Ethiopian-Israeli experience is replicated in the evening's entertainment, a short performance by the Beta Dance Troupe, whose repertoire includes a reenactment of the journey. Based, like *Hamasa*, on collected life narratives, the Beta Dance Troupe in its 2008 iteration is mediated through an Israeli gatekeeper who advocates for the canonizing of the journey narrative. Through the book launch-dance performance, the reenactment of the Ethiopian journey appropriates a top-down citizenship framework from Zionist mythology as a means to renegotiate Ethiopian otherness. While Israeli facilitators of this narrative advocate integration, they somewhat ironically dictate the terms of Ethiopian storytelling.

The Beta Dance Troupe is undoubtedly the most polished Ethiopian dance troupe in Israel, earning international acclaim in the past decade as it has toured the Americas. Until 2011 the troupe was managed by Haifa-based dance scholar Ruth Eshel, and today it is managed by renowned multimedia Ethiopian-Israeli artist Dege Feder (and along with the management change, the troupe is now called the Beta Dance Company). Despite the pedigree, though, its origins are modest. When Beta Israel immigrants arrived in Haifa in 1991 via Operation Solomon, they were living in "caravans" (a Hebrew euphemism for trailers) on the outskirts of town. Eshel spent many hours among the new immigrants, studying their distinctive body movements. She soon formed a troupe at Haifa University, initially called the Eskesta Dance Theater, composed of students from around the country. The troupe has undergone cast changes as dancers have graduated and moved on, and the repertoire has expanded into other East and Central African dance forms. Beta (as it is sometimes known for short) performed to great acclaim in Ethiopia in April 2009. As Eshel explained:

We did three concerts there; we were based in Addis Ababa, and there were a lot of music students there, and there was a lot of original music that we did. The students there were really thirsty for what we were doing, and they requested copies of the music, they wanted to listen to it .... We did one concert for really the Ethiopian cultural elite, and they said to me, "You did it," and [they asked] how did I get their roots, and how did I get their culture. I was really relieved by that because there are people in Israel who say that I don't do that, especially older people say, "What have you done to our dance? We don't recognize this dance." So for me it was important that the Ethiopian cultural elite would think that I had done it the right way, that I hadn't distorted it. (interview, Haifa, June 4, 2009)

The warm welcome in Addis Ababa offered confirmation that the Beta Dance Troupe's experimental style was appreciated alongside their more conservative material. The troupe's repertoire is a source of some trouble for Ethiopian audiences in Israel: Beta performs a diverse prerecorded repertoire, a mélange of Ethiopian traditional (Azmari) and popular standards (such as Aster Aweke songs) and jazz- and "ethnic"-style compositions by Israeli composers Oded Zehavi and Deganit Elyakim.[6]

The "ethnic" and "avant-garde" direction of the troupe dictated the evening's venue: the Inbal Center for Ethnic Dance is part of the prestigious Suzanne Dellal Performing Arts Center in the historic south Tel Aviv neighborhood of Neve Tsedek. Neve Tsedek is the oldest neighborhood in Tel Aviv (beyond the borders of the much older city of Jaffa), and having gentrified in recent years, it is full of sushi restaurants and renovated townhouses. It has no visible Ethiopian population.[7] In other words, it is a world apart from migrant-dominated Levinski Street, which is only a fifteen-minute walk away.

At the launch of *Hamasa*, Beta performed several of its best-known works, including "Opus for Heads." This five-minute routine is performed by four seated women, who "talk" to each other using their heads and shoulders, while Aster Aweke plays in the background (Audio file 20). Eshel's choreography innovates on Eskesta motions, as per her intention to "deconstruct and reconstruct" Eskesta dancing (interview, Haifa, June 4, 2009), but the musical accompaniment is recognizably Ethiopian—the song "Kezira," from Aster Aweke's 1991 album *Kabu*. This selection comes from rather late in the process of Beta Israel migration, the same year as Operation Solomon. The song emanates from an era of transition and hardship for Ethiopian-Israelis: many Beta Israel who remained in Ethiopia following Operation Moses in 1984–1985 had fled Gondar and were living in Addis Ababa at this point.[8] And while Aweke's music is a cosmopolitan product recorded and distributed in the United States, it is closely connected to Azmari music. In the performance's multiple versions online, one can discern at least half a dozen characteristics of Azmari music.[9]

To begin, we hear the main motive in the first three measures of Aweke's solo. Aweke sings a hemitonic pentatonic scale, in this case C D E G A C, probably the most common major pentatonic tuning. Her vocal quality is quintessentially Ethiopian: high-pitched and making extensive use of the vocal ornamentations (such as ululation) practiced in the Horn of Africa, demonstrated in a descending pattern. More influence comes from Ethio-jazz in the form of heavy emphasis on brass that often substitutes for the chorus in a call-and-response pattern with the soloist. Additionally, the alternation between Aweke and her backup singers is characteristic of Ethio-jazz, as is the alternation with a male voice that joins after the second chorus. This male vocalist sings an ascending five-note modal melody just as an Azmari would, and as the krar would do in most recorded versions of the song "Tezeta." The ascending exposition of the main motive is a quintessential Azmari vocal characteristic, as is its descending contour. At the beginning of the song, Aweke ascends and descends quickly. Nevertheless, a chorus of singers is on hand to descend with her so that the descending quality is apparent. The Beta Dance Troupe adds Eskesta dancing to the live performance of the prerecorded song to bolster its essential Ethiopianness, using their heads, shoulders, hands, necks, arms, and abdomens extensively.

Despite a rather avant-garde take on Eskesta in "Opus for Heads," the performance is unmistakably Ethiopian. There is nothing about it that designates it as distinctly Beta Israel, in contrast to the reenactment of the journey in the fifty-minute *Maharo*, which Beta has performed widely across the United States. The reenacted journey in *Maharo* is the one portrayed in *Hamasa*, namely the 1984 descent from Gondar that culminated in Operation Moses. Operation Moses is the moment in Ethiopian-Israeli migration that is imprinted indelibly in the minds of Beta Israel immigrants (*olim*) and world Jewry. Its story is dramatic, and although the majority of Ethiopian-Israelis were not directly involved (it brought eight thousand Ethiopians to Israel), it remains the dominant migration story.[10] However, among Israelis and across the Diaspora, the heroics of the journey are often attributed not to the Beta Israel who risked their lives to cross dangerous terrain (as many as a quarter of those who attempted the trip did not survive it), but to the State of Israel that saved them from starvation. *Hamasa* reconfigures this narrative, portraying the journey from the perspective of the Ethiopian protagonists.[11] Conveniently, the narration of a collective trauma fits into the stories of generations of Jewish immigrants desperate to leave their lives in exile, and in BenEzer's telling, Ethiopian-Israelis are the heroes, their sacrifice portrayed within a recognizable Zionist framework.

BenEzer's narrative was championed early by Tudor Parfitt (1985). In this version of the story, the political situation in Beta Israel villages became especially precarious under the Derg, with young boys being drafted into the military and the Jewish Diaspora holding rallies to lobby for their migration.[12] Hundreds of young Beta Israel began the journey from their villages in small groups, but travel had to be restricted to nighttime; food and water were in sparse supply; the sick and elderly had to stay behind; families were often separated; and the highland terrain was difficult.[13] Those who survived the trip over the border remained in Gedaref (or camps like it) until Operation Moses commenced in November 1984, though many did not live that long. Perhaps as many as twenty thousand people arrived, although only eight thousand left, an undetermined number having died of starvation or malaria in Gedaref.[14] BenEzer approaches the journey narrative as the transformative moment in Beta Israel history, framing it in terms of the liminal state of transition (2002), themes that any Jew can recognize from the biblical Exodus story. In the process, BenEzer makes the case implicitly that Ethiopian-Israelis have earned their place in Israeli Jewish society.[15]

The troupe's performance of journey repertoire implies solidarity with the framing of Ethiopian-Israelis within a national context, but Eshel does not consider herself an activist. Her interest in Eskesta concerns its unique body movements, Eskesta being the most recognizable shoulder dance virtually anywhere, and it is at this level of performance and nonverbal articulation that Beta makes an impact. Predating ethnography's "turn to affect" (Blackman 2012), Hoffman (2005) and Starr (2006) offer diverse and fascinating accounts—the former about war in Sierra Leone, the latter about the decimated Jewish community of Cairo—of the power of nonverbal articulation. They arrive at similar conclusions that nonverbal means of communicating are powerful tools for identity construction and mimicry. Likewise, Tomie Hahn's exceptional work on Japanese dance (2007), which argues for a multisensorial approach to enculturation. While the Beta Dance Troupe does not actually take a political stance, the public performance of black bodies, enacting the centuries-old story of abandoning minority status in exile in favor of freedom in the Holy Land, constitutes a powerful appeal to the Israeli public. Although the top-down effort to convince

Israelis that Ethiopians fit into a national framework tends to be ineffective, it is more compelling rhetorically than any statement of solidarity by politicians.

The complexity of Ethiopian-Israeli social status is particularly apparent at Beta's rehearsals, which take place at the Neve Yosef Community Center in east Haifa. The city of Haifa is multicultural—the population is nearly one-quarter Russian-speaking, and its Palestinian population can trace family lines to well before Jewish immigration (see Carmel 2011). The historic city is built around Mount Carmel, with the three main layers of the city connected by thoroughfares winding around the mountain. The city's neighborhoods are classified colloquially according to position on the mountain, with Carmel at the top enjoying ocean breezes and panoramic views, and Wadi Nisnas at the bottom polluted by fumes from the port. In a city in which status is dictated by "top," "bottom," and "middle," Neve Yosef is located in a part of Haifa that does not fit neatly into categories: "east" Haifa is, literally, around the mountain. In both a metaphorical and actual sense, Ethiopian-Israelis do not register in the fixed social hierarchy.

The people served by Neve Yosef were conspicuously absent from the evening, though. The audience at the launch of *Hamasa* resembled my longtime acquaintance Sharon from Be'er Sheva, university-educated and more comfortable in Hebrew than Amharic. The only white robes I saw—often serving as markers of new immigrants and the unintegrated—were the ones worn by the dancers, and the chatter around me transpired in Hebrew rather than Amharic. Indeed, the incorporation of the journey narrative into a collective ethnohistory can be controversial because it establishes a disparity between the Jewish, more established immigrants who lost family members in the journey, and the Christian or Christian-born, less mobile, recent arrivals who are sometimes called "hitchhikers" (*trempistim*) by social workers. Suffering is a key marker of Beta Israel experience, and it colors how they see the Falash Mura (Seeman 2009: 33, 104). These multiple generations of immigrants live in worlds apart from one another, and the differences between Ethiopian-Israelis expand as some learn to navigate the infrastructures of the state successfully while others fail to integrate.

From the launch of *Hamasa*, complete with speeches and entertainment, I discern two main themes that shape Ethiopian-Israeli life. First, the case for Ethiopian integration into Israeli society is being made at the national level through non-Ethiopian interlocutors (Gadi BenEzer, Ruth Eshel, etc.), who do so by mobilizing a discursive apparatus that the Israeli population understands. The power and effectiveness of the journey narrative do not lie in the empathy elicited by the stories themselves (they are not featured in Israeli documentaries as the festival Sigd is, for example), but in their adherence to a preexisting Zionist narrative of home and return. We have already seen that this narrative can create problems internationally for Ethiopian-Israelis who wish to portray themselves as Afrodiasporic or postcolonial, but in the context of dance, this narrative is both effective in its familiarity to Israelis and troubling in its top-down, mediated delivery.

The second theme that I discern from the evening is that the narrative's power is amplified exponentially when it is performed rather than explained. Beta's audience responds to the urgency of the journey narrative through the "bodies in momentum" (McDonald 2011: 483) on display, even when the underlying story is not explicitly retold. The embodied representation of struggle appeals directly to audiences, who understand the use of Eskesta to narrate Ethiopian marginality as a mechanism for transforming Ethiopian-Israelis into active historical agents.

SIGD: PERFORMING EXILE

November 27, 2008, Jerusalem–Tel Aviv

I spent today constantly recalibrating my assumptions. As I walked to the Tel Aviv Central Bus Station, I noticed that CD emporium Nahum Records was open, which made me nervous. Nahum is religious, so for the store to be trading means that today doesn't count as Yom Tov[16] (a religious festival on which most of the Sabbath rules apply). So, before gathering any data, I had to come to grips with the idea that while Sigd is the most important Beta Israel festival, it isn't Yom Tov. Still, it was important: the queue for the 405 bus to Jerusalem was jam-packed with more Ethiopians than I had ever seen on a public bus. I wasn't surprised, since I expected that thousands of people would be making the trip to Jerusalem. On the bus, though, I noted the second surprise of the day: while some women were dressed in the typical synagogue uniform of a long skirt, most were wearing jeans. *Okay, jeans to services on important festival.* As the day went on, at the Jerusalem bus station, in Talpiyot as I walked to the promenade (*tayelet*), and repeatedly after I reached the promenade, I noted a constant reshifting of my expectations and assumptions. Most of these assumptions were innocuous, and rethinking them was painless. More challenging, however, was the recognition that a quintessential (albeit always changing) Ethiopian Jewish practice[17] might be soon phased out by the prospect of integration, the very social process that researchers like me were advocating.

It was the 29th of Ḥeshvan, a date that doesn't mean anything on the rabbinic Jewish calendar, but which has been an official religious festival in Israel since 2008. The day is Sigd, the most important Ethiopian Jewish festival, and in bringing it into a national forum, the state was granting some degree of approval of Ethiopian religious practice. Supplementing the religious service, secular Ethiopian dancing commenced immediately following the service and continued through the afternoon, thereby ostensibly approving of Ethiopian culture, too. I was fortunate to participate in the first state-sponsored Sigd celebration, and was gratified by the national forum for Ethiopian culture, but the way the Ethiopian-Israeli rite was presented to a national public left me unsettled. I was troubled by a generational split over religious knowledge in the morning, and by an afternoon of dancing that referenced Ethiopian national culture rather than a Beta Israel-specific tradition. I saw in the structure of Sigd, and the use of Eskesta as part of its celebration, the challenge of presenting Ethiopian-Israelis as an *edah* (ethnic community) like any other. The very presence of Eskesta, and the accompanying Ethiopian pop music at the event is interesting, since its reference point is Addis Ababa, a place that many Beta Israel have never visited. Eskesta equates with the performance of Ethiopianness detached from life in Gondar, and its practice at Sigd establishes a connection with an imagined mainstream Ethiopian culture (see Tourny 2007 for a complex picture of Ethiopia's diverse musical traditions) and the urban musical life of Addis Ababa in which Beta Israel have never participated. I found that as much as the crowd enjoyed the dancing, it may at the same time have undercut the main reason for celebrating Sigd publicly. The emphasis on the foreignness of Ethiopian traditions undermined the desired religious legitimacy of the festival, rendering the event a quaint folkloric object of fascination rather than evidence of the seriousness of the rite.

The ritual of Sigd is described extensively in the literature (Abbink 1983, Ben-Dor 1987, Grupper and Nudelman 1995, Parfitt and Trevisan Semi 1999, Shelemay 1980/1981), and Abbink's description is especially detailed. He outlines the service's components: first, the Qessim lead a processional up a mountain and a laying of stones where the Orit (Torah) will be placed. Next, a reading from the Orit is followed by a homily in Amharic. Finally, closing prayers and donations of money precede a recessional down the mountain (or hill). Afterward, attendees break their fast with a ceremonial meal, often followed by secular music and dancing (1983: 793–95).

The rite constitutes a central, but perhaps decreasingly important component of the day. To most Jews, who practice a rabbinic form of Judaism that Beta

Israel do not,[18] Sigd is idiosyncratic, with underlying connections to a variety of festivals. We might think of it as a combination of Yom Kippur and Shavuot that takes place in November. It is a solemn day that starts with fasting and repentance (the Yom Kippur components) and includes ascent of a mountain (like any of the *regalim*, the pilgrimage festivals), praying toward Jerusalem, and reenacting revelation (the Shavuot component). Adding to the Shavuot feel of the festival is that it takes place forty-nine days after Yom Kippur.[19] And like Shavuot, the date represents the end of a harvest season (see Kaplan 1992, Parfitt and Trevisan Semi 2005). In short, the individual elements of the festival are recognizable to most Jews, but the way they fit together is subordinate to the local circumstances of rural life in the Ethiopian mountains.

The Ḥeshvan dating of the festival makes Sigd easy to write off—"It's in MarḤeshvan,[20] it's not a real festival . . ." but Ethiopian-Israelis see it differently. As entertainer Shai Fredu put it in a television interview: "The Sigd holiday is slowly starting to take its place in society. The month that we celebrate Sigd is the only month that there wasn't a holiday in Israel. By immigrating here, Ethiopian Jews brought Israel a holiday in this month. So now, in every month there's a holiday. The Ethiopian Jews secured for Israel, essentially, full celebration."[21] Watching Ethiopians celebrating in Jerusalem, this optimistic positioning of Sigd as the culmination of *kibbutz galuyot* (ingathering of exiles) seems to be the consensus. Everyone I met that day, like Shoshana from Tiberias, confirmed that being able to pray not just toward Jerusalem, but overlooking the Old City, represents the salvation of return. Yet the way the observance of Sigd plays out today—in contrast to how it was observed in Ethiopia, with return narratives subordinate to precise ritual[22]—highlights Ethiopian religious otherness, an issue that has been as marginalizing as bodily otherness. By describing Eskesta performance in the context of other secular and religious musical performance over the course of the day, I describe a state-sponsored event in which Ethiopian Jewish ritual is framed as part of a history of exile that pairs with an imagined mainstream Ethiopian culture, ironically undermining a homecoming narrative.[23]

At the same time, part of Sigd's appeal is its foreignness, the display of exotic African culture represented by the religious ritual. The otherness of Ethiopian ritual is on full display during the morning service. Qessim (or Qessotch in Amharic) in ornate robes carry embroidered parasols and chant in Ge'ez, the language of Beta Israel sacred texts like the Orit. Even Ethiopian-Israelis are struck by the foreignness of the service, most young people (especially those born in Israel) no longer being familiar with Beta Israel liturgy. Abbink's description from Sigd in Israel in 1982 could hold equally true today: "This recital took at least one and a half hour [*sic*], during which the interest of especially the non-Falasha public declined every minute. Neither the Falashas—most of school age—nor the non-Falashas who were present could understand it; a translation was not provided and there was hardly a response of any kind" (Abbink 1983: 805).

For Ethiopian-Israeli observers, the service is a roots experience and a spectacle, but not necessarily one offering the salvation described in the principle of praying for redemption from exile. The appeal of Sigd for a broader audience might be one reason why an abundance of documentaries about it can be found online. In each of the documentaries, the Qessim make up only a small portion of the participating public, and the vast majority of Ethiopian-Israelis in attendance wear their religious and political ideology through white robes, or jeans, or suits, and in a few cases, black hats.[24] Across the mediatized modes of representing Sigd, one cannot help but notice that despite ubiquitous sounds of ululation, most of the participants do not know the liturgy. As more Ethiopian-Israelis join Orthodox (Jewish) congregations, they become detached from Ethiopian liturgy (see Shelemay 1980/1981 or Tourny 2010). Indeed, I doubt that many people will be in the position to lead the Sigd service in several decades' time.

There is no doubt that the public observance of Sigd deserves exuberance as a symbol of official acceptance of Ethiopians, but one can also discern several issues on display throughout the day that warrant serious thought. To begin with, the men in black hats (visible in the aforementioned video clips) have clearly discarded Beta Israel ritual in favor of a normative ultra-Orthodoxy. These men will have spent time in a yeshiva, and some of them probably vote for the Shas Party.[25] Ethiopian immigrants in the 1980s and 1990s were systematically asked by the Ashkenazi rabbinate to undergo a symbolic conversion, and during my fieldwork in Tel Aviv the question of Ethiopian Jewish legitimacy was still ubiquitous. While Israelis accept Ethiopian-Israelis as citizens in principle, some are still skeptical of their religious legitimacy, and one by-product of this attitude is that Ethiopians who seek religious acceptance sometimes turn to Mizrahi forms of Orthodoxy. Most of the people in religious garb were participating in good humor—apart from the national-religious (*dati-leumi*)[26] man shouting "Disgrace! Disgrace!" ("*Bizayon! Bizayon!*"). Religious mainstreaming is one obvious effect of the state's top-down approach to religious life, and the gradual erosion of Beta Israel observance will be one effect for the next generation to consider.

The kind of government intervention on display at Sigd illustrates the complexity of Ethiopian religious life. While the marking of Sigd as national holiday is indeed a sign of acceptance from the government, there is an incontrovertible connection between religious acceptance and the bequeathing of citizenship rights. The Knesset (Israeli parliament) welcomed Sigd into the official Israeli festival calendar in July 2008. This happened just as I arrived for fieldwork, but within the week, I was attending protests outside of the Knesset as an observer. The minister of the interior had decided unilaterally to put an end to Falash Mura immigration, and the community was upset (the law changes frequently, but officially Beta Israel are considered eligible under the Law of Return, whereas Falash Mura are not without converting). The two announcements, taking place within days of one another, demonstrate that the opening of the Jewish calendar to Ethiopians can occur alongside the closing of the border to them. To understand how religion can be endorsed while immigration is curtailed, we must therefore look beyond the logistics of ritual observance, and at the social dynamics of how the observance is organized.

The morning ritual of praying in Ge'ez toward the Old City under parasols is the mechanism through which Beta Israel from across the country encounter "covenant renewal" (Ben-Dor 1987: 141), but the true complexity of Sigd's public observance in Israel becomes increasingly apparent once the service is over around noon, and it morphs into a civic-secular-national celebration. In this afternoon segment of Sigd, Eskesta dance is the central performative gesture of Ethiopianness. The members of the congregation who are wearing white robes break their fast, and many board buses back to Rehovot, Netanya, or Tiberias, while the Scouts set up a stage for Eskesta.[27] Next door to the stage the Scouts have set up a *tukul*, a replica of a hut from Gondar, accepting visitors and serving coffee. For the next several hours the Scouts' sound system plays a continuous loop of recorded urban Azmari music and Ethio-jazz, music that only some young people listen to but that they all support in principle (see Ratner 2015: 112), while people dip in and out of the dancing and the *tukul*. The effect is an afternoon of folkloric pastiche that, despite celebrating the end of exile (*galut*), reminisces about it, rendering it what Abbink calls a "commemorative festival of exile and return" (1983: 802) via Israel's civil religion of national myths.

The Eskesta stage makes sense as a concept, since anyone can participate. To dance Eskesta, a person has to master a difficult set of neck and shoulder movements, but the structure of the dancing usually remains the same. Ruth Eshel explains the basics of Eskesta in the following way:

Originally, I had planned just to analyze the dances. But very quickly I saw that basically there is one dance. The big thing is they have the dance with the shoulders . . . Eskesta. And I saw that this is a musical structure, and a movement structure, and I saw at the wedding that it repeats itself more or less; but in the structure they're basically free to do what they want, it is first and foremost improvisation. And that's it basically. The music changes so my dancers [sic] said to me, "No, there are limitless dances"; what I realized was that there was a lot of different music, but the same structure within the dance. (interview, Haifa, June 4, 2009)

As Eshel asserts, there is room for improvisation in Eskesta, but the dance itself does not change. It is portable and known to all Ethiopians, and it takes only limited local knowledge to recognize. While the movements are difficult to learn, to teach it requires explaining only a limited set of movements.

In other words, there is a legitimate reason to set up an Eskesta stage at Sigd, since it allows the celebration to continue into the afternoon and to showcase Ethiopian culture. A more skeptical reading, though, would interpret the moment of musical transition, between liturgy and folk/pop music, as an ideological cornerstone of the day. The morning is devoted to liturgy in Ge'ez chanted by Qessim as a white-clad congregation prays overlooking the Old City, while the afternoon is spent dancing Eskesta to Amharic-language songs. This path from the sacred to the popular,[28] or the binary method of celebrating festivals, is commonplace in Israel. Many religious (or semireligious) observances that hold civic meaning are observed within a two-part structure that includes both solemnity and frenzy.[29] The tone of the day—from mourning to celebration, as well as public gathering to exchange information (see Salamon 1999 about Sigd as social event)—is built into Israeli public observances, and the structure of Sigd thus has a precedent. From this structural schism, whether we call it religious-secular or Ethiopian-Israeli or past-present, we can extract a confusing set of hierarchies. Even though the public celebration of Sigd represents the welcoming of Ethiopians into Israeli Jewish society, the celebration implies a defined separation between the sacred and the national for this minority population. Rather than blurring the meeting point between Ethiopianness and Israeliness, the two are precisely demarcated. Despite the obvious logistical sense—praying until lunchtime—I read the breakdown of the day as a generational stereotype of Ethiopian religious material (and liturgy) as boring and punishing for the body, and the Scouts' presentations (and dancing) as fun and physically energizing.

As the day continues, the blurring of musical styles becomes increasingly explicit. By evening the celebration usually moves over to Jerusalem's concert halls and clubs, with lineups of prominent Ethiopian-Israeli musicians collaborating on Ethio-jazz covers. One particularly famous example was captured in 2011, involving the most prominent Ethiopian-Israeli musicians.[30] Saxophone virtuoso Abate Barihun plays next to Ester Rada in traditional dress before she was famous. Next to her is then-husband and emerging reggae star Gili Yalo, with acclaimed massenqo player Dejen Manchlot on the left. These musicians perform a wide variety of music: jazz, soul, reggae, Azmari music. But for this performance, they sing Ethio-jazz in a cover by Muluken Melesse, dancing during every chorus. These diverse musicians, who come from the same region (Gondar, mostly), relate to each other today not through the liturgy, documented by Shelemay (1986) and Tourny (2010), that would have organized their grandparents' daily lives, but through the urban music of Addis Ababa, a place most of them have never visited.

Therefore, there is a sense in which Sigd is not a celebration of religious pluralism after all, but an affirmation of difference for a group that has made substantial sacrifices to become mainstream. The specialized textual expertise required to perform the most important service is, past noon, replaced by the embodied knowledge of an essential Ethiopianness that can be acquired by inhabiting the performative stance of Eskesta. Sigd is, effectively, two events connected in time, space, and demographics. Each proposes its own agenda: the first, to observe the preeminent Beta Israel festival, the second, to celebrate what it means to be Ethiopian and Israeli. While most scholars agree that it is a major achievement for Sigd to be accepted by the Israeli establishment as a Jewish festival given the persistence of the question of religious authenticity (Shapira 2012: 459), the day of celebration sends mixed messages to participants. The religious-secular/ Ethiopian-Israeli dichotomy comprising the structure of the day threatens to undermine the festival as a religious observance for immigrants who wish to integrate. And despite Eskesta's consensual association with communal achievement and success, the public performance of it is complicit in a narrative that potentially undercuts Ethiopian religious legitimacy.

The performative theater on display at Sigd demonstrates not only that Ethiopian-Israeli public life requires a great deal of negotiation, but also that the failure to resolve the discursive binaries (black-white, Ethiopian-Israeli, etc.) is the core of the population's continuing social problems. Whether a family can accept interracial marriage—that is, to Jews who are not Ethiopian; if their daughters can wear pants, a sign of secularism; and whether they should send their children to religious schools (where they will likely come to discard Ethiopian religious customs) are some of the most pressing logistical queries that Ethiopian-Israelis face. The communal pride in being Ethiopian displayed by the turnout at Sigd, along with the cultural and generational conflicts demonstrated during the service and afterward, indicates that the integration of Ethiopian-Israelis is affected not only by prejudice from the outside but also by the fact that, despite a government trying to welcome a minority population, this is not a cohesive *edah* like the Moroccans or the Bukharians whose rituals can slot right into Israeli observances as charmingly exotic but ultimately familiar. Ethiopian rituals, like Ethiopian bodies, are conspicuous in Israel, since they do not conform to an agreed image of Jews or Israelis. While I commend the use of Eskesta to empower those othered bodies, I query the utility of juxtaposing bodily otherness with religious marginality as a mechanism for acceptance.

Sigd defines cogently the uniqueness of Ethiopian Judaism. Its individual characteristics align with Sephardi and Ashkenazi festivals, but the composite is unrecognizable to most Israelis. The government declares it a national holiday, but it celebrates a secular culture of the home country that Beta Israel will never return to. And thousands of people travel to celebrate it, but fewer know the liturgy by the year. The people who attend Sigd are moved by the state's inclusive gesture, but the event lacks a focused message about what makes Sigd, or Ethiopian-Israelis, Israeli—or legitimately Jewish. Consequently, Sigd in Jerusalem illustrates the paradox of delivery from exile being disappointing, but it does not address the fundamental question of how to grapple with that disappointment.

INYALINYA: PERFORMING "US"

June 23, 2009, Aḥ Boger graduation, Ashkelon

Certificates are dispensed, and the dance troupe Inyalinya takes the stage— they set up on rugs on the grass as children scurry away to let them through. Naama, an Ethiopian-Israeli program coordinator, turns to the troupe's director to confirm the ensemble's name. He answers "Inyalinya" and she says into the microphone, "I now present Anu Lanu."

This exchange intrigues and puzzles me. Speaking in Hebrew, choreographer-director Zelelew gives an Amharic name for his group, and Naama automatically translates it into Hebrew. The micro-exchange of linguistic and cultural translation is crucial: the Hebrew "Anu lanu" is a direct translation of the Amharic expression "Inyalinya," but there is an agenda in the original title, which translation transforms. The two expressions translate as "we are for us"—or, more loosely, "for us by us," and the expression loses its potency in an acquired language. In Amharic, the meaning is clear: Ethiopian dancers perform Ethiopian music for Ethiopian audiences. In Hebrew, that intention is deflated, and the dynamic of a local interlocutor making the expression Hebrew is an apt example of a minor top-down intervention whose results eradicate the artist's intention. By examining Inyalinya's performance at the Aḥ Boger program's graduation in Ashkelon (a program with which I had no contact apart from attending its graduation), I will pull apart some of the embodied meanings of who "us" means for Ethiopian-Israelis.

Zelelew arrived in Israel in 2006 with his parents, and the whole family moved to Beit Gordon, the absorption center for new immigrants in Ashkelon.[31] The other young people in Beit Gordon live in similar circumstances: most of them were born in Gondar, some moved at a young age to Addis Ababa to await immigration to Israel, and they arrived in the early to mid-2000s. Zelelew's friends in Beit Gordon are often the only Hebrew speakers in their household, and since speaking Hebrew is a mark of integration that offers passage into the labor market, many of their parents are not in the position to leave the absorption center. Zelelew recognizes the social stigma his parents face for not being able to work or communicate in Israel, but he also laments the loss of Ethiopian cultural knowledge among young Ethiopian-Israelis. This is closely connected to family structure: many young people in the 1990s (continuing to a lesser extent today) were sent to study in boarding school (pnimiyah, often translated as "youth village"). Because he is concerned with the decline of conversational Amharic and Ethiopian cultural knowledge in the Israeli-born generation, Zelelew has become a self-styled Azmari of sorts. The first time we met, he had a krar with him, which he purchased in Tel Aviv and learned to play by listening to recordings. He had heard of the well-known Azmari Dejen Manchlot, and had been to Habesh in Tel Aviv. In his enthusiasm to teach the young people around him about Ethiopian music, he organized a dance troupe to perform at weddings and celebrations around Ashkelon. Eventually he called the troupe Inyalinya, and the ten-person ensemble dances to prerecorded Ethiopian music, though Zelelew himself plays and writes music in the Azmari style.

I came to know Zelelew away from the eyes of absorption-center workers, but our first meeting was established and mediated by them. In fact, all of the cultural events that take place at Beit Gordon are heavily mediated through the (mostly) non-Ethiopian workers, who organize special celebrations and everyday activities. At the graduation in June, I counted six administrators and workers responsible for the program, and four of them were non-Ethiopian. Inside Beit Gordon, there are several well-integrated Ethiopian-Israelis who work with the newer immigrants, but the social worker who runs the center is an Israeli of Moroccan descent. Because many of the newer immigrants' language limitations mean that social life is conducted predominantly in the absorption center, they can often be met only by negotiating back channels.

My visits to Beit Gordon were a mixed set of experiences. I had no contact with the older generation, most of whom had arrived in Israel since 2005 and spoke only Amharic, and many of whom had not yet found employment in town. I dealt primarily with friends of Zelelew's, and often chatted with young children while I waited in the courtyard for things to happen. I also spent some time with the social worker charged with the daily running of the center. She was helpful and forthcoming—lending me Malka Shabtay's book (2001) for several months—and eager to introduce me to the better-integrated Ethiopian-Israelis who worked there. But after spending many years at the center, her optimism for the integration potential of recent immigrants was on the wane, which is why programs like Ah Boger are deemed important grassroots efforts. Whereas state-organized events like Sigd highlight the incorporation of Ethiopians into a national narrative, programs like Ah Boger provide day-to-day support for the young people whose parents are not in a position to help them to achieve within an Israeli framework of success.

I attended the Ah Boger graduation by chance—I phoned Zelelew the day before and he told me that his troupe was performing. I didn't know what the occasion was, but he said it would be worth the substantial trip from Tel Aviv because I would see some dancing. The absorption center is located only three or four miles from the train station, but the station isn't accessible to the city on foot, and there is no direct bus route from the station to Beit Gordon. Coordinating the bus with the train involves plenty of waiting. In total, the trip that takes about fifty minutes by car takes nearly two and a half hours by public transport. (An acquaintance in Ashkelon once offered for me to stay at her house after an Inyalinya performance, and was shocked that I said I would manage on public transport. Evidently, middle-class residents of Ashkelon would not bother.) This problem of proximity helps explain why so many of the Ethiopian-Israelis living in absorption centers struggle to become self-sufficient. In smaller cities, public transport isn't particularly convenient (Leitman and Weinbaum 1999: 130), but it's their only option. My massenqo teacher once remarked that he'd come to Tel Aviv by shared taxi (*sherut*), but that the owner of Nahum Records "has a car." Being able to avoid public transport constitutes success in this context.

For that matter, the absorption center itself is hardly a haven from the trouble of urban life: though one must acknowledge its usefulness as a temporary residence for new immigrants who arrive without financial resources, little aesthetic consideration went into its design. As a stone structure accessible through a single main gate and monitored by security, Beit Gordon rather uncannily resembles a prison. Inside, makeshift offices operate out of prefabricated "caravans." In the concrete courtyard, benches and pay phones are surrounded in every direction by high-rise apartment blocks. Only outside the gates does one find a small park with benches and tall trees, which, in the summer heat, was the preferable location for the Aḥ Boger graduation. Ethiopian rugs were laid out on the ground with a microphone and speakers at the front, with plastic chairs set up in a circle around the rugs. The circle was full to capacity for the graduation, and as the ceremony carried on, people trickled out from Beit Gordon's main gate to watch.

The ceremony was scheduled for 6 p.m., and it began at 6:45 with a formal welcome by the program coordinator and a blessing from the rabbi, much like the launch of *Hamasa*. There were about 150 guests, with a non-Ethiopian presence in the single digits. The whole event took place in Hebrew, though white-robe-clad adults were speaking Amharic all around me. After the opening remarks, and a series of short speeches about the success of the program,[32] each teenager who had participated in the mentoring program received a certificate.

Once Inyalinya was introduced, Zelelew came out as part of a ten-person ensemble (five male, five female). The participants were all Ethiopian-Israelis, most of them residents of Beit Gordon. They were dressed in white robes that were belted at the waist, like in an Azmari-bet, and they danced barefoot. When Zelelew indicated that he was ready to begin, one of the male dancers started a CD, and the five males formed a line across from the five females. For the next several songs, they danced Eskesta in a number of familiar formations: individual dancing-in-place; line dancing; and partnered steps. They were well received cross-generationally, with the youngest children (in the four- to seven-year-old age range) all taking the Eskesta stance, hands on hips, moving their shoulders along with the music.

The choreography called for frequent alternation of partners, and the line-dancing setup was heavily geared toward the collective, so it struck me that Zelelew was thinking about what it means to be "one of us" in terms of his multiple subject positions as Israeli, Ethiopian, Jewish, and black. Thinking about whom Zelelew includes in Inyalinya's collective pronouns, he could be referring to his immediate peer group, or to the inhabitants of Beit Gordon more broadly; to recent arrivals from Ethiopia; to Falash Mura; or to a physically indexed identity like blackness. Perhaps his pronouns refer to different subgroups according to the context of performance, but I doubt that they refer simply to Ethiopian-Israelis as a broader group. Indeed, even researchers who know the Ethiopian-Israeli population well mistakenly assume some contiguity to the "community" of people who have arrived from Ethiopia since the 1970s. The group identified in Israel by national origin (*Etyopim* or *yotsei Etyopia*) contains tremendous diversity in religious practice, from religious Jews to "traditional" to ambivalent to secular to converts to Pentecostalism (Kaplan 1999b, Seeman 2009). Likewise, the Ethiopian-Israeli population conceptualizes the boundaries of collective classification with wide variety. In that case, instead of hypothesizing a group that is the subject of Zelelew's pronouns, one should instead unpack the classifications among the performance's attendees.

Inyalinya's troupe members straddle several overlapping Ethiopian-Israeli subgroups. Zelelew's own background is complex. I have never heard a person say, "I am Falash Mura" though I have heard many people say, "I am Beta Israel, an Ethiopian Jew" (the qualification almost always follows the term, since most Beta Israel assume that non-Ethiopians do not recognize the term). It would be impolite to ask whether a person is Falash Mura (Seeman 2009: 99), but sometimes it is clear. Residence in a certain absorption center (ibid.: 122), a tattoo, a personal narrative of coming to Judaism later in life, origins in certain villages, or a cutoff date for immigration are the obvious indicators (ibid.: 34–36). Based on material gleaned in an interview about Zelelew's background, given his recent arrival date and his revelation that his parents learned about Judaism as adults, I was able to put together a picture of Zelelew's family history. In this case, he might be sensitive or even defiant about who counts as part of his own imagined community, because some Falash Mura feel that the better-integrated Beta Israel are unsympathetic to their problems.

The condition of Falash Mura immigrants is even more complex than that of the Beta Israel.[33] Many have converted to Judaism ("returned," as it were), and community workers often imply that the former undercut the religious acceptability of the latter in Israel. Indeed, the term "Ethiopian-Israeli" originates in skittishness about the term "Ethiopian Jew," which assumes a Jewish lifestyle that Falash Mura would not have practiced in Ethiopia. And as a result of the perceived disruption of Falash Mura to Beta Israel integration, many Beta Israel and community workers resent the Falash Mura openly (Seeman 2009: 104). This resentment is recognizable today in the unabashed reference on the part of some social workers to more recent immigrants as "hitchhikers" (*trempistim*) who take advantage of Israeli immigration policy (see Herman 2012: 7–8 on the problem of social workers as mediators).[34] Indeed, the Beta Dance Troupe's emphasis on the Beta Israel journey narrative places the troupe squarely in a position of defending the Beta Israel's noble goals in immigrating, and the national celebration of Sigd actively incorporates Ethiopian Judaism into Israeli/Zionist history. The Falash Mura have little to offer these top-down initiatives other than the potential to be good citizens and sincere Jews.

Admittedly, the differences between the groups will recede in the next generation along with outward markers of ethnicity. The ritual tattoos that adorn the foreheads of Falash Mura women, or the wrists of Falash Mura men, will not be sported by the Israeli-born generation of Ethiopian children. As physical markers and traditional dress give way to modern dress and adornment, the differences between Beta Israel and Falash Mura will decrease in importance, and what will settle in is a more permanent class discrepancy between those who have ascended the educational system and the labor market and those who have not. Zelelew believes that those who learn about their culture will have better odds of succeeding. He explains that all of these social issues are related to musical practice and that Ethiopian social norms are embattled:

> Everything is connected; with language there is also trouble. Little kids who come here study with *faranjim* [Hebrew plural for Amharic word for non-Ethiopians], they go to boarding school, they study with *faranjim*, they go home every other week, they speak a bit of Amharic, but the rest of the time they're with the *faranjim* speaking Hebrew. I will only speak to these kids [motions to the children in the activity room] in Amharic and sometimes they don't understand me, it's frustrating. . . . In our community, by the age of five or six, kids can't really speak anymore. It's up to their parents to educate them, to teach them to read and write and speak Amharic,[35] or it gets lost. It's a real shame. (interview, Ashkelon, June 22, 2009)

Zelelew's words and actions demonstrate concern over racism, but far more, they reject the eradication of history that comes with mainstreaming. "Anu Lanu" is an apt example of the enforced mainstreaming by social workers, which is intended to help Ethiopians integrate but potentially erases legitimate sources of communal self-confidence. In contrast to top-down mainstreaming efforts, Inyalinya embraces its otherness, establishing itself as Israel's others—black bodies being the obvious indicator, but cultural heritage being the real source of difference from Israeli society. Zelelew does not mobilize Afrodiasporic or Ethiopianist mythologies specifically, as much as he pushes back against explicit attempts to incorporate Ethiopians into a Zionist story at the expense of their embedded collective narratives.

Of the three events described in this chapter, the Aḥ Boger graduation is the one in which joy and hope were most palpable. Compared to the grand success of Sigd being declared a national festival, or of a Hebrew-language book being published by a respected academic about the journey narrative, the milestone celebrated by Aḥ Boger was modest. Yet it would have the most direct influence on the lives of the people celebrating it, and the embodied performance of a "mimetic subaltern self" was the most explicit. On the one hand, advocates lament the absence of communal leadership, and the organizers of Aḥ Boger repeated throughout the graduation that this program was a significant first step for all the participants toward becoming successful Ethiopian-Israelis. On the other, the grassroots cultural initiative of a young peer group bypasses the top-down apparatus and initiates a dialogue over Ethiopian heritage rather than integration.

Ruth Eshel describes Eskesta as a single dance that lends itself to infinite variation through improvisation. Ethiopian-Israelis mobilize the unique neck and shoulder movements, taking up the Eskesta stance whenever they intend to enact Ethiopianness publicly. In this way, the dance is a performative permutation of the narratives that aim to incorporate Ethiopians into the Israeli national story, with the mythologies of Zionism meshing flexibly with Ethiopianist histories and Afrodiasporic notions of blackness. In all of the public performances of Eskesta described in this chapter, the public staging of Ethiopian dance accompanies a direct appeal to a national public to acknowledge and accept the Ethiopian presence in Israeli society. The improvised dance, like the appeal to citizenship, is singular but constantly reconfigured.

Using their own strategies, Inyalinya, the Scouts' stage at Sigd, and the Beta Dance Troupe mobilize black bodies in motion to subvert Ethiopian-Israeli marginality. The bodies in motion serve as a visual reminder of the movement of migrants from one nation-state to another, and from one position on the social hierarchy to another. Dancers never state explicitly that they are displaying the very bodies that render them different, but by training those bodies, and exposing their virtuosity and self-mastery in a public forum, they exhibit a comfort in their blackness that undermines the rhetoric of insecurity discernible in their public appeals for acceptance. At these events, Ethiopian-Israelis make the case verbally that their story is part of the Jewish story more broadly—through the retelling of journey narratives, through the display of ritual, and through the assurance that they are working toward mobility—but their embodied displays of collective power indicate acute awareness of difference. While public speeches at national events argue that Ethiopian-Israelis have integrated the myths of Zionism into their collective self effectively, the public spectacle of black bodies negotiating their necks and shoulders through infinite improvisation indicates that blackness and Ethiopian history themselves reconfigure Ethiopian-Israeli citizenship.

FIVE

"What about My Money"
Themes of Labor and Citizenship
in Ethiopian-Israeli Hip-Hop

On three separate occasions in 2014, while perusing new albums and videos coming out of the Tel Aviv Ethiopian music scene, I stumbled upon Israel's best-known Azmari, Dejen Manchlot, who was a new arrival still building name recognition when I got to know him in 2008–2009. I was delighted to see that he was becoming ubiquitous: he was running Azmari workshops in Germany; turning up with dancers on Israeli television;[1] and, most surprising to me, playing massenqo on a dub record (which I will discuss in chapter 6).[2] In fact, the national and international recognition was less surprising to me than his appearance on Zvuloon Dub System's album, since he and I had disagreed in the past about Afrodiasporic popular music. Back in 2009, energized by reading about the power of rap to educate and advocate for marginal citizens (Fernandes 2003, Pardue 2004), encouraged by the global popularity of Palestinian hip-hop (McDonald 2009), and influenced by the developing discourse of rappers as modern griots (what would become Tang 2012), I once asked Dejen whether he thought of an Azmari as parallel to a rapper in his or her position as social critic. Suffice it to say that he did not, and I subsequently kept any views about Azmaris and rappers resting on a continuum within the confines of my doctoral thesis.[3] So while I always expected that Dejen would build a reputation for himself in Israel and maybe abroad, I never expected him to move into the realm of rap and reggae,[4] despite the potential commercial benefits of joining a movement that is, according to Tricia Rose, "transforming humanity's relationship with pre-recorded music."[5]

The Ethiopian-Israeli hip-hop scene, however, is impossible to ignore, since hip-hop is the primary musical style that young people listen to in Israel and Palestine today (Swedenburg 2013). Some Ethiopian-Israeli rappers, like Kalkidan (see Djerrahian 2010) or the contemporary group Produx, are even becoming popular in the national mainstream, though I focus in this chapter on the groups whose songs were popular during my fieldwork. And during that period, specifically the summer of 2008, one song more than the dozens of others playing in the clubs dominated my inbox: a rap-reggae number performed by the duo Axum.[6] I met Axum by accident, patronizing the pizza shop that employed the burgeoning (but at the time, still struggling) rapper Gilor Yehuda on Florentin Street in south Tel Aviv (Reuben Aragai makes up the duo's other half). Axum's flagship song, "Ma Im Hakesef," translated as "What about the Money," was the only Ethiopian rap song I heard that year to earn international popularity (Audio file 21). The song's central dynamic, lamenting financial struggle and the lack of employment opportunities for the urban poor, echoes the concerns of class-conscious performers who have migrated from the global South (Durand 2002, McFarland 2013), by complaining that people write them checks that don't clear, and that they don't have enough money in their bank account. The focus on urban poverty references American hip-hop, but the song makes little explicit mention of the repressive state apparatuses (Althusser 1970:122) that dominate African American male rappers' lives. Instead the figures representing "the man" are bill collectors and customers who haven't paid up, emphasizing the challenges of citizenship and the obstacles to being productive workers.

In this chapter, I will explore why "Ma Im Hakesef" reached such enormous popularity—it is, today, still the best-known Ethiopian-Israeli rap song—by examining some of the social and musical dynamics of Ethiopian-Israeli hip-hop, particularly those that David Ratner does not discuss in his valuable book on hip-hop listening practices (2015). Ratner, like Francophone Canadian anthropologist Gabriella Djerrahian, focuses in his ethnographically rich study on the music of the African American rappers his informants listen to (particularly Tupac Shakur), and he discusses at length the solidarity that young Ethiopian-Israelis feel with African Americans. This chapter takes a somewhat different position, looking at songs written and performed by Ethiopian-Israelis (as opposed to going into depth about what they are listening to on their phones), examining musical style instead of lyrics, and scrutinizing the ways that these musicians encounter Israeli society. I do this by analyzing the music rather than by quoting from interviews or lyrics, though I thank Axum for allowing me to reprint their lyrics, too.

If the performance of a contemporary Israeli Azmari citizenship has a ground zero, perhaps it should be hip-hop, a genre often devoted to critique and wordplay. This book argues that amid the Afrodiasporic and Zionist mythologies that musicians engage dialectically, individuals mobilize wax and gold to navigate Israeli social structures. Indeed, Ethiopian-Israeli rappers invoke Afrodiasporic musical vernaculars largely to explore the Zionist ideologies that they learned in school, the military, and absorption centers. Embracing black identity through musical style, Ethiopian-Israeli rappers' original material unpacks the sociopolitical issues of labor, money, and social status (see Ratner 2015: 119 for corroboration that these issues came up frequently in interviews alongside mention of racial issues). By examining how "Ma Im Hakesef" fits into Israeli codes of cultural intimacy (Herzfeld 1997, Stokes 2010), as well as contrasting it with other Ethiopian-Israeli rap songs released the same year, I trace an underlying current that equates work with the right to participate in public life. The emerging narrative—that a person earns citizenship rights by earning a living—is embedded not only in song lyrics but within the conventions of musical style. Therefore, I present "Ma Im Hakesef" as an appeal to a culturally intimate ethos that labor and service to the state are mechanisms by which an immigrant citizen becomes an insider.

My main point in this chapter—that locally produced rap songs are both a prescriptive and descriptive marker of cultural intimacy for immigrant minorities—makes a broader intervention into the burgeoning field of Hip-Hop studies. A chief critique one might level at the subdiscipline[7] is a tendency to focus exclusively on subversive lyrics at the expense of video production, technological innovations like making beats and sampling, and self-conscious choices of instrumentation, tonality, and vocal style such as articulation and ornamentation. Yet these aesthetic choices reveal an artist's perception of positionality all the same. I will demonstrate that "Ma Im Hakesef" was such a commercial success not only because of the popularity of hip-hop in Israel-Palestine (any number of songs could have been hits), but because it negotiates the Israeli approaches to labor and citizenship that Ethiopian-Israelis must adopt to ascend the socioeconomic hierarchy.

ETHIOPIAN-ISRAELIS WITHIN GLOBAL HIP-HOP

As I try to make sense of "Ma Im Hakesef," I focus in this chapter on labor and citizenship because their thematic exposition by Axum reveals the mechanisms by which Ethiopian-Israelis become enculturated into Israeli conceptions of productivity and value. Were hip-hop the primary focus of this study, though, I might expand my focus to the main themes emphasized in Hip-Hop studies recently, such as masculinity (Bakrania 2013), sociolinguistic nuance (Gaunt 2006, Terkourafi 2010), the quality of improvisation (Morgan 2009), underground music scenes (Burkhalter 2013), or the advocacy and educational applications of hip-hop (Pardue 2011). Ethiopian-Israeli hip-hop can be interpreted from any of these perspectives, but an exploration of labor and citizenship drives this chapter because those are the forces that make it unique, as opposed to an interesting local case study in a growing, important social movement.

Indeed, while I applaud the formal recognition of the legitimacy of Hip-Hop studies within the academy, I query the rise of a literature that surveys new local cases ad infinitum, trumpeting the achievements of rappers as social critics and political advocates. These public figures often provide a service to their societies, though I question the utility of an overly descriptive literature that depicts vastly different musical styles and public personalities as working toward identical goals. Instead I might point to the more cynical work of Hisham Aidi, who queries the assumption that hip-hop is a progressive movement helping to perfect society. In Aidi's work (2014), which is unfortunately selective in referencing style and highly subjective in its conclusions, hip-hop fans are portrayed as social misfits who become rap aficionados because they focus on it single-mindedly, and who go on to apply that same single-mindedness to causes that result in political violence, like jihadism (a cause that Aidi comes short of criticizing). In a climate where rappers are often equated with social workers against their will (Pardue 2011), Aidi's unusual suggestion—that an important social movement that has proven effective as a mobilizing force might not be universally progressive or democratizing—is a useful adaptation of an often-hagiographic discourse of subversion.

At any rate, many aspects of Ethiopian-Israeli hip-hop constitute standard and recognizable fare for rap fans. The innumerable songs that begin with a police officer or bill collector requesting payment,[8] or the provision of identity cards, are an explicit-enough reference to the ubiquity of the repressive state apparatus in black migrants' lives as to remind the listener of the police-brutality theme in African American hip-hop. They likewise might remind Israeli listeners of Palestinian rap, in which poverty, isolation, and individual and collective loss are common themes in young people's lives.[9] The imagery—what Joseph Schloss calls the "aesthetics of disjuncture" (2006: 411)—offers solidarity with a transnational socioeconomic underclass, especially through lyrics and imagery that convey a sense that Ethiopian-Israelis are targets due to their conspicuous appearance and limited social mobility.

The sociocultural milieu of urban deprivation and technological ingenuity is often described as the environment that bore hip-hop (Chang 2005). Indeed, the rootedness of hip-hop in the postindustrial urban decay of the South Bronx, and the catastrophic results of rezoning and austerity measures, account for its popularity among migrant subalterns worldwide (G. Baker 2005: 368) in an era of inequality and export of labor. In her seminal first book on the subject, Tricia Rose explains that, through its function as a surrogate for the atomized family and absent state, hip-hop has become the privileged mouthpiece and the cornerstone of the identity of the disenfranchised:

> Hip hop culture emerged as a source for youth of alternative identity formation and social status in a community whose older local support institutions had been all but demolished along with large sectors of its built environment. . . . At a time when budget cuts in school music programs drastically reduced access to traditional forms of instrumentation and composition, inner-city youths increasingly relied on recorded sound. . . . Artists found themselves positioned with few resources in marginal economic circumstances, but each of them found ways to become famous as an entertainer by appropriating the most advanced technologies and emerging cultural forms. Hip hop artists used the tools of obsolete industrial technology to traverse contemporary crossroads of lack and desire in urban Afrodiasporic communities. (1994: 34–35)

Rose explains that the phenomenon known today as hip-hop is built on a set of innovations by urban youth who lacked access to conventional streams of music education. In this respect one might be scarcely surprised that it has become the performance practice of choice for transnational urban underclasses,[10] and a backdrop of urban decay in "Ma Im Hakesef" cleverly masks an agenda of integration.

The segregation of migrant minorities across the global North, on the other hand, is the backdrop against which hip-hop spread through the 1990s and 2000s. As Laudan Nooshin describes (2011: 93), global hip-hop[11] rose to prominence in many former European colonial peripheries as the popular musical style of choice for economic underclasses expressing frustration with their lack of political and economic power (also see Chang 2007, Elflein 1998, Mitchell 2001, Solomon 2005). The substyles that have emerged in Iran, Turkey, Germany, Brazil, and most recently Sub-Saharan Africa (Charry 2012) adapt the now-ubiquitous practice of rapping over homemade or downloaded beats to local musical context. Certain styles have proven more exportable than others — French and Arabic-language hip-hop being especially popular abroad (Charry 2012: 17, Mitchell 2001) — and many more have emerged in populations for whom injustice, inequality, and disenfranchisement are quotidian realities. In Africa, hip-hop often fuses with traditional styles as a modernizing symbol of pan-African solidarity (Charry 2012: 18).

In each of these cases, the most direct avenue to recognizing the common dynamic of urban deprivation is through lyrics expressing disillusionment, and Ethiopian-Israeli hip-hop is no different. Much like other localized genres such as reggaeton in Puerto Rico or Cuba (E. Baker 2005, G. Baker 2011), Ethiopian-Israeli hip-hop — particularly the work of Axum, Jeremy Kol Habash, and Cafe Shahor Hazak examined in this chapter — is rooted in local context and vernacular. Crucially, all of the music presented in this chapter is sung or rapped in Hebrew.

As a genre, Ethiopian-Israeli hip-hop consists of a unique combination of styles, revealing the conflicting positions that Ethiopian-Israelis occupy: African American hip-hop implies a connection to other black minorities in a white society; Israeli popular-music samples demonstrate some enculturation of the second generation into local popular culture; reggae, which draws on Afrodiasporic notions of cultural capital and constructions of authenticity; and Azmari music. These diverse lyrical, musical, or gestural cues are sometimes explicit, such as rhythmic emphasis on a measure's second and fourth beats coming from reggae. In contrast, the Azmari influence is opaque, resembling Patricia Tang's argument about the rapper as modern griot (2012: 79).[12] To an Israeli listener, though, the only element of most Ethiopian-Israeli rap songs that would be immediately accessible is language, with nearly all Ethiopian-Israeli hip-hop performed in Hebrew rather than Amharic or Tigrinya, or English.

Hebrew lyrics are an important element separating rap from reggae in Israel, both of which are often grouped together on the club scene, along with R&B under the umbrella of *musiqa shehorah* (Ratner 2015, Shabtay 2001, 2003). In addition to their common origins among a black diasporic underclass, and their belonging to the same black Atlantic sphere of cultural exchange (Gilroy 1993), there are formal congruencies between the two styles that have been explored extensively by Greenwald (2002), Hebdige (1987), Rose (1994), and Walser (1995). Both African American and Jamaican popular music in the late 1970s involved an MC speaking rhythmically and in rhyme over music played by a DJ on a sound system; both value wordplay and improvisation; employ sampling and musical referencing; do not require live performance from musical instruments; and incorporate lyrical themes of frustration that are the effects of subaltern status.

Nonetheless, despite convergences and common origins between rap and reggae, and the common categorization of them on the Ethiopian-Israeli club scene (Shabtay 2003), the two styles diverge widely in their reception among international audiences, perhaps providing a clue as to why hip-hop offers such particularly local, community-based appeal to Ethiopian-Israelis. In the culture wars of the 1990s, rap polarized American audiences, with listeners either lauding its powerful social critique or lambasting its ambivalence toward violence, misogyny, and risk-taking behavior (Rose 2008). Reggae, on the other hand, with slow, hypnotic rhythms and what is perceived to be a tolerant ethos, was more palatable to white audiences in North America and Europe (O'Brian Chang and Chen 1998: 52).

Hip-hop scholars often acknowledge the popularity of rap and reggae among white teenagers with a tone of scorn or mockery, although the mainstreaming of *musiqa sheḥorah* at least offers individual Ethiopian-Israelis a path to cultural capital. The Israeli market consumes reggae voraciously, so Ethiopian-Israeli musicians often join reggae bands. These individual musicians benefit from having a national platform, while their backing bands earn access to markets that would otherwise ignore Israeli musicians, such as the U.S. and Caribbean markets.[13] There is intense negotiation of blackness going on here, although the Ethiopian-Israeli self-identification as black really only materialized in Israel. Back in Ethiopia they might have referred to their skin as "red" (or *qey* in Amharic; see Salamon 1999: 8 for the Ethiopian classification of skin tones in detail) to demarcate themselves from dark-skinned slaves, or from their neighbors in Sudan and southern Ethiopia.[14] Blackness is therefore a state of being that is contingent on being surrounded by white people, and a social structure that places black skin at the bottom of the social hierarchy.[15]

Indeed, in the Ethiopian-Israeli experience, skin color has come to signify various sources of otherness, from phenotype to religious practice. The controversy over Ethiopian-Israeli Jewish lineage, and thus their right to Israeli nationality, has been co-opted in a less arcane but more superficial discourse of racial difference (Seeman 2009: 168). Steven Kaplan argues that much of the challenge for Ethiopian-Israelis adjusting to their new circumstances and neighbors since arriving in Israel can be understood as a process of "becoming black," where blackness signifies a new identity at the margins (1999b).[16] Many Ethiopian-Israelis recognize that they are disadvantaged not only because of any inherent official prejudice regarding skin color, but rather because race is a key issue along a constructed class-poverty axis that determines who will or will not succeed economically in Israel. It is reassuring that in this narrow context, some young people can use skin color to their advantage in claiming authority over reggae, even if there is little evidence of positive economic impact on the wider Ethiopian-Israeli population.

"Ma Im Hakesef" demonstrates the widespread acceptance of Ethiopian musicians in bands that perform Afrodiasporic repertoire. Axum is a rap-reggae group, and a multiethnic one, with one Moroccan and one Ethiopian member. While the other groups I discuss in this chapter are entirely Ethiopian-Israeli, they likewise collaborate with high-profile Israeli media figures as a way of counterbalancing their modest origins. Apart from "Ma Im Hakesef," I will discuss two other songs in this chapter: Cafe Shahor Hazak's "Eizo Medinah" (Audio file 22) uses the beloved standard of the same name by Mizrahi singer Eli Luzon (Audio file 23) as its base. Third, Jeremy Kol Habash's "Lemi Ikhpat?" (Audio file 24) pays homage to R&B-influenced rap from the 1990s. None of these groups is tremendously profitable yet, but they command a following in clubs and on the Internet. Most of them began their rap careers in Ethiopian-Israeli community centers or in the network of Ethiopian nightclubs in south Tel Aviv, such as Club Ethiopia or Club Menilek.

All three groups perform a repertoire of original songs, covers of reggae standards (I saw Axum play Black Uhuru's "Guess Who's Coming to Dinner" on the beach in Tel Aviv in August 2008), and the occasional Israeli megahit. I noted with confusion during fieldwork that the musicians preferred to play standards when performing reggae but original material when rapping. I was puzzled by the stark contrast between rehearsed Kingston material and original beats and rhymes from Tel Aviv or Netanya, but I soon concluded that far more than expressing "rage" as constantly overstated in the literature, these rappers were improvising and composing new material in Hebrew as a mechanism for becoming Israeli and identifying with Israeli modes of cultural intimacy.

"WHAT ABOUT MY MONEY"

Like most of their contemporaries, Axum released their first hit on YouTube. I met the Moroccan Israeli Gilor Yehuda, known onstage as Jackson, only a few weeks later in August 2008 during my first month of fieldwork. I saw Yehuda perform with his Ethiopian-Israeli partner, Reuben Aragai, known onstage as Tedross, the following week, while the duo was still under the radar. Axum's big break was not long in coming. In late 2008 they played Barzilai, a gargantuan nightclub at the epicenter of the alternative scene in Tel Aviv, and in March 2010 they performed their first gig in the United States. "Ma Im Hakesef,"[17] which translates as "What about the money?" or, more loosely, "Where's my money?" turned out to be their first and biggest success to date.

If the name Axum and the images associated with it resonate with the group's fans, it is because the city in northern Ethiopia of the same name holds immense symbolism for Ethiopians. In pre-Islamic times, Axum (more common spelling: Aksum) was the capital of the powerful and prosperous Axumite Empire, which controlled a vast swath of territory along the Red Sea comprising modern-day Eritrea and the Ethiopian highlands, and parts of Sudan (Levine 1974). The antiquity of the Axumite Empire, along with the distinction of being among the first empires to adopt Christianity as the state religion (ca. 325 CE) and Ge'ez as its liturgical language (Ullendorff 1968: 125) not spoken by laymen (Salamon 1999: 85), confers symbolic power on the city that gave Tedross and Jackson their stage name. For centuries, kings and pilgrims have flocked to the city for its claim to the Ark of the Covenant (ibid.) and for its capacity to confer legitimacy on the polities that succeeded it. This tradition continues today in a modified form. To the Ethiopian nationalists who lay claim to its heritage, Axum represents a trope of sovereignty, power, and glory of almost mythical proportions, rooted in a past that is ever impinging on collective consciousness (Levine 2004: 2). Indeed, notwithstanding whatever misgivings about the primordial nationalist use of history one may harbor (Hutchinson 1996: 374), it is reasonable to consider Axum a historical and ideational foundation of Ethiopian civilization (Levine 2000).

The Axumite Empire's name recognition across the African diaspora contributes to one of the great ironies of life in Israel for Ethiopians: that *musiqa shehorah* is, thus far, the first niche area where they have been embraced by the Israeli mainstream. This is interesting: Ethiopians have no direct historical connection to the Middle Passage or to the Afrodiasporic musical styles that incubated rap and reggae. However, by virtue of the Rastafari focus on Ethiopia, Ethiopia is considered a heroic mythical nation when filtered through Marcus Garvey's early black nationalism.[18] It is somewhat bittersweet for Ethiopian immigrants who buy into Zionist ideology that Beta Israel should have come to occupy a marginal status that—to Israelis if not to anyone from the black Atlantic sphere of influence—enhances their credentials as a branch of the African diaspora. For Israelis, Ethiopians occupy a position of custody over black music and identity.

The reference to Ethiopian history piqued my interest in Axum, but "Ma Im Hakesef" stands on its own as a fascinating exposition of the complexities of life for Ethiopian-Israelis. In stark contradistinction with the idealized mountainous landscape of Ethiopia, the visuals for the "Ma Im Hakesef" video consist of short shots of people in a dilapidated cityscape (Netanya, Axum's hometown). Throughout the video, Aragai, Yehuda, and a multiethnic cast of poor Israelis sing and gesticulate against a backdrop of crumbling Bauhaus buildings. The imagery is both a literal and metaphorical indictment of Israel's mounting social inequality and failed welfare policies: the high-grade, cutting-edge social housing conceived by the European architects and urban planners of the Bauhaus school in the 1930s (Cohen 2003: 10) embodied for many residents of the Sharon region and Greater Tel Aviv hopes of an advanced, egalitarian Jewish welfare state. That these buildings are crumbling signifies not only official neglect of Israel's poor minorities, recent migrants, and the working class, but also the demise of a socialist dream inseparable from the origins of the state.[19]

Through the song, the duo bemoans a state of affairs in which the poor are buried under an avalanche of bills and subject to intense financial pressure, as the camera surveys the faces of Ashkenazi ("Russian"?), Mizrahi, and Ethiopian-Israeli youth. The song begins with a brief introduction on the accordion and the sound of a woman ululating, a classic Ethiopian iconic nonverbal sound.[20] The introduction then picks up a reggae beat, with a guitar, a bass, and percussion playing a 4/4 rhythm that emphasizes the second and fourth beats. The singers' voices are laid over the instruments, chanting "money money money" (*kesef kesef kesef*) for four measures. On the pickup, the ululating voice returns along with brass playing a minor ascending pattern that evokes Ethio-jazz modality. In the fifth measure, the rappers come in with the first verse. The song style alternates every four measures: one through four constitute the introduction; five through eight are sung over a reggae beat; nine through sixteen make up the song's main refrain. In the seventeenth measure, Tedross and Jackson break into rap for the first time, and the rest of the song alternates in four- to eight-measure segments between rap, heightened speech, and declaiming the main refrain. The gist of the lyrics is economic hardship based on not being compensated for one's labors. The introduction announces the song's theme adeptly:

Kesef kesef kesef kesef kesef kesef
Kesef kesef kesef kesef kesef kesef
Kesef kesef kesef kesef kesef kesef
Kesef kesef kesef kesef kesef kesef

Money money money money money
Money money money money money
Money money money money money
Money money money money money

The first verse presents the challenges of poverty equally convincingly:

Anashim samim li chekim, dapim
Mismakhim mesubakhim
Yipui koaḥ, bilbul moaḥ
Omrim ze shotef tishim
Kol hazman
me'arbevim oti beḥartot
Mevin rak mezumanim,
Az bo daber eilai . . .

People give me checks, pages
Complicated documents
I don't have the strength, driving me crazy
They say "it clears 90 percent"
They're always
stressing and confusing me with problems
Only understand money [cash]
So talk to me. . . .

The main chorus reinforces the point of trouble in making ends meet:

Beshkalkalim metsaltselim,
Paḥot milim—ma im hakesef
Haadumim, gam yerukim
Hakol holkhim—ma im hakesef
Beshkalkalim metsaltselim,
Paḥot milim—ma im hakesef
Hadolarim, gam uro'im
Hakol olim—ma im hakesef

With coins ringing
Fewer words—where's my money?
The reds, also greens,
All go—where's my money?
With coins, ringing
Fewer words—where's my money?
Dollars, also Euros
It all costs—where's my money?

And, finally, the second verse summarizes the narrative struggle:

Moḥrim lokshim meshalmim bekoshi
Yala teshaḥrer ya'abu kamun
Ani lo Rotshild, shtok, sim
Shkalim bimkom milim
Lo ḥol, lo diburim
Ḥalas im hastaras mah jaras
Ḥalek lainyanim
Lamah ma zeh meanyen oti
Kol haprotzedurah, ḥalturah
Ani lo shar rak le'arak
Po zeh lo flora falfura
Bekhol minei milim gvohot
Kemo kisui hotsaot
Menayot yeridot, aliyot she'arim
Mevin rak mezumanim
Az bo daber elai

Sell dearly, barely pay
Fine, let me go, old man,
I'm no Rothschild, shut up, give me
Shekels instead of words
Not work, not words
Enough with words, stop the cover-up
Break it up
Why do I care?
About all the procedure
I don't sing just for arrak
This isn't a flora farfura
With all these big words
Like "cover," "expenses"
"Stocks go down, shares go up"
Only understand money [cash]
So talk to me . . .

Tedross and Jackson have no trouble conveying that they are cash-strapped. Yet rather than sounding angry, a sense of playfulness is assured through their vocal inflection, as when they sarcastically absolve the state of any discrimination at 2.09 by rapping, "Ve'khulanu Yisraeliiiiiiim," or "And [after all], we're all Israelis. . . ." On "Israelis," their voices drop and ascend quickly in faux arpeggiation, mocking a neoliberal all-in-this-together trope. Indeed, even here, the lyrics on their own only make the point together with tone and delivery.

If we ascribe to Axum some vestige of wax and gold, it would be fair to say that the wax is contained in the apparent critique of Israeli society within the lyrics of "Ma Im Hakesef." But if we dig down to the gold, the refrain appears to be infused with irony. Indeed, there is a widespread perception in Israel of Ethiopians as welfare scroungers, which, in my experience, social workers at absorption centers sometimes perpetuate (Mevasseret Tzion absorption center, personal communication, June 23, 2009). The hammering of "Ma Im Hakesef" and, at the opening of the song, "money money money" (*kesef kesef kesef*) is an instance of tongue-in-cheek appropriation of a xenophobic trope associated with both Jews and rappers (Hisama and Rapport 2005).

The song's laden visual imagery, its lyrics and stylistic hybridity, are not coincidental. Just as Axum's name evokes themes of Ethiopian nationalism and transnational Rastafari-style pan-Africanism, Ethiopian-Israeli hip-hop bears the markers of a struggle between Zionist and Afrodiasporic mythologies, and the journey that immigrant and Israeli-born musicians take to resolve the ideologies behind those myths.

THEMES OF LABOR AND CITIZENSHIP
IN "MA IM HAKESEF"

The dominant tension that shapes the lives of Ethiopian-Israelis today is partly about race—what Du Bois terms "the color line" (1904)—but more broadly is about a struggle to ascend a social hierarchy that renders them illegitimate as citizens. A collective anxiety over remaining civic outsiders in Israel manifests itself in the journey narrative, the story of Zionist homecoming that frames Ethiopian-Israelis as yet another branch of Israeli society that has returned from exile. Yet while a credible journey narrative explored in previous chapters draws the connection between Ethiopian migration and the previous waves from Europe and the Arabic-speaking world, it has failed to convince Israelis that the state's most substantial black population is authentically Jewish. What makes "Ma Im Hakesef" effective is that it circumvents questions of religious authenticity and addresses directly the question of what it means to be Israeli insiders. By framing citizens as productive workers, in the century-long tradition of Labor Zionism, Axum makes the case that, over and above any indignity of being subject to racial epithets, Ethiopian-Israelis are deprived of their citizenship rights by being denied the right to contribute to the economy productively. By invoking the key criterion of productivity under the tenets of Labor Zionism, "Ma Im Hakesef" hides a plea for civic inclusion inside a song that might sound on the surface like any other hip-hop anthem to conspicuous consumption. The message, informed by Israeli (Ashkenazi/European) notions of what makes a valuable citizen, demonstrates a vacillating dialectic of competing Zionist and Afrodiasporic mythologies.

The connection in the Israeli imagination between labor and citizenship stretches back to decades before the establishment of the state, with roots in the nineteenth century (Avineri 1981). The secularists who founded the kibbutz (collective farming) movement advocated that European Jews could achieve emancipation through toil, rather than prayer and study (Segev 1986). The ethos of the movement can be summarized handily in the poet Hayim Nahman Bialik's children's poem, "Shir Ha'avodah Vehamelakha," or "The song of work and toil":[21]

Mi yatzileinu meira'av
Mi ya'akhileinu leḥem rav
Umi yashkeinu kos ḥalav
Mi ya'akhileinu leḥem rav
Lemi todah, Lemi brakha
La'avodah velamelakha
Mi yitein lanu ksut bakar
Umi baḥoshekh yitein or
Mi ya'aleh mayim min habor
Umi baḥoshekh yitein or
Lemi todah, Lemi brakha
La'avodah velamelakha
Al kein na'avod, al kein na'avod
Tamid, bekhol yemei haḥol
Kaved ha'ol, naim ha'ol
Uve'et hapnai nashir bekol
Shirei toda, shirei brakha
La'avodah velamelakha

Who will save us from hunger,
Who will feed us ample bread?
Who will water us with a cup of milk?
Who will feed us ample bread?
Whom do we thank, whom do we bless?
To work and toil
Who will give us a morsel of beef?
Who will give light in the darkness?
Who will draw water from the pit?
Who will give light in the darkness?
Whom do we thank, whom do we bless?
So we will work, we will work
Always, on all the days [of the workweek]
The burden is heavy, the burden is pleasant,
And in a free moment we sing out loud
Songs of thanks, songs of blessing
To work and toil
To work and toil

Many of the idioms from this text are direct quotations or loose paraphrases of biblical language. Even though it is an ostensibly secular poem, it will be stylistically familiar and referential to anyone who had a religious education. More importantly, though, it reveals the values of the "pioneers" (*halutzim*) or early legal settlers in Palestine (Weitz 2007): that following the trauma of European pogrom violence, Jews might not reasonably rely on God and might instead work toward self-sufficiency, and that honest, manual labor would bring about modern redemption.

To a religious person, though, Bialik's poem would have been subversive and surprising. Someone raised to believe that God will provide might be taken aback to hear that giving thanks to labor and toil is the answer to the problems of the *shtetl*, the Eastern European peasant milieu of many early immigrants to Palestine. To the Jews of Central and Eastern Europe who were never granted the rights of citizenship and land ownership, the aspirational notion of working one's own land was a pathway to self-determination (Laqueur 2003). While giving full consideration to today's postcolonial problem of occupation, and the sectarian violence across the Levant that is in part attributable to the mid-century displacement of populations in Israel-Palestine (Morris 2009), I might note that in the prestate era, the Labor movement strove to achieve salvation for immigrants and refugees for whom working the land was the sole route to realizing a state in which they could be citizens. As Regev and Seroussi explain (2004), the literary allusion in music to a biblical landscape here is not metaphorical, but quite a literal secular attempt at salvation.

ETHIOPIANS AND MIZRAHIM

By the 1920s, though, the immigrant population was no longer arriving exclusively from Europe. Yemenite immigrants were coming in small numbers, too. Musicians like Nahum Nardi began to set Yemenite oral/aural tradition to notation. An early example of collaboration between Ashkenazi and Mizrahi Jews was the Yemenite singer Bracha Tzefira, whose vocal rendition of Bialik's poem is highly stylized (Audio file 25). Tzefira is staged as a "pioneer" woman of the prestate era, most of whom were literate, European, and secular. In Tzefira and Nardi's performance of the poem,[22] her nasal vocal style and Arabic-inflected accent are tempered by a minimalist ornamentation style, absent the *silsulim* or ladders of grace notes that characterize Yemenite singing.

This collaboration is iconic, but reveals an asymmetric collaboration between

Ashkenazi and Mizrahi musicians. The integration of most Mizrahi immigrants was complex and often problematic (Segev 1986). After the establishment of the state, which followed the arrival of an influx of Jews from the DP camps of Eastern Europe, the population grew quickly with the mass emigration/expulsion of Jews from Edot Hamizrah (the Mizrahi communities) (ibid.). New immigrants from Yemen, Morocco, and Iraq had a harder time integrating, in part because the founding Ashkenazi elite considered them to be "quantitative citizens" (Shafir and Peled 2002: 44), immigrants who expanded the population but did not improve the quality of the state's output. As defense of borders and a war of demographics became chief concerns for the Israeli government, women and Mizrahim were targeted as sources of cheap labor who could also build up the population. In development towns today, Ethiopians and Mizrahim often feud, competing for resources, and indeed there is a case to be made that Ethiopians constitute the "new Mizrahim" at the bottom of the Israeli Jewish social hierarchy.

By the 1970s the ingathering of the Mizrahi Jews was virtually complete, and Israel was transformed demographically. Mizrahi culture was stigmatized, but once the recording industry realized how much business it was losing by ignoring this important demographic, Mizrahi musicians slowly moved into the mainstream (see Horowitz 2010 for a thorough examination). Some musicians even went through the channels of the military's music troupes (*lehaqot*) or trained in SLI style. Ofra Haza, perhaps Israel's biggest Mizrahi star internationally, emerged during this period. Haza became an international name, performing at Eurovision (1983),[23] touring Japan in the 1980s,[24] lending her voice to a Dreamworks children's film soundtrack,[25] and eventually becoming Israel's first high-profile casualty to AIDS.[26] Her image was carefully managed during her lifetime as a wholesome daughter of the nation, and her performance can be framed in terms of female work and Mizrahi participation in the public sphere.

Her repertoire ranges from the squarely SLI-influenced, such as her Eurovision hit "Chai" (Alive), pronounced in modern Hebrew that could easily come from Ashkenazi liturgy, to the traditional/exotic rendition of "Qalbi" (My Heart). Her first international hit, "Im Ninalu," runs the spectrum stylistically (Audio file 26). She first performed the song in 1978 with a local theater group from the Hatikvah neighborhood of Tel Aviv, where she is seated as part of an ensemble, including guitars, in the collective-song (*shira betsibur*) tradition of SLI. As she was developing a public profile, her style accommodated mainstream taste when necessary. In 1984, though, she recorded the song on her album *Yemenite Songs*, where she sings seventeenth-century Yemenite poet Shalom Shabazi's poem in the Yemenite dialect, bolstered by Mizrahi instrumentation and ornamentation, and a melismatic vocal style full of *silsulim*. The album is sometimes considered evidence of a wider cultural acceptance of Mizrahim in Israeli society. Yet when she recorded the song for a world audience in 1988, she elided the religious lyrics in the Yemenite dialect and replaced them with English lyrics about a romance, the whole song accompanied by a synthesizer. The composite of staging—collectively in 1978, communally in 1984, and in a romantic relationship in 1988—portrays a transformation of the Mizrahi subject position in Israel between immigration (1950s and 1960s) and the 1988 recording.

Mizrahi status changed with the radical transformation of Israeli society. In the first decades of the state, Israel was inhabited and managed by Ashkenazi Jews (Arab-citizen minorities and Palestinians over the Green Line not being considered for any kind of leadership contribution). The Labor Party administered the country, ostensibly under the principles of Labor Zionism, and those Ashkenazi Labor elites were resented by the newer Mizrahi immigrants scattered across the country's development towns and urban slums. In 1977 the Mizrahim voted overwhelmingly for the Likud Party, and the liberalization of markets that followed contributed to the individualization of Israeli society, which Regev and Seroussi characterize as the shift from the first-person plural (we) to the first-person singular (I) in song lyrics (2004). The electoral result and cultural shift also contributed to the rise of ethnic-identity politics in Israel, and the three versions of "Im Ninalu" draw from the culturally intimate framings of labor, nation, and family as initially interchangeable but shifting over a short time.

Following the radical transformation of Israeli society, Mizrahi social status improved slightly: a key component of a racialized hierarchy in Israel is the ascent of the bottom rung upon the arrival of a newer, darker group of immigrants. The arrival of Ethiopians in the 1980s allowed Mizrahim to ascend the social ladder by default, aided by high-profile public figures and effective collective organizing. Today the Mizrahi working class is kept afloat by the ability to do unskilled labor that many Ethiopian-Israelis cannot because of underdeveloped Hebrew skills (see Ratner 2015 for an explanation of how this leads to bitterness against Mizrahi neighbors). The language barrier that prevents some older Ethiopian immigrants from joining the workforce keeps them from becoming full-fledged citizens, as they have failed to prove their productivity. The result of the language barrier and labor crisis is that many Ethiopian-Israelis remain in absorption centers for years after arrival. Perhaps intentionally, or perhaps not, Axum identifies the nerve center of Ethiopian-Israeli anxiety and makes it public. The narrator's lament that their employer from a gig two months ago keeps saying about payment, "Bado'ar, ba'doar," or "In the mail, in the mail," or that "Kvar esrim veshmoneh, ve'ein maskoret," or "I'm already 28 and have no salary" might have some resentful subtext, but a dominant affect is shame over debt and inadequacy.

In this context, the musical style in "Ma Im Hakesef" is satirical and resentful. It opens with an accordion, a sarcastic auditory reference to SLI, and ululation at the end of the reggae introduction. Forgoing the typical hip-hop convention of rapping the verses and singing the chorus, the chanting style throughout presents as sing-speech with high tonal stability, making ornamentation a melodic focal point. The ornamental counterpoint between Zionist folk song and Afrodiasporic popular music juxtaposes the nation-building contributions of the ideal types of qualitative and quantitative citizens, types initially directed at Mizrahim but fitting equally well for Ethiopians.

Axum is undoubtedly channeling a critique of inequality in the lyrics, but perhaps the Afrodiasporic influence on rhythm and vocal style is consistent with the examples of Bracha Tzefira and Ofra Haza performing a syncretic — in their cases, Mizrahi — style that blends the immigrant-minority popular style of the day with embedded hints at irony and alternative storytelling. Axum projects the anxieties that have plagued immigrant minorities for a century, using the musical convention of rapping to disguise the most standard trope of immigrant minorities, that an uncontested citizenship can only come through toil and service (even if there might be racial factors at play, too). The musical style is a red herring, occluding the ideology of Bialik's poem, and also a hook to draw audiences in. The familiarity of this trope might be one reason this song has been so popular. Axum's second hit, "Pocket Full of Money,"[27] sung in English and glorifying conspicuous consumption, did not reach nearly the level of popularity of "Ma Im Hakesef."

We return then to the central question of why this song, rather than the dozens of others produced in 2008 and since, earned international acclaim. The song carries particular resonance because it invokes a narrative that all Israelis recognize, and that young Ethiopian-Israelis struggle with — that work is the route to civic legitimacy. Axum borrows from the musical vernacular of the African diaspora to repeat the most fundamental value of Zionism, thus appealing to Israelis who might not even recognize the song as particularly Israeli. And while Axum's dialectical tension between Afrodiasporic and Zionist mythologies stimulates the song's appeal, what is more striking is that Axum's contemporaries draw on the same dynamic to varying degrees.

"WHAT A COUNTRY": CAFE SHAHOR HAZAK

A conflict between Afrodiasporic and Zionist mythologies manifests itself frequently in Ethiopian-Israeli rap songs. Axum's success might have been a bit of a surprise, but their main competitors demonstrate the difference between a runaway hit and satisfactory local success. By examining another Ethiopian-Israeli rap song that hit YouTube in 2008, called "Eizo Medina" (What a Country/State) by the group Cafe Shahor Hazak (Strong Black Coffee), I demonstrate that Ethiopian-Israeli hip-hop commonly invokes citizenship narratives, but that small stylistic differences make a tremendous difference in crafting a message for the wider Israeli public.

The group Cafe Shahor Hazak, henceforth referred to as CSH, comes from the coastal city of Netanya, where they went to the same school as Reuben Aragai and Gilor Yehuda. Today only two members of the group remain;[28] when I first encountered CSH in 2008, they were teenagers who could hardly believe that they were touring North America and putting videos on YouTube.[29] Over the next several years the band members completed their compulsory military service, and thus did not record. After leaving the army, some of the original members made different life decisions, and the only rappers left are Ilak Sahalu and Uri Alamo. Like many of the musicians profiled in earlier chapters, they met in a community center in Netanya, so their name references political consciousness-raising.

The name Strong Black Coffee pays homage to Ethiopia's main cash crop (*buna*). Ethiopians take pride in their coffee-preparation techniques, which are honored with their own ceremonies (see Brinkerhoff 2011) and sometimes associated with possession rituals (Seeman 2015). Yet they use the Hebrew (*cafe*) rather than the Amharic term, setting the stage for a civic engagement based around integration. The "black" part of "Cafe shahor hazak" sounds sarcastic here, considering the racial hierarchies mentioned previously: the group is referring to the coffee being black, but also to their own label in Israeli society. The "strong" part of their name (*hazak*) is, presumably, a call to arms as well as a beverage descriptor. The band's name, filled with double meaning and allusions to history and circumstance, is classic wax and gold. The name is thoughtful, but it also implies resentment over being labeled as different, and a preference to join the establishment rather than to critique it as such.

Back in 2008, CSH had just returned from concerts in North America.[30] They had performed in Cincinnati, San Francisco, and other cities with significant Reform Jewish communities, courtesy of lobbying group AIPAC.[31] All of the group's members were still in high school, so their music seemed, to adult audiences who generally did not follow hip-hop, charming and nonthreatening—in other words, different from the hip-hop being produced in the United States (see Rose 2008 for the baggage-laden positive and negative stereotypes about hip-hop). Their message was an autobiography of integration, their songs narrating the process of becoming well-adjusted Israeli citizens through a strong command of Hebrew rhyme.

"Eizo Medinah" quickly became CSH's flagship song. It involves collaboration with a beloved Mizrahi singer, Eli Luzon; includes a professional video; and raises some similar concerns to "Ma Im Hakesef." The song deals with local (Israeli) concerns like road accidents, military anxiety, and unemployment, and through its association with Luzon it explicitly frames Ethiopians as the "new Mizrahim" in Israeli society. However, it falls short of Axum's popular potential in two ways: first, whereas Axum's agenda is hidden inside a musical style that is a cool and contemporary staple of youth culture (reggae), CSH collaborates with a veteran (beloved) musician who appeals primarily to an older generation. Second, CSH frames their grievance against the state in oppositional terms: while Axum's lyrics read as though they are driven by a desire to be better citizens, CSH's lyrics sound like complaints. As a result, while Axum is effectively asking the Israeli populace for a chance to prove themselves through work, CSH sounds like they are accusing the power structure of exclusion, a nuance that really only comes through after careful analysis.

One can contrast the commercial success of "Ma Im Hakesef" with "Eizo Medinah" to the detriment of the latter, but I find "Eizo Medinah" rather touching, especially because of Luzon's contribution. Perhaps the world's most famous Jewish albino, Eli Luzon is something of a racial outsider in Israel himself, perhaps making him sympathetic to the Ethiopian-Israeli experience. He is also a native of Netanya, so he might have been inclined to boost the profile of the city's young people. To come from Netanya is very different from growing up in the cosmopolitan privilege of Tel Aviv or its suburbs. And to ascribe even more notoriety to it, during my fieldwork Netanya dethroned the Tel Aviv suburb of Rehovot as the center of Ethiopian-Israeli life. For decades the Gush Dan[32] had been the main artery of Ethiopian-Israeli populations, with Rehovot's 6,400-strong Ethiopian-Israeli population making up 6 percent of the town's occupants, or four times the national Ethiopian-Israeli average.[33] In recent years, however, Rehovot's importance as a center of Ethiopian-Israeli life has declined:

Kiryat Malakhi, a remote development town in the Negev Desert, possesses the highest proportion of Ethiopian-Israelis in Israel, and Netanya (Ethiopian population: 10,500) has the most in absolute numbers.[34] The dispersal of the population away from suburbs and toward rural areas or poor immigrant cities is an important component of the song's narrative, in which melody and lyrics work in tandem to frame Ethiopians as Israel's "new Mizrahim." This teenage group from a small coastal city inhabits a position, unusual in global hip-hop, of the rapper peering inward.

The original source material for "Eizo Medina" is a Mizrahi standard. Eli Luzon's 1986 hit[35] begins with a qanun (Middle Eastern zither) and his melismatic voice singing in the Arabic *bayyati* mode as characterized by the flatted second (Marcus 1992: 173). Whereas many of the Mizrahi hits of the 1970s and 1980s were literary, borrowing medieval poetry or composing in metaphor (Horowitz 2010, Regev and Seroussi 2004), Luzon sings explicitly about a corrupt government that brings hardship on its citizens. Luzon's version is beloved for evoking both a jaundiced view of the state as a bed of corruption, and contrasting affection for land and country. The chorus describes a government that foists pressure on a choking nation: "What a country, singularly special / The government presses, a country under pressure, what a country" ("Eizo medina meyuhedet beminah / Memshala lohetset, medina nilhetset, eizo medina"), concluding that he loves it anyway. This is a dominant trope in Israeli hip-hop, too, to be found in any song by Hadag Nahash, the preeminent left-leaning rap/funk group. The chorus forms the basis of CSH's version, though they substitute the verses that lament the government ministers who take kickbacks with rapped original material.

Luzon also appears in CSH's music video, walking around Tel Aviv's business district with CSH's members interspersed with shots of Israelis and Filipina migrant workers dancing at bus stops. The focus on occupying urban space is a crucial theme of early hip-hop videos from the 1980s (Rose 1994), and equally powerful in the context of Tel Aviv, where one does not often see groups of Ethiopian teenagers. The video makes a statement by connecting different generations of migrants to Israel, from the Mizrahi to the Ethiopian to the Asian labor migrants who fuel Tel Aviv's service sector.

The emphasis on diversity in the video implies a connection between ethnic minorities and labor migrants as subalterns struggling to succeed in tandem, or occasionally in competition with one another. In today's Tel Aviv, these three groups (Mizrahim, Ethiopians, Filipina labor migrants; and I would add to this Palestinians in Jaffa, who are absent from the video) compete for a share of the city's ever-increasing wealth, even as it appears to consolidate in the hands of media and technology professionals. Indeed, the resentment that comes from economic exclusion drives a secondary message of the song: that Ethiopian-Israelis, as new immigrants, occupy the social status that Mizrahim did a generation ago, and that they would do well to align themselves with Mizrahim. CSH accepts this point tacitly, by borrowing Luzon's song rather than, say, Mahmoud Ahmed's, and through their proximity to Luzon they make the case that they are Israel's preintegrated new migrant underclass.

The song's basic structure is heavily indebted to Luzon's original: it begins with a sort of abbreviated *taqsim* (a Turkish-derived nonmetrical introduction that displays virtuosity of the main melodic instrumentalist), followed by a standard pop song structure. Luzon's chorus plays once for eight measures in 4/4, which remains the pulse for the whole song. After eight measures of the main motive/chorus, CSH raps for sixteen measures, emulating the *wahdah* rhythmic style of "improvisation over a rhythmic/melodic . . . pattern" (Rasmussen 1992: 70) for two verses. In each verse they name-check key problems within Israeli society, mentioning in particular the number of people who die in road accidents (a common Israeli lamentation) at 1.02.[36] Luzon's chorus comes back in for eight measures, after which CSH raps for another sixteen measures, this time about the anxiety of military service and unemployment. After these verses, CSH raps Luzon's chorus for eight measures, followed by a twice-repeated Luzon chorus for sixteen measures. In the entirety of the song, there is almost no mention in the lyrics of Ethiopia, blackness, or immigration.

The theme of civic critique carries through the first CSH verses. The second verse discusses the trouble of finding decent work: "A single mother with two [children] searches for work / She tries with all her might to save her dignity / She feels like working, always worrying" ("Hahorrit plus shnayim meḥapeset avoda / Menasa bekol hakoaḥ lahatsil et kvoda / Margisha avodah kol hayom beḥarada"). It then goes on to express the anxieties of Israeli teenagers about serving in the army (at 1.46), and the responsibility of the government for "the situation" (at 1.37). Meanwhile they expand on Luzon's theme of governmental corruption (at 00.46). That CSH feels comfortable enough to criticize the government for standard corruption and incompetence, and to highlight Israeli social problems, is unusual because the concerns are national, as opposed to local complaints. CSH's gesture toward Israeli cultural intimacy represents a move away from discretely Ethiopian identity politics.

When comparing "Eizo Medina" with "Ma Im Hakesef," many similarities emerge immediately, such as Hebrew lyrics and Israeli points of cultural reference.[37] Both involve collaboration between Ethiopians and Mizrahim, Mizrahim often being seen as proximate adversaries (Ratner 2015). In addition, both groups adopt Luzon's distinction between the powerful political class and the powerless citizenry. But the way the two groups work with the stratification of society diverges at the point of where their critique is directed. Whereas CSH places the blame for the nation's significant problems directly at the feet of the government, Axum's indictment of the government is, rather subtly, simply that the government has not given Ethiopians a chance to be the productive citizens they want to be. So, somewhat paradoxically, the main difference between their approaches is in the way they evaluate who is a desirable citizen.

"Eizo Medina" has earned CSH significant accolades, and the degree of international exposure afforded a group of teenagers riffing on a Mizrahi standard was amazing to watch. It seems to me that CSH achieved this unprecedented level of adolescent success by engaging a musical style and political ideology that Israelis could understand. And yet their critique, pointed directly at the same institutions that in other chapters are described as refusing to accept them, may have prevented them from gaining the kind of national recognition that "Ma Im Hakesef" achieved with its language of the aspirational virtues of work and earning.

Nonetheless, while Axum has been eclipsed commercially by groups like Produx, CSH is back on the Israeli recording scene with songs like "Yihye Beseder" (It Will Be Okay) (Audio file 27). They have decided to position themselves at hip-hop's more commercial end, and it has worked, winning awards and earning tremendous media attention.[38] Their success or failure as professional rappers, though, depends on their ability to engage legibly with a wider Israeli body politic.

"WHO CARES?": JEREMY KOL HABASH

One Thursday in May 2009, I went to Habesh for Menilek and Avi's weekly performance. Whereas many weeks I took a friend with me, or sat at Menilek's table, this week I sat alone. A group of three young men invited me to join them, and although I wouldn't have considered it in the UK, I felt comfortable enough at Habesh to be approached instead of, as usual, being the person to approach strangers and ask them questions about their lives. All three young men had recently left the army, and Moshe (a Kenyan, I later learned) had just returned from a trip to Ethiopia. The second member of the group, Avera, was Ethiopian, and the third, Gadi, was Israeli, a dreadlocked "honorary" Ethiopian like Gilor Yehuda or Idan Raichel. It was a fascinating evening, because though I had grown accustomed to being an object of amusement and confusion in Ethiopian venues (to say nothing of Azmari-betoch in Addis Ababa), this was really the first time I felt that I was being scrutinized ethnographically, as a paradigm of what an Ashkenazi woman thinks about Ethiopian culture.

For two hours we ate, talked, and listened to music, and I introduced them to Menilek. They weren't terribly interested in Habesh, though. It was a stopover for them: they had come down from Hadera (a town halfway between Netanya and Haifa, which has a substantial Ethiopian population) to meet some friends from a Facebook group and to hang out on the *tayelet*, the Tel Aviv boardwalk, which is only steps from Habesh. I joined them briefly, and met a dozen or so Ethiopian-Israeli teenagers (two were female), some of whom became Skype friends. Each of them sought the same outcome in conversation: to show me their *klippim*, the collection of Ethiopian music clips they had amassed on their mobile phone. None of them listened to the IRP, nor to Axum or CSH, but almost every one of them listened to a rapper I hadn't encountered yet: Jeremy Kol Habash.

The dozen teenagers I met that evening described Jeremy as "a giant" (*anak*), or "all over the Internet," and the two descriptors seemed basically interchangeable. The reason I didn't know Jeremy was that while he did produce hip-hop videos, he was best known on the club scene around south Tel Aviv, where he has established a successful career as an MC, independent of formal affiliation with record companies.[39] His name basically advertises his advocacy approach: his name effectively translates to a Hebrew speaker as "Jeremy the voice of the Ethiopians," and in English he often spells it Jeremy Cool Habash, which is roughly a homonym with the word for "voice" (*kol*). Leaving his live club performances for others to parse, I focus on his flagship song, "Lemi Ikhpat?" (Who Cares?), in contrast to Axum and CSH's songs.[40] In describing the song and his approach, I highlight a recognizably early-1990s aesthetic that links the African American experience to the Ethiopian-Israeli one directly. Jeremy's position works from an advocacy perspective, but his *j'accuse* stance toward the power structure limits his appeal among non-Ethiopians.

"Lemi Ikhpat?" is the only song in this chapter that includes some Amharic, which is spoken in the video's dramatized introduction. The video begins with the unmistakable pounding on the door of an enforcer, seemingly collecting an electricity bill.[41] An Ethiopian family member tries to wake Jeremy in rushed Amharic, while the faceless RSA (Repressive State Apparatus) orders him in a deep voice to open the door. The imagery of foreignness and of the RSA frames Jeremy as an enemy of the state before we hear his voice.[42] The cue of the black man evading the RSA frames Jeremy in the lineage of NWA or Public Enemy rather than alongside his Ethiopian-Israeli cohort, and this message of being disappointed by Zionism is delivered in the song style and lyrics. His implied connection with the African American experience shapes the viewer's interpretation of Jeremy's positionality vis-à-vis the dialectic of Zionist versus Afrodiasporic mythologies that contribute to his sense of citizenship.

The song follows the same formula as "Eizo Medina" of rapped verses and sung chorus. Following the brief conversational introduction, a common opening in the Native Tongues Collective in the 1980s,[43] the four-minute song cuts between Jeremy's rapped verses and an R&B chorus sung by an unnamed Ethiopian-Israeli woman. One verse appears to have perhaps been filmed inside Nahum Records in Tel Aviv. In other words, the musical style skews toward African-American musical taste, without any influence from SLI or *musiqa Mizrahit.*

The lyrics are the most critical among the songs surveyed in this chapter. Jeremy directs his critique unambiguously at the state's failure to absorb its Ethiopian population. He subverts several mainstream Zionist tropes, such as "the nation in bloom" (0.48) or, in an explicit reference to the Passover festival liturgy, "Avadim hayinu, avadim nishaer," or "We were slaves, slaves we will remain."[44] The chief literary mechanism that he draws from throughout the song is to borrow common Zionist or Jewish imagery and note Ethiopian-Israeli exclusion from the metaphors of self-determination and liberation. In a somewhat dour call-and-response, the woman singing the R&B chorus sings, "Hotsaot gedolot hakhnasot ketanot," or "Large expenses, small income," to which Jeremy raps back, "Lemi ikhpat, lemi lemi ikhpat?" or "Who cares, who who cares?" Immediately after, he raps from behind a gate, apparently implying prison, self-identifying with the victims of the RSA, and drawing an explicit association with the African American experience.

Ethiopian-Israeli youth look reasonably to African American recent history as an example of music offering an alternative avenue to acclaim as described poignantly by David Ratner (2015). When traditional routes to prosperity are tied to the economic resources that a migrant underclass cannot access, entertainment offers a path to prosperity that has, historically, benefited African Americans who might not be given the opportunity to study law or medicine. But the African American musical tradition was not always as critically and commercially accepted as it is today (though it was frequently co-opted), and hip-hop has had an especially difficult journey to respectability (Rose 2008). As recently as the mid-2000s, hip-hop had not yet even earned widespread academic attention (Rose, Walser, and Keyes were early advocates of the genre), and its musical characteristics were frequently written off as noisy or violent.

Among the rappers I followed, Jeremy takes the most assertive stance that Ethiopian-Israelis are outsiders; that it is because they are black; and that the state is to blame for their exclusion. Many residents of absorption centers take this view; some of the teenage boys I met on Thursday nights or at Eskesta performances have been conditioned to believe that their life prospects are curtailed "because I'm black" (*biglal/mipnei she'ani shahor*). To be sure, racism abounds in Israeli society, and the economic disadvantage that most Ethiopian-Israelis experience stacks the decks against them regarding employment and educational prospects. But one could argue that the comparison with African Americans, and the focus on the RSA instead of a celebration of Ethiopian success, effectively dictates that Jeremy's focus remains communal instead of national, since his commentary often involves placing blame squarely with the institutions that exclude Ethiopian-Israelis. This might be the reason that his appeal remains local, with Jeremy all but unknown in the broader Israeli rap scene.

Part of Jeremy's clarity lies in his use of pronouns. Whereas Axum narrates a first-person struggle to be productive (*li, eilai*), and CSH uses mostly third-person-singular points of view (*hee, hu*), Jeremy's position is first-person plural (*anahnu*). In a video that features an entirely Ethiopian cast of backup dancers, where the only non-Ethiopians are the bill collector in the opening sequence and two police officers who cross Jeremy's path at 0.55, an "us-and-them" construction abounds, as in "Anahnu po, v'hem sham," or "We are here, and they are there" at 1.14.[45]

As Ratner's book demonstrates (2015), the African American experience informs Ethiopian-Israeli life in some salient ways: both constitute a racial minority in a state with a dominant white immigrant majority. Both groups live within a state that is officially democratic, but that has a history of ongoing civil rights abuses against people of color deemed inferior. Both groups constitute nodes of an African diaspora, and they have an experience in common of their culture being denigrated and also appropriated. However, there are also many critical differences between the two groups' experiences. Crucially, Ethiopian-Israelis came to Israel by choice as opposed to by force (having immigrated rather than been brought as prisoners and enslaved); they have been citizens since they arrived; they are "above" Arab minorities in the social hierarchy; and they have never been subject to the extreme kind of violence and oppression that African Americans have. Indeed, the people who are still left in Addis Ababa, the Falash Mura awaiting visas, have engaged in a lengthy legal battle on behalf of their right to live in Israel (Seeman 2009: 28).

Jeremy has articulated effectively the attitude, commonplace among the multitude of club-going Ethiopian-Israelis, that hip-hop culture is an effective means of identifying with African Americans, and with a global economic underclass more broadly. He appeals to Ethiopian-Israeli young people because they can relate to his explicit association with African American hip-hop culture. He directs his critique at the powerful infrastructure of the Israeli state, which proves to be the recipe for amassing solidarity among disenchanted young Ethiopian-Israelis, but limiting appeal for wider Israeli audiences.

In a sense, each of the three songs described in this chapter engages in a critique of the State of Israel: CSH at a corrupt government, Jeremy at the police, and Axum at the inner workings of a welfare state that cannot accommodate immigrant minorities. Through a race-class axis that drives the infrastructures of global inequality, most Ethiopian-Israelis are marginalized intersectionally despite efforts to be good citizens. Yet in each of these three songs, the mechanisms whereby Ethiopian-Israelis realize their rights and responsibilities as citizens are described in starkly contrasting terms. Jeremy Kol Habash wears baggy clothes and raps behind a gate about how he does not have rights, while CSH roam the streets of Tel Aviv lamenting government corruption. Axum, meanwhile, channels the medium of rapping to survey poor neighborhoods and request the opportunity to be productive.

In the songs and in the groups' images, cultural references to Ethiopia arise sporadically, but the crux of each song is a negotiation between the Afrodiasporic and Zionist mythologies of exile and belonging that battle for control of the Ethiopian-Israeli conception of citizenship. Unlike in the IRP's songs that display sometimes veiled but recognizable Zionist agendas, or in neo-soul, or in dub music described in the next chapter, which represent a reorientation toward the African diaspora, Ethiopian-Israeli hip-hop offers a critical look at the real problems that Ethiopian-Israelis encounter when they try to resolve the two narratives, in which they alternately return from or join the diaspora.

The battling messages come through in both music and lyrics. Axum uses reggae to convey a point of nonaggression, while CSH frame themselves through collaboration as "new Mizrahim" who will integrate after a generation, whereas Jeremy makes no apologies for resenting his outsider status, displayed through his '90s R&B style. These musicians use instrumentation and syncretism as mechanisms within their compositional style that drive their dialectical negotiation of participation in the public sphere.

In particular, Axum's aesthetic schema is consistent with the convention of incorporating new immigrants' musical styles into songs about labor, drawing a distinct line from a nineteenth-century Bialik poem to today's popular rap songs. For Ethiopian-Israelis, as for a century of immigrants to Israel-Palestine, popular music is a central vehicle through which immigrant populations demonstrate their mastery of Israeliness through culturally intimate musical language. "Ma Im Hakesef" made it to the top of the charts, above all, because Axum's audience recognized a wax-and-gold dynamic whereby immigrant minorities mobilize cultural intimacy as a mechanism for becoming qualitative citizens.

SIX

Levinski Street,
Tel Aviv's Horn Mediascape

It's 10.30 a.m., and I am lost. I had turned from Begin Street onto what I thought would eventually become Har-Zion. But I wasn't on Har-Zion, and I could tell that I was quite a distance from where I wanted to be. There were mechanics standing out on the street smoking on every side of me, and the first pedestrian to pass was a Russian speaker. These are the hallmarks of working-class central Tel Aviv, and I was trying to get farther south (to working-poor labor migrant Tel Aviv). The roads don't move like that, though; Tel Aviv was built up in the 1920s and 1930s by predominantly German architects who needed to accommodate European refugees quickly, so the roads were built mostly on a slant. Unlike in the grid pattern of my hometown, New York, a Tel Aviv pedestrian can almost never see either the beach (the westernmost marker) or the Ayalon Expressway that cuts off the central neighborhoods from Greater Tel Aviv. I look for Hashalom Tower—it's north of where I wanted to be, but from any angle I turned it still looked like it was north. *I know my way around. I don't need help,* I tell myself as I walk in circles, passing mechanic after mechanic. I search for socioeconomic markers that I'm going in the right direction (that is to say, looking for a "worse" neighborhood). Finally, I stop at a lottery kiosk and ask the proprietor which way to Levinski Street. Furrowing his brow, he says, "But Levinski's . . . south." He means south Tel Aviv. He means that's not the neighborhood for me. Not prepared to get into it, I reply, "Yes, which way?" and he answers, "After Hamasger." I take it as a compliment that he presumes I know what that means. "So, *that* way," I confirm, pointing. He shrugs dismissively, so I head off in the direction that I hope is south.

Geographical disorientation and existential angst go together in Tel Aviv, because the city is built along a socioeconomic hierarchy befitting its political complexity (see Azaryahu 2006 or Mann 2006). Politicians and doctors live in Ramat Aviv (far north, by the university), wealthy Russian speakers and *Yekkes* (the descendants of Germans) live in Tsafon haYashan, the Old North, students and new French immigrants live central, Mizrahim and hipsters live south, and '48 Palestinians and bohemians live in Jaffa. Alongside the north-south axis, though, an east-west axis separates those who neighbor the beach from those who neighbor the expressway, and the working-poor labor migrants and asylum seekers who live south and east have the roughest time economically. The area where they live is known to all Israelis and tourists because its centerpiece is the Tel Aviv Central Bus Station (Taḥana Merkazit), the heartland of Israeli otherness. The bus station, in all its ethnographic richness, is a source of fascination to researchers because of the convergence inside of Tel Aviv's citizen and migrant subalterns (Hankins 2013, Horowitz 2010, Shokeid 2015, Webster-Kogen 2011). As an American teenager using the bus station to transit from kibbutz to Jerusalem, I wouldn't have been much interested in the Russian pop music, Filipino minimarkets, Bukharian bakeries, or Eritrean Internet cafes (to say nothing of the graffiti—see figure 6.1), the empty and abandoned bottom levels, or the AIDS clinic discreetly tucked away, because I possessed many of those class biases reflected in aesthetic taste.[1]

Because of those biases, I also would not have ventured out of the bus station to the thoroughfare that later became a focal point for me: Levinski Street.[2] Levinski runs east to west, and all the way down, it offers a glimpse into the complex matrix of migration and citizenship in Israel. As I describe the Ethiopian businesses and musical institutions that animate Levinski, the only major thoroughfare in Tel Aviv with substantial Ethiopian representation, I contend that race, class, and legal status converge around the cultural production that drives citizenship narratives of otherness and belonging.

For an enthusiast of Ethiopian culture, Levinski is actually rather confusing. For every Ethiopian restaurant with a proprietor wearing a *kippah*, there is another where nobody speaks Hebrew. Likewise for record stores and nightclubs. This is because Levinski, having been a hub for Mizrahi immigrants in the past and for labor migrants from Asia and Africa in the present (Fenster and Vizel

FIGURE 6.1 Graffiti in the Tel Aviv Central Bus Station (author photo)

2007), exists as a liminal space in Israeli history and culture. Ethiopian-Israelis occupy that space, too, as Israeli citizens at the bottom of the socioeconomic ladder, who are, through their black skin and origins in the Horn of Africa, phenotypically connected to the asylum seekers from Eritrea who live along Levinski today. So while mapping the Ethiopian-Israeli culture in south Tel Aviv necessarily involves discussion of the subjectivities of nationalism and exclusion that Ethiopian-Israelis inhabit in Israeli society, it also requires an understanding of Israel's minorities and non-Jewish refugees (see Kemp and Rajiman 2004). Ethiopian-Israelis are an in-between population in south Tel Aviv, sitting uncomfortably between citizens (like Mizrahim) and noncitizens (Eritreans). On Levinski, Ethiopian-Israelis are both insiders and outsiders, their connections along the avenue deriving from a state infrastructure that welcomes them but keeps them marginal.

In this chapter, I map the Ethiopian mediascape along Levinski, and examine the influence of mass migration of Eritrean asylum seekers on Ethiopian-Israeli status in the city of Tel Aviv.[3] I argue that the vibe along Levinski—the demographics, the businesses, the sounds—contributes to the sense that Ethiopian-

FIGURE 6.2 Concert advertisements at the Red Sea Internet Café (author photo)

Israelis are outsiders in the city, aspiring to join the infrastructures of state power but retaining reluctant links with the asylum seekers who are not Israeli (despite sometimes speaking excellent Hebrew). All up and down Levinski, Ethiopian-Israelis participate in the life of the city in ways that alternately connect them to the power structures of mainstream Zionism on the one hand, and to the subcultures of alterity on the other. To illustrate the former, I might mention the train station, in which young Ethiopian-Israelis work as security guards, a common job for working-class military veterans. To demonstrate the latter, I highlight the Red Sea Internet Café, an establishment that caters to the Eritrean asylum seekers who populate Neve Sha'anan, the neighborhood around Levinski, where promotional flyers for live music sit alongside phone plan deals (figure 6.2).

The Horn-dominated spaces along and around Levinski illuminate key issues in Ethiopian-Israeli public life: military service, language barriers, religious controversy, and generational class conflict. From the bus station to the train station, from Nahum Records to Afroshop, from the Red Sea Internet Café to Tenät restaurant not two hundred meters away, and from the Azmari-betoch on

Hamasger to the "black music" clubs on Harakevet Street, Ethiopian and Eritrean spaces in south Tel Aviv are composed of subcultural soundworlds that navigate the insider status of citizenship alongside the outsider positioning of minorities. With Azmari citizenship hovering in the foreground, this chapter surveys a local Horn mediascape that, for Ethiopian-Israeli citizens and for Eritrean asylum seekers, conveys often-diverging perspectives on similar musical material because of its symbolic power to connect them to the nation. The presence of Ethiopian-Israelis among the mix of labor migrants, and the tensions that arise between the groups, demonstrate some of the more mundane ways that music functions in the everyday life of the city's most marginal residents and visitors.

Walking down any street in Israel, an Ethiopian is immediately recognized by his or her skin color, but on Levinski, Ethiopians mark their space with the sound of Eskesta music and the imagery of red, yellow, and green (the Ethiopian flag's colors). Creating space for poor immigrants in a rich city, musical consumption and entrepreneurship transform citizenship from subaltern into participatory. All along Tel Aviv's most insalubrious district, Ethiopian-Israelis are represented, whether as agents of the security apparatus or as merchants of a sensorial world reaching out to visitors from the north of town. In these spaces, Ethiopian-Israelis move up the citizenship scale by bringing music into a national forum, and this chapter tracks the multiple subject positions they occupy alongside the people who share their phenotype but not their legal status.

TEL AVIV'S BINARY CITYSCAPE

The hierarchies and power imbalances propelled by the political dynamics of the State of Israel present themselves in microcosm in Tel Aviv's cityscape. Officially called Tel Aviv-Jaffa, the city's name bears the state's often-confusing binaries (see Azaryahu and Troen 2012). On the one hand, biblical lineage (the prophet Jonah set sail from Jaffa in his eponymous story) and primordialism (the *tel* part, which refers to an archaeological hill covering remains) ascribe to the city/cities a sense of prehistory. On the other, Arab alterity ('48 Palestinians live in a virtually segregated city within the municipality) and symbolic modernity (the "spring" part of the city's name — *aviv* — connotes awakening) invoke a new political order. This set of binaries is bolstered by a long-standing feud between secular, liberal Tel Aviv and religious, conservative Jerusalem (Ram 2005). Finally, the city was divided for decades between the rich Ashkenazi north of town, the center of the Israeli power structure composed of politicians, intellectuals, and

החניה אסורה

FIGURE 6.3 Construction boom in Tel Aviv (author photo)

entertainers, and poor south Tel Aviv, dominated by Mizrahim. Scholars like Benjamin Brinner (2009) map the directions of influences between Mizrahi musicians—upward, making inroads in an Ashkenazi mainstream, and across to Arab musicians living in Jaffa and East Jerusalem. In a complex matrix of relations between the foreign-born and displaced locals, Mizrahi music created an underexploited link between Jewish and Arab culture, in part because of the challenge of dividing resources in poor migrant Tel Aviv.

As Tel Aviv becomes increasingly removed from the surrounding State of Israel, though, with a skyrocketing cost of living and a soaring high-tech industry, the pockets of poor, migrant, and ethnic minority populations, what Sharon Rotbard calls the "black city" (2005), are isolated from the life of the city. As lawyers move into Kerem Hateymanim—the formerly rundown Yemenite quarter by the beach that is under mass renovation (Golan 2009: 126) (figure 6.3)—hipsters into Greek-founded Florentin, and Jewish creative types into Jaffa (see Monterescu 2015), the poor move over the expressway and farther from the beach. Walking the length of Levinski, one sees the full spectrum of Tel Aviv otherness, from the Ethiopian-Israeli citizens working as security guards at Hahagana train station overhanging the Ayalon Expressway, to the Eritrean migrants working for the Mizrahi merchant selling bourekas and almonds at the spice market around Herzl Street.

Today virtually the length of Levinski is dominated by the lowest rung on the social ladder—asylum seekers from Eritrea and Darfur (see Kritzman-Amir 2015)—but the area around the bus station has been a commercial center for working-class immigrants for decades. Amy Horowitz describes poignantly in her book on Mizrahi music the hierarchical judgments of class conflict in the fledgling state through the soundscape of the bus station, and outlines the set of social prejudices that caused elites to write off Mizrahi music as "bus station music" (2010). As the Mizrahi immigrants integrated into Israeli society, they moved out of the neighborhood, their denigrated music becoming part of a national soundscape. And today they have been replaced along Levinski by more recent arrivals, the poorer minorities whose civic status is unresolved.[4]

ETHIOPIAN-ISRAELI CITIZENSHIP IN THE NEWS

The political events of the past few years (since 2015) demonstrate that the Ethiopian and Eritrean position in Israeli society remains unstable. A series of social protests over the spring and summer,[5] or the murder of an Eritrean in Be'er Sheva who was confused for a Palestinian,[6] illustrate their unresolved integration and physical otherness in the body politic. The unrest highlights the importance of myths and symbols in connecting Ethiopian-Israelis to their cocitizens rather than to the Eritrean asylum seekers often called "infiltrators" by the media.

The unrest began on April 27, 2015, with social media reports that Demas Fekadeh, a young Ethiopian-Israeli, had been roughed up by police in Holon (a suburb in Greater Tel Aviv) the previous evening. The event was captured on closed-circuit television but still debated,[7] prompting an initial reaction of exhausted resignation. It came not from Fekadeh's skin color (black), but his clothes: he was wearing a military uniform and a *kippah*, perhaps the two most important sartorial symbols in the State of Israel (perhaps in addition to the Palestinian kaffiyeh). Ethiopian-Israelis have grown wary defending their religious credentials over the past twenty years, especially as more Ethiopians join rabbinic synagogues and attend yeshiva (Talmudic college). At any rate, the religious question has grown quiet over the past several years, as Ethiopian-Israelis seemed to be moving, slowly, up Israel's social ladder. Replaced by Sudanese and Eritrean asylum seekers at the very bottom of society, Ethiopian-Israelis counted themselves lucky for the mobility (albeit at others' expense) they possessed as citizens. And unlike the much larger minority population of '48 Palestinians, they were Zionist, serving in the military at the very highest rate among Israeli citizens (Cohen 2008: 114, Shabtay 1999). Having engaged in substantial efforts to become members of Israeli society, young Ethiopian-Israelis enrolled in universities and tried to demonstrate that their skin color was not an insurmountable problem in the state they supported.[8] So the image of Fekadeh, a visibly religious Jew on active military duty, being assaulted by police officers who apparently saw neither a Jew nor a soldier, but a *kushi* (derogatory term for a black person), soon unleashed collective defiance.

As the week progressed, the news reports spread—from Facebook, to local news, to *Haaretz,* to *The Guardian* and the *New York Times.*[9] Nightly protests in Jerusalem and Tel Aviv were growing violent, with both the president and prime minister stepping in to calm down the protesters and the police.[10] What became clear as the protests grew louder was that the "Ethiopian issue" in Israeli society had not yet been resolved, despite some years without controversy. Although they officially possessed all the rights of citizenship, Ethiopian-Israelis were demanding a sense of belonging that had not materialized. In effect, they wanted to be differentiated from noncitizen recent immigrants like the Eritreans.

Since the "blood affair" of 1996, Ethiopian-Israelis have tried to learn the rules of Israeli citizenship, advocating for their rights through community support organizations. When the interior minister called for an end to Falash Mura immigration in 2008[11] (that is, the immigration of Ethiopians who have recently returned to Judaism from Christianity, or who have a claim to citizenship on the basis of family reunification), the reaction was somewhat muted, the Ethiopian-Israeli population concerning itself with accumulating the qualifications necessary to secure employment. When consecutive Netanyahu governments launched military campaigns in Gaza, they participated. And when African migrants made the front pages of the newspapers because their appeals against deportation were deferred (Shokeid 2015: 216), they thought that they had earned a place of appreciation in Israeli society, perhaps considered a relative success story in the tidal wave of public relations disasters for the state. The problems of the Eritrean asylum seekers, and the '48 Palestinians feared to be "voting in droves,"[12] could not be the fault of institutional racism considering that the Ethiopians caused no such problems.

But in May 2015, the Ethiopian-Israeli population realized that their complicity had not yielded the mainstream recognition they expected, and they demanded the attention of the government. They turned to collective action, and their grievance was simple: that after arriving in Israel without the language, without job skills applicable to the Israeli economy, and with a family unit dismantled by a housing policy that favors the nuclear family over the extended family (see Westheimer and Kaplan 1992), their contribution as quantitative citizens (Shafir and Peled 2002)—as soldiers, and residents of border towns—was not sufficiently compensated by the government or acknowledged by society. Despite often voting for right-wing Zionist parties (Seeman 2009: 164), they were still suspect religiously. And despite full military participation, they were still looked upon with suspicion as criminals.[13] If there was resonance with the Black Lives Matter movement in the United States, that is not because people were being killed by the police (they were not), but because young people believed that the status quo was transforming Ethiopian-Israelis into Israel's equivalent of African Americans (see Salamon 2003 for a critique of the context of racializing Ethiopian social issues).

Walking down Levinski brings the crisis of Ethiopian-Israeli citizenship into focus. In juxtaposing Ethiopian record stores and restaurants with the bus and train station, hair salons and Internet cafes for Filipino and Nepalese labor migrants and Eritrean asylum seekers, along with clubs and unlicensed bars, a visitor gets the sense of Ethiopian-Israeli alterity through their proximity to other subalterns. Throughout this book, I have uncovered the processes through which musicians connect Ethiopian-Israelis to Israeli society, but here I identify areas of proximity with noncitizens. Indeed, the sheer concentration of non-Ethiopian Horn migrants in Tel Aviv today would have been a surprise to me during my 2008–2009 fieldwork, since the Eritreans, too, occupy a complex space in Tel Aviv's urban fabric, as Habesha people who are not Jewish. If Ethiopian-Israelis are in some ways closer to the Eritreans than to Israelis, it is not because they seek connections with them. By describing an emerging Horn mediascape, I highlight some of the ways that the fight for Ethiopian integration has been losing ground in the intervening years since I conducted my initial fieldwork.

CENTRAL BUS STATION

"Why would I be carrying a weapon?" Simon whispers to me.

"Just say no. It's fine," I respond, hurrying him along without bothering to go into detail, or to enumerate all of the things about this interaction that aren't fine.

It's my husband's first trip to Israel—he has come to visit me on fieldwork, and he is thoroughly bemused by the interrogation process that precedes entrance to any commercial or transport center.[14] At the entrance to the Tel Aviv Central Bus Station, like in front of malls and public buildings, young men in white shirts, and usually a *kippah*, guard the flow of people via turnstiles and metal detectors. We get through without any trouble, but behind me, an African American family speaking excellent Hebrew is detained, the father told that he can't bring in his suitcase, or that he has to open it up first to display the contents. "Then how am I supposed to make my bus?" he asks the guard. I tell him in English that the guard isn't going to budge, and I can help him take his bags to the next entrance if he likes. "Nah, these racists are all the same," he says, referring to the Ethiopian-Israeli security guard giving him trouble. I don't know how long he had been in Israel, but it was long enough to recognize that dominant racial hierarchies converge with citizenship hierarchies, and thus, that he can be discriminated against on racial grounds by someone with black skin and an Israeli passport.

Inside the bus station, everyone is carrying big bags that hadn't been opened up at the entrance. Russian pop music blares, and a long line for McDonald's spills into the hallway blocking the escalator. Filipina women prepare to make their weekly call home, and groups of giggling Ethiopian teenage girls in religious garb congregate around Café Aroma. Soldiers in every direction hurry to their bus platforms. Commuters avoid the abandoned bottom floors and the aggressive calls of cab drivers.

This is the Tel Aviv Central Bus Station, one of Tel Aviv's most iconic brutalist buildings (figure 6.4), and a notorious center for gray-market trade. At seven stories high, it was the biggest bus station in the world for nearly two decades until being overtaken recently by Delhi.[15] It has a lot of storefront property, and perhaps most of it was in use at one point. Today, though, the bottom two floors are virtually out of action, and university theater groups offer "bat tours" on Fridays (tours to see the bats) and graffiti exhibitions perpetually.[16]

The third floor—located at street level—is dominated by McDonald's and by Internet cafés and compact food stores frequented by the city's Filipino and Thai population.[17] The fourth-floor shops are owned and operated by Russian speakers, and the pirated CD and DVD stands are often the first impression of the Bauhaus city for many tourists, leading middle-class Anglophone tourists to think that Tel Aviv is grimy and dangerous. The fifth floor appears to be little more than a plateau to change escalator, which makes it a conveniently discreet location for the STD clinic that cares for the neighborhood's Russian-speaking sex-worker population.[18]

FIGURE 6.4 Interior of the Tel Aviv Central Bus Station (author photo)

To find people from the Horn, one should make a beeline for Afro-shop, the record store on the third floor in the loud and busy commercial center. Afro-shop sells all kinds of Ethiopian and Eritrean music, but its specialty is *musiqa sheḥorah*. Young people spend time thumbing through Tupac albums and the latest Eskesta videos from Addis Ababa, but a favorite local band of the day is Zvuloon Dub System, the reggae band that started out at the Afrodiasporic venues like Club Menilek and Club Rastafari, and that has earned enough of a following online that it toured the United States in summer 2014. Afro-shop is the kind of establishment that sells their records and promotes their concerts, proud that Israelis are interested in Ethiopian-Israeli singers.

Zvuloon Dub System is fronted by Gili Yalo, who was born in Ethiopia, but the rest of the band—Inon Peretz, Ilan Adiri, Ilan Smilan, Tal Smilan (the two brothers founded the band), Simon Nahum, Lior Romano, and Tal Marcus—is Ashkenazi or Mizrahi. As a frontman, Yalo offers the band some credibility playing reggae, thanks to the decades-long Rastafari connection to Ethiopia (he is currently testing the extent of that credibility by branching out into a solo career). The band incorporates Ethiopian instruments on its albums to lend it textural richness, but they sing in English about Zion, which comes off as notably un-Zionist. For any Ethiopian-Israeli fans for whom life in Israel has been a disappointment, Zion can take on alternative meanings—meaning Ethiopia in Jamaican symbology, but perhaps not the Ethiopia they or their parents left.

The proper noun in the band's title is the name of Leah's sixth son to Jacob in the biblical book of Genesis, Zevulun, whose name was eventually lent to one of the tribes that settled biblical Israel in the Galilee. When the Assyrians conquered in the seventh century BCE, the tribe was absorbed, thus being known as one of the "lost tribes of Israel." The rationale behind the name, therefore, ties in both to the Sephardi former chief rabbi Ovadiah Yosef's proclamation that the Beta Israel are the lost tribe of Dan (Salamon 2003: 6), but also to radical black narratives of the lost tribes. In choosing the name Zvuloon (note the more phonetically accommodating spelling), the reggae group ties together Israelite/Jewish, Beta Israel-specific, and pan-African/Afrodiasporic connotations of lost tribes being redeemed through return.

Zvuloon Dub System (henceforth referred to as ZDS) released their second album in 2014, called *Anbessa Dub*, which includes local Ethiopian favorite musicians like Azmari Dejen Manchlot, and especially the krar player Tigrinya Lilay, sometimes known to Israelis as Yaakov. The idea behind *Anbessa Dub* is the triangulation of the Ethiopian-Israeli mythologies that I have already unpacked, which the band frames as a sound that mixes Tel Aviv, Addis Ababa, and Kingston. The group strives for an Afrodiasporic sound resembling a product of Kingston or New York City, but they rely on a narrative of intersections of source materials. To that end, one song on the album samples Mahmoud Ahmed, and the group cites the *Kebra Negast* in its liner notes.

The musical style is rooted in reggae (and its stylistic successor, dub), with melody in the bass, emphasis on the second and fourth beats of a measure, and a slowed-down tempo. The lyrics to their best-known songs like "Going to Mount Zion" (Audio file 28), equally typical for the genre, bespeak a trip to Mount Zion and the request that "Jah" will "Protect I and I from all evil."[19] The adoption of Rastafari theological terminology for God ("Jah") and self ("I and I") is funny for Israeli listeners, who took compulsory Bible classes in school, and the references to Mount Zion might seem somewhat silly to the band's fans in and around Jerusalem. But the group doesn't seem self-conscious about the contextual strangeness of the English-language Zion trope as much as concerned with speaking in the Rastafari vernacular as a way of demonstrating their fluency in the musical language of reggae.

Tigrinya Lilay plays the krar on the 2014 album. ZDS often stages Lilay's krar right next to Gili Yalo,[20] creating the impression that despite English lyrics, Ashkenazi songwriters, and mostly rock instrumentation, the repertoire is heavily African- and Afrodiasporically influenced. The addition of the krar might not substantially change their song structure, but it yields audience interest in Ethiopian culture. The appearance or referencing of Mahmoud Ahmed, Dejen Manchlot, and Tigrinya Lilay on this album demonstrates that ZDS is serious about spotlighting Ethiopian music.

This is music conceived and produced by and for a mixed audience of Ethiopian-Israelis and the wider Israeli population, who basically sympathize with Ethiopian-Israeli social problems but whose orientation is outward toward national tropes. The bus station is a space of alterity, comprised of migrant minorities of all types, but the music coming out of places like Afro-shop often situates Ethiopians in Israel as a citizen minority that has something to offer Israeli society.

NAHUM RECORDS

One need only step outside the bus station for the picture of overlap between Ethiopian-Israeli citizens and Eritrean asylum seekers to appear substantially more complex. Across the street sits Nahum Records, the definitive emporium of Ethiopian music, magazines, and hair products. An Ethiopian music enthusiast might recognize the name from the Ethiopian record label based in Washington, DC, of the same name. For anyone familiar with the Israeli affinity for referential multilingual punning, this name for the store is mildly funny.[21] The shop is barely noticeable from the street since its storefront is only a few meters wide and its sign is written in Ethiopic script (*fidal*). Most of the store's clientele reads or recognizes *fidal*, but for anyone who can't, the red, yellow, and green-striped awning signals Ethiopia (figure 6.5). Inside, the store is barely ten square meters, and its walls are lined with CDs covered in Amharic and Tigrinya. The density of material available makes it pointless for a neophyte to navigate without assistance. As a non-Ethiopian there, the dominance of Amharic is striking—a Hebrew speaker wouldn't be able to choose a disc without guidance. The store's employees, who run the spectrum from expert curators to total indifference to customers, therefore become tour guides to everyone who enters the shop. As an archive of Ethiopian culture, Nahum Records offers more of a history lesson than a consumer experience.

FIGURE 6.5 Nahum Records from Levinski Street (author photo)

The store has been around since the 1990s, founded by immigrants who came over in Operation Solomon (1991), including Nahum. The clientele is made up of Ethiopian-Israelis passing through town, sometimes Eritreans who live in the neighborhood, and Israelis who want to learn more about Ethiopian culture. I was fortunate that the first time I visited, the late proprietor (who died in 2016) was sitting at the counter; on many subsequent visits he was in the office or unavailable. On other occasions I dealt with his deputy, Avi, who kept me informed about Azmari performances at temporary restaurants, or with a pair of women who failed to recognize me even after a dozen visits.

It wasn't until my fourth visit or so that I actually got a look at the vast stacks of discs that cover the interior walls. The owner wasn't around, and the women on the desk greeted me as a lot of Ethiopians do in that context—with amusement and skepticism. Defiant, I huddled in a corner and left with CDs chosen at random. Unwrapping the CDs at home, I understood their confusion—the choice was vast, the customers learn best about Ethiopian music by following the experts' advice, and I had chosen poorly. I listened to the synthed-up Azmari disc once and left it to collect dust. I realized after that visit how important an ambassadorial role the store was fulfilling. Assigning a record a place on a shelf is, for a visible minority establishing its own space in a rich city, not an isolated action, but the final step in a process of classification and evaluation that enables Ethiopian-Israelis to process the meaning of a text, and to navigate public representation.

The employees of Nahum Records are responsible for thinking about how to place and promote the music of different regions and ethnic groups, which presents differences that some but not all patrons appreciate. Gurage folk music, Bolel (urban Azmari), and Tigrinya pop might share the same instruments, but they hold distinctions for their listeners that matter a great deal in conceiving of life "back home." Or even more confusingly, how might one classify Tigrinya Lilay, the krar player who collaborates with ZDS? He works within traditional and popular networks, dealing with Ethiopian-Israelis and non-Ethiopian-Israelis in about equal measure. Lilay hosts a YouTube channel that promotes his business,[22] performance at Ethiopian weddings. His videos are usually closer to the Eskesta material—that is, national dance—than to the commercial, mediated music for broader national consumption. In his wedding material, his performative identity is a Tigrayan krar player. When he plays with ZDS, though, he often goes by Yaakov, using the Hebrew name that would have been assigned to him upon arrival or at boarding school in his childhood. He transitions seamlessly between his Tigrinya-self and his Yaakov-self according to the style of music for which he is contracted.

Should a musician like Lilay develop a wedding business, maintaining a band, perhaps eventually teaching krar students, and sticking to Tigrayan repertoire, he has the potential to establish financial mobility. Wedding work is reliable and consistent, since Ethiopian-Israelis invest as much of their assets as they can in enormously celebratory weddings, though the repertoire today comes from Addis Ababa rather than villages (Seeman 2009: 210). Since Lilay's reputation has spread by word of mouth, and he is respected on the Ethiopian wedding circuit, he has plenty of earning capacity in this part of his performance life. Having a CD in a place like Nahum Records would be a mark of honor for the shop, since there isn't much material there that is locally made. Nahum Records wouldn't sell ZDS, for example, since the lyrics are in English—that is material for Afro-shop—but it might sell anything put out in an Ethiopic language.

The decision of how and when to stock local musicians renders Nahum Records influential over south Tel Aviv's Horn mediascape. One part of that influence is initiating people into the history and content of Ethiopian music, chatting with visitors about what they like, and sending them away with material that provides an overview of the diverse musical climate in Ethiopia. But at the same time, Nahum Records and its employees control the way that music is classified and categorized, with religious and Afrodiasporic styles noticeably absent. Ethiopian Jewish liturgy, somewhat overrepresented in the scholarly literature thanks to the work of Kay Kaufman Shelemay (1986) and the French and Israeli scholars who sought different conclusions based on her work (Atar 2005, Tourny and Arom 2005), is absent from the store. That is because the shop's remit is, in addition to providing the raw material to learn about Ethiopian culture, to preedit it so as to offer a repertoire that is contemporary and respectable. On Levinski, the editor-shopkeeper who ultimately decides which aspects of a fractured and elusive "back home" will be remembered is responsible for the practices of choosing and disseminating repertoire that initiates Ethiopians, Eritreans, and a small number of non-Ethiopians into the vast set of popular and traditional styles that comprise popular music of the Horn. The seemingly modest Nahum Records plays no direct role in musical performance, but its editorial fingerprint on Tel Aviv's Ethiopian musical climate is distinct.

In a country where the news is dominated by demographic data, "facts on the ground," and the political ramifications of building permits,[23] Nahum Records situates Ethiopian-Israelis within the power structure. In Tel Aviv, where securing a few square meters of real estate translates into upward mobility, Nahum Records has created a space for Ethiopian culture in a city from which Ethiopians are more or less excluded. This exclusion, which manifests itself through denigrating comments about religious credibility, the immigrant generation's shaky command of Hebrew, and failure to be absorbed successfully into the workforce, is sometimes explained away with the culture-wars catchphrase of "cultural differences," and specifically, the notion that Ethiopian-Israelis came to Israel without culture or heritage. To a vast majority of the musicians, audience members, and community workers I encountered in my time in and around Tel Aviv, like for Fantahun the young self-taught Azmari, music is indeed a source of pride, but also of material gain, cultural capital, and upward mobility. A place like Nahum Records, in which a whole roomful of texts (CDs with liner notes) demonstrates the existence of long-standing tradition, contributes in its own way to the impetus to participate in civil society.

RED SEA INTERNET CAFÉ

By the time one leaves Nahum Records and walks two blocks down Levinski, one recognizes a paradox: that despite the charges in the media that Ethiopian-Israelis encounter discrimination and marginalization, one comes face-to-face with a lot of people with a phenotype from the Horn of Africa in south Tel Aviv. At first glance, a visitor might then think that Tel Aviv is full of Ethiopian-Israelis. But the East Africans on Levinski are more often than not Eritrean asylum seekers, who now dominate the bottom of Tel Aviv's service sector. As recently as my first year of fieldwork in 2009, the jobs washing dishes in restaurants and stacking chairs at the beach were mostly occupied by Palestinians, but as the population from Jaffa has become educated (Rabinowitz and Monterescu 2008: 213), some Arab citizens have moved on to more lucrative jobs. Meanwhile Eritreans have moved into those jobs, and at any café or restaurant in town one finds a few migrants from the Horn working in the background. Many of them speak Hebrew now, and they send their earnings home. On Levinski, it can be difficult to tell the difference between an Ethiopian-Israeli citizen and an Eritrean asylum seeker because they often code-switch between Hebrew and Amharic or Tigrinya (the latter being more or less mutually intelligible for an Amharic speaker). And for an Ethiopian music enthusiast who wants to know where the gigs are happening, the first stop should really be the window of the Red Sea Internet Café on Levinski (see figure 6.2).

Just off the intersection with Har-Zion, Red Sea Internet Café is a central Horn mediascape in town. The windows are covered in ads for live Ethiopian and Eritrean music happening around south Tel Aviv, mostly in small unadvertised bars around Hamasger. The words "Red Sea Internet Café" are written in English only, and inside, most everyone is young, male, single, and Eritrean. They are there to socialize, once they've made contact with their families back home. The Eritrean asylum situation is well known by now in Europe following the media coverage of the rogue state's compulsory military service,[24] often served indefinitely and usually involving menial and manual labor. At present, 3 percent of Eritrea's population has fled (see Poole 2013), most going north to seek safety in Europe. The Eritrean population in Israel is older, most of them, including some from nearby Darfur, having arrived in 2008 and 2009. They came up via the Red Sea and Sinai with great difficulty, nearly everyone arriving with a horror story about economic exploitation (for the men), sexual assault (for the women),[25] or bearing witness to organ harvesting (for the most severely exploited) by smugglers.[26] Today there are 55,000 Eritreans in Israel, or nearly half the number of Ethiopian-Israelis, and a majority of them live in Tel Aviv.[27] Actually, most of their asylum applications are still pending, because the courts have slow-walked their files, afraid to set a precedent. Several thousand have been rejected, another few thousand have been offered incentives to travel to a third country such as Uganda or Rwanda, and still more have been detained in the Holot or Saharonim centers in the Negev Desert. There is some crime in the community, but for the most part this population has tried to make life in limbo work. Part of the reason they are at the Internet café is to alert their families to remittances they will be sending back (Feinstein International Center 2012).

Inside, the only language exchanged is Tigrinya, the most widespread Eritrean language, which is also spoken by the small minority of Ethiopian-Israelis whose families originated in Tigray, the region bordering Eritrea. There is no Hebrew or Amharic to be heard anywhere inside—not among the customers, and not coming from the dance music blaring out of the speakers.[28] The music is recognizable to any Ethiopian, though, because the vocal style, dancing conventions, and synthed-up instrumental accompaniment are similar to the styles favored across Ethiopia. The pastoral scene and domestic metaphors in Eskesta-style videos remind the asylum seekers of an idealized life back home that they know they aren't actually missing out on, but the sounds of the krar and the solo male vocal accompanying the harvest dance offer recognizable imagery from the Ethiopianist narrative of a glorious, independent African history.

TENÄT

And finally, less than two hundred meters from the Red Sea Internet Café, Tenät caters to a relatively upmarket crowd (see figure 6.6). The restaurant is vegan, which is a smart choice considering its location and the ongoing dispute over Ethiopian religious credibility. In the shadow of the rabbinate's hopelessly corrupt supervisory system to ensure that food is kosher,[29] proprietors of Ethiopian restaurants in Israel deal with the wider population's doubt by brandishing their rabbinic certification (te'udat kashrut). Veganism is a good alternative so that customers know that they are at no risk of eating nonkosher meat. By being vegan Tenät can attract a moderately religious crowd, to say nothing of the hipsters from nearby Florentin. On a typical visit to the restaurant, technically located just off Levinski on Tchlenov Street, there are usually some bohemian or academic types at the next table.

FIGURE 6.6 Tenät Restaurant by day (author photo)

Tenät doesn't offer live music often, instead having a screen in the corner that projects soccer. But on a lucky evening at multiple places like Tenät around Hamasger, or indeed at Habesh's new location on Hanegev Street, a patron might catch a set with someone like Dejen Manchlot. Dejen plays the massenqo, and while he trained to accompany himself as a solo singer, in Tel Aviv, performance usually requires a drum machine to facilitate dancing. After playing as a sideman in Addis Ababa for prominent musicians like Mahmoud Ahmed, he came to Israel in 2006 (personal communication, 2009), and today he performs frequently with Ethiopian saxophonist Abate Barihun (and appeared on the ZDS album) in addition to weekly gigs around the country.

On a night where someone like Dejen performs, a restaurant becomes more like an Azmari-bet. Virtually every city in Israel has an Ethiopian restaurant that occasionally doubles as an Azmari-bet, and with the Horn population being as concentrated as it is in south Tel Aviv, there are several that pop up for short periods on Hamasger by the highway, or in private houses in Neve Sha'anan, the neighborhood around Levinski. But this is the place in all of Tel Aviv where one is most likely to find Israelis, Ethiopian-Israelis, and Eritreans occupying the same space, and also where the differences between them are starkest. The symbols of belonging on display there code alternately as indexes of belonging to the Israeli nation, to the neighborhood, and to the Horn mediascape.

In each of these distinct spaces, and many others documented in the work on south Tel Aviv (see Hankins 2013 or 2015 or Shokeid 2015), Ethiopian-Israelis encounter the migrants of Tel Aviv, the Israeli residents of Tel Aviv, and the other population from the Horn in different mixes. In the four locations, one hears a variety of genres of Horn-derived popular music, almost all of which use a synthesizer and circulate digitally. On Levinski, which forms a single Horn mediascape today, musical performance and recordings are cultural currency for two groups separated by legal status.

This portrait of Levinski doesn't convey Azmari citizenship fully, because (apart from ZDS) it ignores the nationally consumed material like the Idan Raichel Project, national Eskesta dance troupes, or musical exports like Ester Rada. But this sketch of Levinski's Horn mediascape offers a profile in the kinds of social issues the different strands of new immigrants face, and a picture of a music scene that stays within the community and for the most part doesn't engage national tastes. That in itself offers a commentary on what many Ethiopians think of the hybrid material that Israelis consume more readily.

For the State of Israel's marginal citizens and residents, the alternative mediascape of south Tel Aviv offers a textured commentary on inequality in a rich, modern city. The aesthetic manifestations of political upheaval and transnational migration are embedded in the urban mediascape of Neve Sha'anan that narrate the lives of young Ethiopian-Israelis. The Tel Aviv Central Bus Station, Nahum Records, the Red Sea Internet Café, and Tenät, in addition to the clubs around Harakevet or the unlicensed Azmari-betotch on Hamasger, are creative spaces for an immigrant minority still insecure about its status in a society where they remain conspicuous. When they find themselves traveling and working alongside migrants of the same regional background who will likely never be citizens, their status is reconfigured along musical lines, with live performance on Ethiopian instruments offering a direct route to articulating what they want their place to be in the national narrative. Levinski is a confusing but productive space for Ethiopian-Israelis to work through national (Israeli), regional (that is, the Horn), and subcultural (or Afrodiasporic) subjectivities that form the basis of a multilayered citizenship.

Conclusion

Mishkenot Sha'ananim, Jerusalem, September 9, 2014

It is my first time at the Jerusalem Festival of Sacred Music (2014), and a diminutive, solitary figure in white robes emerges under a spotlight. Visibly moved, Alemu Aga sets his lyre on the stage overlooking the Old City walls. This is Aga's first invitation to perform in Jerusalem, the city sanctified in the imaginaries of Ethiopian Christianity. For musician and instrument—the Ethiopian lyre is commonly known as "the harp of King David"—this is a homecoming, a pilgrimage to the city where Jesus is said to have died, where Ethiopian civilization's imagined progenitor king, Menilek, gained God's favor by stealing the Ark and transferring the sacred source of power and authority to Ethiopia (Levine 2000). Unlike many professional musicians who travel to the State of Israel to perform, Aga has not spent months agonizing over the cultural boycott, nor does he consider himself to be taking sides in an intractable conflict. Nor does he intend to soothe the audience's nerves with uplifting statements about conflict resolution or building bridges between cultures. Aga introduces his selection: "This piece . . . is about the futility of life."

These resonances are lost on the audience, a generally left-leaning crowd of older Jewish Jerusalem residents. They came to the concert because they knew that Aga was featured in the Idan Raichel Project's "Bo'ee" or they wanted to hear African music, perhaps not expecting the paraliturgical verse of the Tewahedo Church, the world's second oldest (Ullendorff 1968).[1] Aga's performance conjures the formulaic, rigid liturgy of monks and priests, arcane and impenetrable to many Western and world music audiences but vaguely familiar to an ear trained in Jewish liturgy. Yet despite an insurmountable language barrier and little sense in the audience of what the music means, Aga somehow channels his Christian faith to this audience as though Menelik had never left Jerusalem.

Aga's performance can be framed as a spiritually charged return, yet it is also part of an exchange that has expanded in the past decade between Ethiopia and Israel. Ethiopian musicians who come to Israel are not coming for pilgrimage as such. Rather, they perform in Jerusalem or Tel Aviv, as did international star Aster Aweke in 2014,[2] for Ethiopian-Israelis (Kaplan 2005: 389). Visiting Ethiopian musicians are often requested to perform nostalgic work that reminds their audience of life "back home," or some approximation of it. Strikingly, there was no Ethiopian-Israeli presence at this highbrow performance of a Christian musician. The interest in this particular act seemed to emanate purely from a national (Israeli) interest in learning something about Ethiopian culture. It would be imprecise, however, to explain Aga's invitation to Jerusalem as the expression of mere curiosity on the part of the Israeli public, or as an effort to replicate show-cases of exoticism occasionally promoted by Western European venues such as London's Barbican Centre or Paris's Cité de la Musique. The significance of this concert is twofold: on the one hand, "Aga in Jerusalem" constitutes in itself a small but telling sign of two nations opening themselves up to each other, politically, socially, and culturally. The signs of this budding relationship are many: trade relations are flourishing[3]—including the import of herbs for traditional healing (Danino and Amar 2009: 113)—and visiting Ethiopia is becoming a rite of passage after completing military service as the counterpart to the Israeli postarmy phenomenon of traveling around India, Thailand, or Brazil.[4] On the other hand, Aga's visit can be taken as evidence of the tentative but tangible social advancement of Ethiopian-Israelis and the internationalization of their cultural scope.

When I began my research in Tel Aviv in 2008, the only prominent Ethiopian musicians coming through town were so-called "sidemen," or musicians who played in the bands for Ethio-jazz greats in the 1970s and 1980s. Like Dejen Manchlot or jazz saxophonist Abate Barihun (whom I haven't discussed in detail in this book, but whose jazz-fusion album *Ras Deshen* is highly acclaimed), these musicians were often themselves immigrants to Israel, and they didn't tour so much as find venues to host weekly gigs. Indeed, Tel Aviv and Jerusalem were completely off the grid for Ethiopian performers who, like many other Ethiopians, resented Ethiopian-Israelis for relocating during a famine (Karadawi 1991), subsequently remaining cut off from Ethiopian culture. For that matter, Ethiopian-Israelis never had much money to spend on leisure activities, so they had little pull as a diasporic market. Yet only a few years after my initial research the situation is transformed. Ethiopian-Israelis may remain at the bottom of the socioeconomic ladder in Israel (Elias and Kemp 2010), but young people are graduating from university and finding employment in increasing numbers. Whereas the young people I met early in my research were concerned first and foremost with visible signs of betterment such as education and employment, this new class of university educated and better-integrated Ethiopian-Israelis has shown interest in exploring their parents' premigration lives. And like all Israelis, they are increasingly drawn to the idea of traveling for extended periods and living and working in the United States or Western Europe, where it can sometimes be easier to establish peer networks among other Ethiopians than among Israelis. In a pleasantly surprising turn of events, these sociological changes, as well as the impetus to travel to Ethiopia and to encounter fellow Ethiopians in Rome or Harlem, has rendered Tel Aviv a stop on the itinerary of touring Ethiopian musicians, even world-famous artists like Teddy Afro in 2010 and 2013 and Mahmoud Ahmed in 2012.[5]

The most recent musical events that I have described in this book (from 2014 and 2015) — Ester Rada's success on the European jazz-festival circuit, visits by Ethiopian pop stars to Israel — confirm the entry of Israel into the Ethiopian diaspora, and a preliminary resolution of the dialectics of Zionist, Ethiopianist, and Afrodiasporic myths. The arrival of Aster Aweke and *Éthiopiques*'s ambassadors in Israel demonstrates, in effect, that Ethiopian-Israelis have arrived. After decades of marginality, they are now visible enough in both Israeli society and the Ethiopian diaspora to bring in the best-known Ethiopian musicians (such as those mentioned in Shelemay 2006a), and to frame those performances in local terms, i.e., Jerusalem's local musical culture. The mutuality of exchange — the offer from the musicians to perform, and the offer of sponsors to pay their travel — demonstrates a multidirectional upward mobility of Ethiopian-Israelis. The revamped, adult configuration of Cafe Shahor Hazak that performed in December 2015 at Limmud, the British annual Jewish-studies conference, were ambassadors of Israeli difference and astute employers of Jewish blackness as a rarefied form of cultural capital. As the State of Israel becomes increasingly isolated abroad, such cultural capital may even be deployed to political ends. The mobilization of reggae and hip-hop musicians might cynically serve the state's image caretakers as concrete proof of openness to diversity. Israel joining the Ethiopian diaspora via the musical touring circuit represents, above all, the reconfiguration of entrenched hierarchies that Zionist and Afrodiasporic mythologies enact and represent.

THE FUTURE OF INTEGRATION

Throughout this book, I have illustrated the multiple voices that Ethiopian-Israeli musicians take on as they articulate their place in Israeli society, arguing that subtle codes function as alternative political frameworks. Over the past decade, musicians have become often-inadvertent political spokespeople, since the usual pathways to political change have proven ineffective. As traditional routes to integration have led to dead-ends, individual Ethiopian-Israelis have found a route into Israeli society documented in this book, one whereby the mainstream considers their contribution legitimate and valuable. It was a surprise to me in 2008, when I first arrived in Tel Aviv, to field constantly the dual set of questions over Ethiopian religious legitimacy and musical representation that I have mentioned previously. The juxtaposition of "So, are they really Jewish?" with "Have you heard of the Idan Raichel Project?" may have been jarring, but it was an early clue as to the potential music has to make the case for Ethiopian-Israeli belonging. It is no small achievement for the population to have found a path to representation that cuts out powerful but ultimately ineffective state infrastructures.

It would be incomplete, however, to let this positive account stand without qualification, especially in light of the events of the summer of 2015, when a highly publicized social protest movement erupted over the mistreatment of an Ethiopian-Israeli solider by the police. As I described in chapter 6, the closed-circuit-television-captured manhandling of Demas Fekadeh was troubling for the Israeli public but somewhat expected for Ethiopian-Israelis. What took the country by surprise was the course of events that followed: the protests in major urban centers that turned violent, with tires burning and police using force to disperse crowds, and the public apologies from politicians in high office; the acquittal of the police;[6] and the eventual subsiding of the mass protest without tangible results. While the pain of Ethiopian-Israeli exclusion has been acknowledged unambiguously over the past year or two, the state has made it clear that easing that pain will only be prioritized under threat of violence.

These events remind us that the process of integration still has a long way to go. Ethiopian-Israelis remain at the bottom of the socioeconomic hierarchy, with half of all Ethiopian-Israeli households having no breadwinner (Ben-Eliezer 2008,

Shapira 2012) and more than 60 per cent of Ethiopian-born men never having worked in Israel (ibid.). There is a real danger that the events of 2015 are early fissures that threaten to undermine, if not undo entirely, the modest successes of an Ester Rada or Cabra Casay in forging a critical but productive dialogue with a reticent Israeli mainstream over civil rights and belonging.

The association of Ethiopian-Israeli civil rights with the African American movements against police brutality like Black Lives Matter could have an integrating or a deintegrating result. Unlike the American movement that has gained steam since the summer of 2014, protests in Tel Aviv that claim similarity to the Ferguson experience have earned little critical mass or recognition in the corridors of power. From a musical standpoint, I have already explored how the dynamic plays out in hip-hop material that identifies explicitly with the black experience in the United States of dealing with the repressive state apparatus. More broadly, if musicians really do play a key role in effecting social change and political inclusion, there is a legitimate argument to be made that Ethiopian-Israeli comparisons to black life in America are spurious or, in the worst case, self-fulfilling prophecies. Only time will tell if the ideologies of black authenticity are an asset in accruing cultural capital.

The condition of Ethiopian-Israelis vis-à-vis the Israeli state and society has, moreover, been vastly complicated by the arrival of Eritrean asylum seekers, several thousand of whom reside in the Negev Desert's Holot and Saharonim detention centers, and far more of whom staff the Tel Aviv service sector. The shifting demographics of blackness in Israel require of Israelis to draw ever finer distinctions of culture, nationality, and religion and come to terms with the nonreligious and nonideological pull factors that bring migrants to Israel. In conscious contradistinction to Eritrean economic migrants, Ethiopian-Israelis are presently asking to be rewarded as Jews and committed Zionists, yet an uncomfortable reality is now developing in Tel Aviv in the wake of Eritrean migration. Some of the asylum seekers engage in petty or violent crime, but many of them speak excellent Hebrew and send their children to Israeli schools where they learn the norms of Israeli society. In contrast to some of the Ethiopian-Israeli immigrants living in absorption centers, supported just enough by the state not to need to learn Hebrew but not enough to be able to find work or to equip their children with the tools they need to succeed in Israel, some of the asylum seekers who arrive as able-bodied young workers are actually integrating more efficiently. Around the Tel Aviv city center, most of the black faces one encounters these days are Eritrean, whereas Ethiopian-Israelis are often confined to marginal spaces and neighborhoods. In the Israeli center of economic and cultural power, black faces remain underrepresented when they are the faces of citizens who have relied on the government to absorb them.

What we see emerging is an increasingly complex sociological picture with some Ethiopian-Israelis forging ahead and many left behind, with the forces of cultural and diasporic globalization working to increase the community's prestige but also deintegrating Ethiopian-Israelis along the lines of their racial (black) identity. Embracing a narrative of blackness can bring social mobility when it opens the door to European jazz festivals (as in the case of Ester Rada), while it can invoke the despair of the global urban underclass (as in the case of Jeremy Kol Habash). Likewise, Ethiopian source material can be leveraged into a token of exoticism in the world music market as it is for the Idan Raichel Project, or it can invoke nostalgia for a life of rural poverty back home, as Azmari music often does. As performers, dancers, and audiences use source material from Ethiopia, Israel, and the African diaspora to define their positions on religion, politics, and their bodies, the population is becoming more internally divided along class lines while also failing to be absorbed into Israeli society. In this sense, Ethiopian-Israelis bear a remarkable similarity to their adopted nation, growing ever more partisan and divided.

In light of these contradictory forces rending the community, the future of Ethiopian-Israeli music may lie in its rarely acknowledged and modest aims. The music examined in this book sometimes deals directly with the issues of integration and belonging, but most often not. Instead, the musicians I worked with, interviewed, and followed online, as well as their audiences, are less concerned with making explicit political statements than with building an audience and creating a discernible musical signature. Those musical signatures, individually, draw from diverse source material and make modest statements about society, but as a composite, they articulate a political agenda that, in practice, translates directly into public advocacy. As a singer building a following in Europe, Ester Rada might not intend for her individual aesthetic choices to amount to a worldview or political ideology, just as Axum or the leftist Idan Raichel might not intentionally invoke ubiquitous Zionist tropes in their inclusion of Ethiopian samples and sounds. But their choices of instrumentation, language, tonality, vocal timbre, source material, and iconic nonverbal sounds contribute to the construction of a soundworld in which sound has discernible political meaning.

———

I have articulated those meanings as myths, or sounds that are assembled and invoked to build a narrative. The three dominant narratives that I have gleaned over the years of working with Ethiopian-Israeli musicians—Ethiopianist, Afro-diasporic, and Zionist—are sometimes performed individually, or more often in combination with one another to construct a profile of Ethiopian-Israeli citizenship. I have thus proposed that Ethiopian-Israelis engage in Azmari citizenship, or the consistent rehearsal of wax and gold in their dealings with the state. They do so by often refraining from explicit critique of the Israeli government and society, instead inserting critique into musical style in a manner that can be immediately recognized by listener-insiders. These critiques can be as outright as Jeremy Kol Habash's lyrics, such as, "Where is *our* nation in bloom?," or as subtle as Inyalinya's preference to keep its Amharic name.

It is irrefutable, though, that Ethiopian-Israelis seek the rights and responsibilities of citizenship, from the right to migrate (and for the Falash Mura, to complete the immigration of the several thousand awaiting permission in Ethiopia) to the fulfillment of military duty. These rights and responsibilities bear directly on the possibility of upward mobility, for which there is a renewed urgency today. Along with high-profile achievements, like Ethiopian-Israeli singer Hagit Yaso winning *Kokhav Nolad* (A Star Is Born, Israel's version of *American Idol*) come new challenges.

The Ethiopian-Israeli musical scene has changed substantially in the years since I commenced research in summer 2008, and one can assume that even more apparent musical evolvements are still to come. For example, I have made little mention of jazz saxophonist Abate Barihun, a virtuosic innovator who brings Ethio-jazz to jazz collaborations, and the next generation might yield conservatory-trained musicians equipped to bring their own interpretations to jazz and Ethio-jazz. So far, Ethiopian-Israelis have almost no profile in the fields of classical and art music, but as the Azmari and Ethio-jazz traditions earn acclaim nationally, there will no doubt be demand for composers from within the tradition. For those musical mediums to be left in the hands of Ethiopian performers, rather than Ashkenazi/Mizrahi facilitators, would be a considerable development.

Some of these musical developments will come at a cost, and others will render Ethiopian-Israeliness even more complex. I have mentioned the decline of Ethiopian Jewish ritual in Israel, a result of the rabbinate's delegitimization of Qessim, and of the desire to integrate. With the decline of Ge'ez scriptural knowledge and expertise in Beta Israel liturgy, one can only guess what will happen to events like Sigd. At the same time, the rise of Pentecostalism among Horn migrants all over the world is already affecting Tel Aviv, with some Falash Mura and Eritrean asylum seekers seeking out a more direct religious experience than the Orthodox Church provides. Most of the Pentecostal networks exist beyond the reach of religious overseers, but the rise of the religious right as a political force in Israel, combined with the encounter of Ethiopians and Eritreans along Levinski Street, could yield fascinating cultural collaborations or familiar religious problems.

Finally, the dynamics of Ethiopian-Israeli society will inevitably change as the Israeli-born generation comes of age. Many of the musicians I consulted live in absorption centers, and some younger musicians behave as de facto caregivers to their parents. As these young people leave the absorption centers and enter the workforce, they will encounter many of the typical problems of urban migration across the Global North involving the ghettoization of minorities. Yet many of them are equipped for this, and resolutely determined to join the Israeli middle class by acquiring a university degree. They will no doubt be better integrated than their parents, but it remains to be seen what kinds of ties they will want to maintain with Ethiopia in the long term. The musical soundworld that I have presented is therefore a work in progress, and the cultural and political processes by which Ethiopian-Israelis navigate their positionality as citizens will be affected by the current political climate in Israel, and to a lesser degree by trends in Ethiopian music in Addis Ababa and the Ethiopian diaspora. The ongoing process of subject formation and reformation is facilitated by locally specific but intersecting and overlapping subjectivities of gender, religion, blackness, ethnicity, and citizenship. For Ethiopian-Israelis as for other Israeli minority immigrants and for many Ethiopians across the diaspora, social mobility requires the transformation of self and the contextually appropriate destabilizing of fixed identities. In the meantime, the often-imperceptible ideologies behind Ethiopian, Israeli, and Afrodiasporic musical cues amount to a dramatic remapping of this postexile/ newly diasporic group's collective understanding of nation, speech, and power.

NOTES

INTRODUCTION *Symbolic Codes of Citizenship*

1. The naming of Ethiopia's Jews has a troubled history. The Beta Israel (House of Israel) come from northwest Ethiopia, where their history traces back some six centuries by scholarly accounts (Shelemay 1986: 203), or as far back as three thousand years according to fanciful local lore (Parfitt 1985: 8). They lived in villages in the mountains of Gondar and Tigray, often in punishing poverty, maintaining minimal relations with world Jewry. Throughout this book I refer to them as Ethiopian-Israelis, a term that includes all Ethiopian immigrants regardless of the nuances of their family's religious background.

2. The affair is still widely referenced today, and Don Seeman devotes substantial attention to it in his book *One People, One Blood* (2009). Officials were concerned about potentially high rates of infection among Ethiopian immigrants with HIV and hepatitis B, but did not want to shame Ethiopian soldiers donating blood on military bases. So rather than turning them away as donors, or testing the blood for infection, they discarded all Ethiopian blood. A long period of protest followed the revelation of this policy decision.

3. The term "soundworld" is used occasionally in musicology, and while it implies a holistic impression of sonic references, it usually goes without being defined precisely. Deborah Kapchan uses it as a substitution for "sound economy" (2009 for the latter, 2017 for the former); she does not define it, but it sounds in context much as I define it. In this book I define a soundworld as the complete range of source material that shapes my informants' sensory life, including soundscape (an important but discernibly incomplete part of a soundworld), live music, recorded music, and language/speech. Indeed, the term "soundscape" has taken on a life of its own in the fledgling subdiscipline of Sound studies, where it refers to the sounds associated with a certain place. Kay Kaufman Shelemay's definition of soundscape in her textbook of the same name (2006b) defines a soundscape much as I define soundworld.

4. The Jerusalem citadel was refinished by Suleiman the Magnificent in the sixteenth century. The attribution to King David makes it a major tourist destination for pilgrims.

5. The musical style that was popular in Addis Ababa in the 1970s, and which is popular today among "world music" audiences. The *Éthiopiques* CD collection offers exhaustive coverage of the genre, including material by Mahmoud Ahmed, Alemayehu Eshete, Mulatu Astatke, and other musicians who have earned acclaim at home and abroad.

6. This is a commonly used expression of anxiety that Ethiopian-Israelis frequently repeated to me.

7. Statistics indicate that a majority of Ethiopian-Israelis receive some form of government assistance (Elias and Kemp 2010, Weil 2004).

8. Moreover, I do not argue that individual musicians have the power to effect direct political change. A krar player whom I do not name in this book has engaged in a fight with the Israeli government for over a decade over the expropriation of his prefabricated home in a Jerusalem absorption center. Despite protests on his behalf, and his increasingly desperate circumstances, the government has refused to return the trailer.

9. Scholarship on myth offers a wide variety of definitions of the genre. Joseph Campbell's formulation of the hero narrative is perhaps the best known. William Doty describes myth as a precursor of science, while Carl Jung defines it as a transformative symbolic journey. The differences of opinion across disciplines are somewhat beyond the scope of this discussion, but I note the debates over, for example, rationalism and comparativism (Doty 1996, 1998, Segal 1987, 2002, 2005).

10. I use three main sources for statistical information (all available online): first, "The Ethiopian Community in Israel," Israel Ministry of Foreign Affairs, accessed July 28, 2017, www.mfa.gov.il; second, "The Ethiopian Population in Israel," Central Bureau of Statistics, accessed July 28, 2017, www.cbs.gov.il; third, "Research" (*meḥkar*), Israel Association for Ethiopian Jews, accessed July 28, 2017, www.iaej.co.il.

11. According to the demographic data offered by the Central Bureau of Statistics, fewer than 1 percent of Ethiopian-Israelis live in Tel Aviv: "The Ethiopian Population of Israel: Basic Demographic Details," Central Bureau of Statistics, accessed July 28, 2017, www.cbs.gov.il.

ONE *Afrodiasporic Myths: Ester Rada and the Atlantic Connection*

1. Ben Shalev, "You Have to Listen to Israeli Soul Singer Ester Rada's New Album," *Haaretz*, August 24, 2017, www.haaretz.com.

2. Interview, Jerusalem, September 10, 2014.

3. David Ratner's book about Ethiopian-Israeli hip-hop subcultures (2015) frames a similar geographical circuit, and his work will come into focus in chapter 5. A key difference between his work and this chapter's perspective, though, is that I frame the African

diaspora as one influence among several, instead of as the chief lens through which to understand the Ethiopian-Israeli experience.

4. Gilroy devotes substantial space in *The Black Atlantic* to discussion of the historical and discursive connections between the Jewish and African diasporas.

5. There is a precedent for this association in Israeli society, since some Mizrahim have identified as black since the 1960s.

6. The deceased rapper Tupac Shakur is the towering antiracist role model for Ethiopian-Israeli teenagers today. I will return to his legacy briefly in chapter 5, but David Ratner (2015) goes into much more depth.

7. Kay Kaufman Shelemay has published widely about musicians in North America's Ethiopian diaspora (2006a).

8. See Chivallon's introduction (2011) for a succinct overview of the debates around diasporic hybridity as framed by Appadurai (1990), Clifford (1994, 1997), Gilroy (1993), and Hall (1990).

9. Some scholars are unconvinced by the designation of Israel as a white society. See Kaplan (2010) to query concepts of whiteness in Israel and Ethiopia. I will refer to Israel as a white society occasionally, though I acknowledge its ethnic diversity.

10. As Boyarin and Boyarin argue (1993), the culmination of *shivat Tziyon* in the founding of a nation-state is paradoxical. They argue that the state of exile is central to the modern Jewish experience.

11. Ben Shalev, "Israeli Soul Sister Chooses to Sing in English," *Haaretz*, accessed July 28, 2017, www.haaretz.com.

12. Kiryat Arba is the Jewish settlement adjacent to Hebron; the settler movement fights to retain it because of the religious importance of the Tomb of the Patriarchs. Palestinians who live within Hebron outnumber Jewish residents by a factor of more than ten, while the settlers are protected by an often-ambivalent military apparatus. The presence of small numbers of Ethiopian-Israelis in the territories adds a dimension of complexity to framing the occupation strictly in terms of race and racism.

13. In these interviews, Rada is often explicitly critical of the state of Israel in her words, if not in her music and lyrics.

14. I have seen European musicians struggle with Ethio-jazz in high-status concert halls like the Barbican Centre in London (2008) and the Cité de la Musique in Paris (2011).

15. "Ester Rada—Four Women (Official Video)," YouTube, accessed July 28, 2017, www.youtube.com.

16. "Ester Rada—Four Women—Montreal Jazz Festival 2014," YouTube, accessed July 28, 2017, www.youtube.com.

17. "Ester Rada vs Nina Simone—Four Women," YouTube, accessed July 28, 2017, www.youtube.com. In the minute before beginning the song, she explains briefly in Hebrew what it is about, mentioning the intersection of race and gender. She says that she loves

Nina Simone's songs for their simplicity (*pashtut*), and that the song describes paradigms of African American women.

18. Liberal Zionists often avoid discussing the occupation onstage, especially internationally. Criticizing the state can alienate Diaspora Jewish audiences, while even calling oneself Israeli can lead to boycott in Europe. If she stays out of Israeli politics onstage, she can sometimes slip below the radar abroad.

19. "Sorries—Ester Rada—Indie City," YouTube, accessed July 28, 2017, www.youtube .com.

20. "Ester Rada—Life Happens (Official Video)," YouTube, accessed July 28, 2017, www.youtube.com.

21. The language of the *edah* (singular for *edot*) is usually applied to Mizrahim, and rarely to Ashkenazi Jews or to Palestinian Arabs.

TWO *Ethiopianist Myths of Dissonance and Nostalgia*

1. "Fasting" food means that it does not contain the animal by-products that are forbidden on the Ethiopian Christian fasting calendar. In the Ethiopian Orthodox tradition, adherents decline a variety of animal products in certain months of the year, or on certain days of the week. Rather than calling oneself a vegetarian in Ethiopia, it makes sense to order fasting food—the fasting fir-fir, a chickpea (*shiro*) puree, is a perennial option. I habitually asked for fasting food in Addis Ababa, and once I was served fasting macchiato—coffee made with powdered milk.

2. See *The Khat Controversy* (Anderson, Beckerleg, Hailu, and Klein 2007) for a fuller account of its effects and uses. Danino and Amar (2009) argue that Ethiopian folk medicine is enjoying a revival in Israel.

3. Donald Levine (1965) and Edward Ullendorff (1968) examine the epic at length. It is the basis for some Beta Israel lineage myths, but at the same time promotes theological supersessionism, arguing that religious power was transferred from Israelites to Ethiopians through the usurping of the Ark of the Covenant.

4. The drum machine and synthesizer are widespread in Addis Ababa today, but reviled by purists. At the extreme end, Ethiopian-Israeli saxophone virtuoso Abate Barihun refers to the latter as a "cancer": "The Cancer of Ethiopian Music: The Synthesizer," *Haaretz*, accessed July 28, 2017, www.haaretz.com.

5. In the limited but still-definitive book-length study on Ethiopian traditional music in English, Michael Powne warns that we might reconsider calling the Ethiopian scales pentatonic since they rely heavily on minor-second intervals (1968: 47).

6. The word means "nostalgia," and it is the name of a song from which a mode of the same name descends. However, in common understanding, all three of these concepts are mixed together—the song, and indeed the mode itself, inspires nostalgia.

7. Sociologists have determined that a higher proportion of Ethiopian-Israelis live below the poverty line than any other Jewish minority, and approximately equivalent to the Palestinian Israeli population. Seeman discusses the difficult economic conditions of Falash Mura life in Ethiopia (2009: 44–47), and Yiftachel and Meir compare the Ethiopian-Israeli experience to the Palestinian Israeli one in terms of housing policy (1998: 51).

8. Many Beta Israel immigrated around the period of the Derg (1974–1991), Mengistu's military dictatorship, when musical life was halted abruptly. As a result of an official curfew in Addis Ababa, musicians made virtually no living for the regime's duration (see Shelemay 2009: 177, or a longer explanation in Shelemay 1991). The recording industry was paralyzed, and many Ethio-jazz greats emigrated (Falceto 2002). The reopening of the *Azmari-betotch* (plural for Azmari-bet, or music house) and the revitalization of the music industry in 1991 was a boon to urban life.

9. Patricia Tang explains that in the griot context of West Africa, self-taught musicians are often hesitant to self-apply a professional label, even if they are authorities in their genre (2007).

10. It should be noted, though, that Weisser and Falceto credibly contest the portrayal of *qignit*, the modal system, as fixed (2013). Most of the material has never been transcribed, written down, or orchestrated on Western instruments, and the tuning is often relative. Musicians who play the krar or massenqo tend to be less concerned with pitch than musicians who notate their repertoire would be. And since the tradition is oral, there are variants—regional variants, and major and minor variants. In short, there is no consensus on the repertoire's musical rules, so a description of the modal system should probably never be presented as definitive.

11. The massenqo has scarcely been written about in English, but I have extensive anecdotal evidence that American, British, and Israeli audiences do not respond to the massenqo as they do to the krar. In festivals and concerts, I have seen world music fans put off by the massenqo even as they were eager to give Ethiopian music a chance. Our ears simply are not attuned to the timbre and tonality.

12. Statistics on the Ethiopian-Israeli population are rare, but researchers estimate that fewer than half of Ethiopian-Israelis ever lived in the Beta Israel villages of the Gondar region. And only a small fraction of the population ever lived in Addis Ababa, the place from which contemporary Azmari influence emanates.

13. Gadi BenEzer (2002) and Hagar Salamon (1999) narrate their informants' stories of exclusion sensitively. BenEzer frames the memory of the trip from Ethiopia as trauma, while Salamon examines conspiracy theories about Jews casting spells on their neighbors.

14. "Aklilu Seyoum," Facebook, accessed July 28, 2017, www.facebook.com.

15. "Interview with artist Aklilu Seyoum part 1," Ethiotube, accessed July 28, 2017, www.ethiotube.net.

16. The casual attitude spills over into a general scarcity of scholarly literature in English

about contemporary Azmari music. The work of Asheknafi Kebede (1975, 1977) and of Cynthia Tse Kimberlin (2009) are notable exceptions.

17. "Common—The Game," YouTube, accessed July 29, 2017, www.youtube.com.

18. There is plenty of academic precedent for overstating the place of Beta Israel in Ethiopian society. As the distinguished historian Steven Kaplan claims, the Beta Israel might be the "world's most-researched people per capita" (Westheimer and Kaplan 1992: 3).

19. Some people visit regularly to see family or tend to business matters. Among the Israeli-born generation, though, visiting is more of a rite of passage. Cabra Casay, the Ethiopian-Israeli singer discussed in chapter 3, featured in a documentary about her first trip to Ethiopia (2006's *Black over White*), while Ester Rada told me in our interview that she intended to visit en route to a tour stop in South Africa. Among many young people, visiting Ethiopia may be part of a postarmy trip abroad.

20. Ethiopia's government is currently a single-party system, and press freedom is curtailed through the imprisonment of dissident reporters.

21. Shalva Weil has written extensively on the subject of the difficulty of relying on interviews alone (1995).

22. It is a shame that there have been so few studies on the subject (Seeman 2015 on coffee rituals being noteworthy), because the rise of Pentecostalism among Ethiopian immigrants in Israel is fascinating. There is a high rate of conversion in Ethiopia and the diaspora, and despite a dearth of scholarship one can easily find clips of church services on YouTube.

23. Without drawing any substantial conclusions from this single observation, one should note that women have fared far better in Israel than men have in this population (Anteby-Yemini 2004). But it is worth considering a race-gender-ethnicity axis of power relations in the reshaping of migrant musics cross-culturally. In certain cases, migrants with hyphenated identities are torn between identification with home and host culture, while in others, two sides of an identity can coexist peacefully. Trinidad is a multiethnic society, where South Asian and Afrodiasporic populations mix together, with calypso music and its descendant soca yielding offshoots like Chutney soca that negotiate the relationships between a population's constituents. More often, though, popular music reveals instances of internecine conflict: Arabesk and salsa emerged as a result of warring identities within a subgroup (Manuel 2000, Stokes 1992).

24. Menilek used this expression, too. It means to take them to the next level of professionalism and opportunity.

THREE *Zionist Myths and the Mainstreaming of Ethiopian-Israeli Music*

1. I have interviewed only Azmaris about the Project, and have never conducted a formal interview with a member of the band. Therefore, my conclusions are based on

discussions with Azmaris, Ethiopian-Israelis, and Israeli world music fans of the Project. I have also spoken with some of the Ethiopian musicians whose work he has sampled, and they have a separate set of opinions.

2. Prior to the arrival of the Idan Raichel Project on the music scene, the best-known example of Ethiopian fusion projects was the work of Shlomo Gronich and the Sheba Choir from the 1990s (Ester Rada was a member as a child). Gronich, a nationally recognized star in Israeli music, recorded a CD with a group of young Ethiopian singers, who were at that point referred to as Ethiopian Jews. The Sheba Choir's music is not connected stylistically to the music I describe in this chapter, but it should be mentioned as the first large-scale national exercise in popular representation.

3. Raichel made the statement quoted here in a Hebrew-language television interview in Oslo when he was selected, together with India.Arie, to perform at the Nobel Peace Prize award ceremony. Since the 1980s Ethiopian-Israeli children have systematically been sent to *pnimiyot*—loosely translated as boarding schools, but often without sufficiently informed consent of new-immigrant parents—for the purpose of faster integration. The phenomenon is still widespread, with children speaking Hebrew during the week and returning to their Amharic-speaking parents on weekends. See Marilyn Herman's discussion of the institution (2012: 6).

4. He has also put out a collaborative album with Vieux Farka Touré (2012), to generally favorable reviews.

5. This narrative allows Ethiopian-Israelis to claim cultural similarity with other Jewish groups who fled their native lands.

6. For a thorough explanation of cultural intimacy, see Herzfeld (1997). Stokes (2010) explains how the concept of an intimate national culture applies to popular music in societies that imagine themselves as an East-West hybrid such as Greece and Turkey (and Israel).

7. Casay discusses her feelings about Israel and Ethiopia in the documentary *Black over White*: "Black over White—A film by Tomer Heymann," YouTube, accessed July 28, 2017, www.youtube.com.

8. "Cabra Casay in Paris at the Cirque d'hiver with Yannick Noah, Yael Naim, Ayo, Oxmo Puccino, Fefe, Mathieu Chedid, abd EL Malik," Facebook, accessed July 28, 2017, www.facebook.com.

9. Her solo work from 2014 onward has been produced in Paris (yielding mixed reviews).

10. Despite common ground in musical interest and shared Jewish/Israeli roots, Raichel's socioeconomic circumstances differ significantly from his bandmates'. He comes from the affluent suburb of Kfar Saba, whereas Avi Wassa, as the lore goes, was "discovered" while working as a security guard at the Haifa train station.

11. These binaries have been a useful mechanism for the state power structure in

determining that only certain immigrants are acceptable. Since a small middle class of university-educated Ethiopian-Israelis is emerging in major urban areas, the government and community workers can claim that they have tried their best but that some immigrants cannot be helped—particularly those of questionable religious legitimacy and those who do not speak Hebrew or achieve gainful employment. Marilyn Herman's study on the immigrant generation exposes these binaries adeptly (2012).

12. The Israeli anthropologist Malka Shabtay has written widely about the niche area "between reggae and rap" (2001, 2003).

13. The Israeli government has been known to confiscate material deemed subversive from Palestinian singers (Al-Taee 2002: 50). Or, even closer to home, Ted Swedenburg writes about the panic that ensued across Egypt when transsexual pop star Dana International (Saida Sultana in Arabic) became a Cairo cassette-culture phenomenon in the mid-1990s (Swedenburg 1997).

14. According to a recent survey by Israeli newspaper *Haaretz*, a majority of American Jews support the state of Israel while being critical of policies like occupation: Gabi Sheffer, "Listen to American Jews' Stand on Israel," *Haaretz*, accessed July 28, 2017, www.haaretz.com.

15. Cordelia Hebblethwaite, "World Music Israeli Style: Idan Raichel Project," *BBC News*, accessed July 28, 2017, www.bbc.co.uk.

16. See Regev and Seroussi (2004) for a definitive explanation of SLI style, history, and ideology. The musical style dominated the recording industry, which was operated by elites who were connected to the government and the military. As a result, for the state's early decades of existence, music, politics, and the military were inextricably linked through the state apparatus and institutions of cultural production.

17. "Mima'amakim," the Idan Raichel Project, accessed July 28, 2017, www.idanraichel project.com.

18. Official translation by Yali Sobol for album liner notes. Author's transliteration of Hebrew lyrics, reprinted with permission by the IRP.

19. While Kartun-Blum examines biblical imagery as a vehicle for nationalist discourse, this connection is not unique to Israel and finds resonances in South Africa (Erlmann 1996), Turkey (Stokes 1992, 2010), and Brazil (Stround 2008).

20. Since political and religious forms of Zionism developed in Central and Eastern Europe (Aronson 2003), Ashkenazi Jews dominated early forms of Zionist ideology. Early Zionist thinkers were influenced by European ideas of self-determination and civic nationalism that were popular in nineteenth-century Europe, such as perennialism, modernism, and ethnosymbolism (Smith 2004) and blended them with Jewish tropes of home and return such as exile (*galut*) and love of Zion (*ahavat Tziyon*) (Friesel 2006: 297).

21. This contrasts with the perception that Israelis think they "came without culture."

22. The beganna is a ten-stringed lyre used in Ethiopian Orthodox religious and

paraliturgical music. Morphologically it somewhat resembles a larger version of a krar (Kimberlin 1978).

23. Transcriptions by the author, reproduced with permission by Alemu Aga.

FOUR *Embodying Blackness through Eskesta Citizenship*

1. This genre is also projected ubiquitously on screens in restaurants and record stores: "Balazena—New Ethiopian Eskista Music 2015," YouTube, accessed July 28, 2017, www .youtube.com.

2. In a groundbreaking discussion of the kinds of prejudices that demean and marginalize female creativity, Marcia Citron explains the scarcity of female composers through the lens of nineteenth-century notions of creativity (1993). Within her framework, women's roles are separate from men's, and denigrated as not being important because they do not leave a textual record.

3. Important work on recording and mimesis may help to understand the denigration of the prerecorded. Walter Benjamin pioneered this pursuit (see Kang 2014), and in twin articles, "On the Mimetic Faculty" (1933) and "The Work of Art in the Age of Mechanical Reproduction" (1936), he examines aura and mimesis, two components that distinguish the live from the recorded. He argues that an original work of art has an aura, a uniqueness or magic; that reproducing an aura is impossible; and that reproduction is inevitably inferior. On the other hand, reproduction provides the opportunity for mimesis, or the imitation of something "authentic." Susan Buck-Morss (1989) frames Benjamin's argument as a dialectic among the Frankfurt School, and Michael Taussig's *Mimesis and Alterity* (1993) applies ethnographic methods to Buck-Morss's interpretation of Benjamin.

4. This is the era Francis Falceto identifies as "Swinging Addis," before the emperor was deposed in 1974.

5. Hagar Salamon's groundbreaking work on Ethiopian-Israeli humor argues that communal jokes help to process life in Israel (2011). She also argues that jokes reveal truths that interview material cannot (ibid: 16).

6. "Ethnic" style in Israel means Mizrahi.

7. In wealthy Tel Aviv, sushi restaurants and Ethiopian-Israelis appear to function as opposing signifiers of mobility, with the former representing upper-middle-class cosmopolitanism and the latter representing poverty. This dichotomy was stated convincingly by the proprietor of an Ethiopian restaurant I patronized in central Tel Aviv in August 2008. When I asked her how business was, she replied, "People here only want sushi restaurants." When I passed the restaurant in late September, it had closed.

8. In the years following Operation Moses, most remaining Beta Israel villagers moved to Addis Ababa to await transport to Israel, which came in 1991 with Operation Solomon. So while the 1984 immigrants never lived in Addis Ababa, many of the 1991 immigrants did.

9. "Beta Dance Troupe—Opus for Heads," YouTube, accessed July 28, 2017, www.youtube.com.

10. The story of sacrifice draws on the themes of the biblical Exodus myth, and many Israeli immigrant groups share in common stories of the traumas of fleeing their countries of birth, or of the massive loss of life that was suffered before or after reaching Israel. A revealing example is the Zionist myth of the "draining of the swamps," the stories in which many Eastern European prestate immigrants died of malaria while cultivating the land for farming.

11. The migration from Gondar to Israel via Sudan was dangerous, and "the journey" is a source of literary and musical inspiration for younger generations. The story has been examined and described extensively by Parfitt (1985) and BenEzer (2002, 2005).

12. Parfitt (1985) provides detailed explanations of the multiple perspectives of world Jewry, while various African political science journals portray the escape of the "Falasha" as part of a Jewish conspiracy (Karadawi 1991, Wagaw 1991).

13. Ibid.

14. According to the Ethiopian-Israeli narrative, Operation Moses took place in 1984, which is when the trek took place. The airlift in 1985 is often the date assigned by the Israeli government.

15. BenEzer based his analysis on his informants' stories. My own interviews and conversations corroborate the importance of the journey.

16. There is no scholarly consensus on how old Sigd is; Shoshana Ben-Dor explains that the festival was first referenced in the fifteenth century but not described in detail until the nineteenth century (1987: 145).

17. Abbink argues that, like the Moroccan Mimouna, Sigd could be transformed successfully into a widely observed Israeli ethnic holiday (1983: 799).

18. Rabbinic Judaism, particularly its ritual and law, is based on the Talmud (a sixth-century compendium in Aramaic), while Beta Israel follow biblical laws that are sometimes contradicted by rabbinic law.

19. Shavuot takes place at the end of a seven-week counting period after Passover. Known as Pentecost in English, Shavuot literally translates as "weeks."

20. A diminutive for the second month of the Jewish year, so named because of an ancient Semitic cognate—the eight month of the year in Akkadian—but popularly named because the month is "bitter" (*mar*), uniquely containing no special days of observance.

21. See the following national broadcast about Sigd: "Israel Celebrates Ethiopian Jewish Holiday," YouTube, accessed July 28, 2017, www.youtube.com.

22. The extensive literature on Sigd addresses the introduction of a return narrative in the postimmigration context.

23. Abbink draws a similar conclusion, namely that the festival might soon be rendered obsolete since so much of its observance has been taken out of context (1983: 808). Since

Beta Israel clergy are not ordained in Israel, there will eventually be few Ethiopians with sufficient knowledge of the liturgy. There is a strong chance that this tradition will do far more than change, as most traditions do; it could well be eliminated from Israeli religious life within this century.

24. "Sigd 2013: un film en noir et en couleurs," YouTube, accessed July 28, 2017, www .youtube.com.

25. The ultra-Orthodox party for Mizrahi Jews. They have seven seats in the current parliament.

26. "National-religious" is the term for religious Zionists. Closely associated with the settler movement, they are recognizable by their knitted head coverings (*kippot*). They currently have eight seats in parliament.

27. No longer politically active, the Scouts were known historically as a secular Labor Zionist movement.

28. Actually these musical styles are not so far apart. From Beta Israel liturgy, only a few permutations of instrumentation, language, and ensemble transform Ge'ez prayers into Ethio-jazz. Shelemay provides dozens of transcriptions of Beta Israel liturgy, and her analysis concludes that the tradition developed alongside church music (1986). The two styles (Jewish and Christian) employ the same language and instrumentation. Church modes served as the basis for folk music as well, with a transition from the beganna to the krar (Beta Israel liturgy is accompanied by its own instruments, such as the *senassel*, a sistrum). Ethio-jazz replaced the krar with the guitar.

29. On Purim in March, and Simḥat Torah in October, prayer (or fasting) and revelry are juxtaposed. But the most salient comparison among the Jewish festivals is Yom Ha'atzmaut, Israeli Independence Day, usually observed in May. It immediately follows Yom Hazikaron, a memorial day for "fallen soldiers." The civic has taken on religious proportions among Zionists in Israel and the Diaspora: many congregations have set aside a Torah reading for the day and chant Hallel (a set of Psalms), rituals typically reserved for the festivals dictated by the Torah. Today Yom Ha'atzmaut is one of the most animated days of public celebration in Israel.

30. "Gili Yalo—Tenesh Kelbe Lay," YouTube, accessed July 28, 2017, www.youtube.com.

31. Name and absorption center anonymized.

32. Aḥ Boger is similar to Big Brother programs in North America. It was established in 2007 by the Jewish Agency, an umbrella organization that disburses funds to Israeli charities. In the program, a teenager mentors a young person for an academic year, serving as a companion. The young person is given a role model to admire and emulate, while the teenager is trained in leadership and responsibility. Since many of the participating children's parents are unfamiliar with Israeli social mores, the program mainstreams the children into Israeli social practices—for example, the teenager can advise about supplies for school (see Anteby-Yemini 2004).

33. When Beta Israel villagers left Gondar in 1984 to escape starvation or military conscription or to fulfill an ancient covenant, they did not consider Ethiopianness to be an essential component of their identity as it is today. Shoshana Ben-Dor calls them "historically isolated and embattled" (1987: 141). Marginalized by the predominantly Christian Amhara, Beta Israel saw immigration to Israel as marking completion of the covenant. Many of the newer immigrants take a different view, though, and appear less interested in integrating (Kaplan 2005: 390). Some are Jewish, while others practice Orthodox Christianity or Pentecostalism; some view aliyah (Jewish migration to Israel) through the prism of covenant, while others are economic migrants who became eligible through family reunification laws. Like Palestinian Israelis, some yearn to be accepted as Israelis, others complain of being excluded by default (Seeman 1999). While Israelis impose on the groups the single category of *Etyopim*, the reality is one of differing values, memories, and rites that render difficult the "imagining," let alone the formation of a cohesive Ethiopian community.

34. It must be noted, however, that Israel's immigration policy is far from forgiving. The imminent deportation of a non-Jewish Ethiopian divorcee whose children had served in the military made headlines in 2015. Although technically eligible for permanent residence as the parent of soldiers, he was nevertheless scheduled for deportation for initially filing the wrong papers of appeal: Ilan Lior, "Father of Israeli Soldiers Faces Deportation Despite Being Eligible for Residency," *Haaretz*, accessed July 28, 2017, www.haaretz.com, or Ilan Lior, "Immigration Authority Freezes Deportation of Father to IDF Soldiers," *Haaretz*, accessed July 28, 2017, www.haaretz.com.

35. This is an ideal; in reality many of the parents arrived in Israel nonliterate, so they will not teach their children to read and write Amharic.

FIVE *"What about My Money": Themes of Labor and Citizenship in Ethiopian-Israeli Hip-Hop*

1. "Old School Guragna and Amharic Song by Dejen Manchilot Live from Israel," YouTube, accessed July 28, 2017, www.youtube.com.

2. "Anbessa Dub," Zvuloon Dub System Bandcamp, accessed July 28, 2017, www .zvuloondubsystem.bandcamp.com.

3. The continuum idea is also the basis of the scholarly appraisal of Beta Israel religious practice. Steven Kaplan advocates thinking of Ethiopian Judaism in concert with Christian and animist beliefs practiced alongside it in Ethiopia (1992), and Don Seeman advocates thinking of the Falash Mura not as apostates but as moving closer to Christianity on the spectrum of religious practice (2009: 28).

4. I usually distinguish between rap and reggae. David Ratner argues that young people prefer one over the other based on emphasis on lyrics or beat (2015: 104). I focus less on

lyrics than Ratner does, but like him I consider them as distinct genres, in contrast to earlier, much-appreciated work by Malka Shabtay that often conflates the two as Afro-diasporic popular music (2001, 2003).

5. "Hip Hop Wars," YouTube, accessed July 28, 2017, www.youtube.com.

6. The song contains elements of each genre.

7. Ratner's book is an important contribution and the most comprehensive work dealing with hip-hop among Ethiopian-Israelis, but it, too, claims that hip-hop is mostly about lyrics (see 2015: 80, where his informants distinguish between hip-hop and reggae, introducing the lyrics-beat dichotomy already mentioned).

8. In "Ma Im Hakesef," it is an employer who has not paid them yet.

9. Many Palestinian songs invoke the military or police force, and the theme is especially common among '48 Palestinians, as evidenced in DAM's song "Born Here": "DAM, 'Born Here,' Hebrew/Arabic with English subtitles," YouTube, accessed July 28, 2017, www.youtube.com.

10. Incidentally, this is also the function that connects hip-hop to Azmari music: to get the audience to reconsider circumstances through double meaning and suggestive lyrics that shock and/or amuse. According to Cheryl Keyes, rap is part of a long line of West African and African American musical traditions that exploit the polymetric interplay between speech and rhythm in forms of heightened, dynamic speech (1996). Azmari music belongs to this tradition to the extent that Azmari singing is detachable from the base melody (which is often played in a repetitive and cyclical 6/8 meter), and a song's lyrics are frequently spoken. Both forms demand lyrical improvisation.

11. This term can be interpreted in several different ways, but I borrow the term from Chang (2007) and Mitchell (2001), and for the purposes of this chapter it refers to hip-hop that is non-Anglophone and/or "non-Western."

12. The idea that opaque references can be found within a musical genre has been advanced by Chris Washburne in his examination of the *clavé* rhythm in jazz (1997: 59). He argues that a Caribbean influence overall is readily apparent only to those who know both genres. Kelly Askew's work on *dansi* and *ngoma* demonstrates that there may be strong connections between musical styles that are not readily apparent but that emerge through analysis (2003: 611).

13. In chapter 6 I discuss Zvuloon Dub System, a group who performed at a reggae festival in Jamaica in 2014. It is all but impossible to imagine their doing so without a black presence up front.

14. With the influx of large numbers of non-Jewish Africans into Tel Aviv from such places as Senegal, Sudan, and Nigeria, many Ethiopian-Israelis have demonstrated ambivalence toward the term "African."

15. Ashkenazim constitute the paradigm because they dominate Israel's power structure, but anecdotal evidence and personal communications indicate that Ethiopian-Israelis

sometimes identify with the Mizrahi experience, or often feud with them for local re-sources due to their closer proximity in the color hierarchy. Some Ethiopian-Israelis vote for the religious Mizrahi party Shas, whose primary platform is to redress the balance of perceived Ashkenazi hegemony.

16. As mentioned before, several scholars challenge the strict black-white paradigm altogether (Ballantine 2004: 111). And while Israel is sui generis in terms of its history of Jewish immigration and expulsion of Arab populations, there is no doubt that the state of Israel operates a strict social hierarchy, and that skin color often dictates an immigrant's starting point in that hierarchy.

17. "Axum—Ma Im Hakesef," YouTube, accessed July 29, 2017, www.youtube.com.

18. This is in addition to the long-standing Mizrahi association with blackness, starting with a local Black Panther movement in the 1960s.

19. I will leave aside the demise of the Zionist dream, but refer to the work of Tom Segev, especially *1949: The First Israelis* (1986) and *Elvis in Jerusalem* (2002).

20. Ululation is a common lyrical ornament in the Horn of Africa, and also among certain Mizrahi Jews.

21. Bialik grew up in the Russian Empire and wrote in Hebrew before it was widely spoken as a revived language. He is considered a "father" of modern Hebrew literature, and to the Israeli public, a key figure in the revival of Hebrew (Bialik and Hadari 2000).

22. "Israel Music History Singer Bracha Zefira The Mother of the Composer & Singer Ariel Zilber," YouTube, accessed July 28, 2017, www.youtube.com.

23. "Chai Eurovision Song Contest 1983—Ofra Haza," YouTube, accessed July 28, 2017, www.youtube.com.

24. "Ofra Haza—Live in Japan 1989_behind the scenes," YouTube, accessed July 23, 2017, www.youtube.com.

25. "Ofra Haza—The Prince of Egypt film clip—Deliver us," YouTube, accessed July 28, 2017, www.youtube.com.

26. Avi Shilon, "The Double Life of Ofra Haza," *Haaretz*, accessed July 28, 2017, www.haaretz.com; Deborah Sontag, "A Pop Diva, a Case of AIDS and an Israeli Storm," *New York Times*, accessed July 28, 2017, www.nytimes.com.

27. "Axum—Pocket Full of Money (official video)—אקוס," YouTube, accessed July 28, 2017, www.youtube.com.

28. Amos Harel, "Hot, Black Israeli Rap Duo Bubbles over on YouTube," *Haaretz*, accessed July 28, 2017, www.youtube.com.

29. "קפה שחור חזק ואלי לחזון איזו מדינה קליפ," YouTube, accessed July 28, 2017, www.youtube.com.

30. "Café Shachor Chazak in San Francisco—My Baby," YouTube, accessed July 28, 2017, www.youtube.com.

31. It is common practice for Jewish organizations to send Ethiopian-Israeli musicians

on tours of the United States. In 2013, the JNF (Jewish National Fund) sent pop singer Hagit Yaso to North America. Still known as "Ethiopian Jews" in the United States, musicians are well received, and their sponsoring organizations often call upon their diversity as a defense of more controversial geopolitical stances. AIPAC is among the more politicized of American Jewish advocacy groups, aligning itself closely with the Israeli government.

32. So named after the area served by the Dan Bus Company that operates across the Greater Tel Aviv region.

33. "Research" (*meḥkar*), Israel Association for Ethiopian Jews, accessed July 28, 2017, www.iaej.co.il.

34. Figures are taken from the 2008 demographic data from the Israel Association for Ethiopian Jews (ibid.).

35. "אלי לחזן ויצפאן - איזו מדינה," YouTube, accessed July 28, 2017, www.youtube.com.

36. This material is common fodder for the popular newspapers *Yediot Achronot* and *Maariv*. Among the most prevalent clichés in Israeli political discussion is the rate of deaths in road accidents compared to terrorist attacks.

37. Perelson explains that Palestinian Israelis could break into the recording industry only by accepting the Israeli canon as their own (1998: 114). For CSH, bringing in a beloved Israeli standard is an appropriate way of rendering themselves recognizable to Israelis.

38. Amos Harel, "Hot, Black Israeli Rap Duo Bubbles over on YouTube," *Haaretz*, accessed July 28, 2017, www.haaretz.com.

39. The musical subcultures around Tel Aviv that develop without the support of the recording industry are well documented by Horowitz (2010), Regev (1996), and Regev and Seroussi (2004).

40. The video's life on the Internet has been troubled. Since February 2011 it has been removed and reinstated periodically. Although this is frustrating for readers following a link, perhaps it conveys a sense of the vulnerability of musicians working outside of the recording industry.

41. "גרמי קול חבש \ הוצאות גדולות הכנסות קטנות למי איכפת," YouTube, accessed July 28, 2017, www.youtube.com.

42. The paradigm of the minority that is hounded by authority figures is widespread in African American hip-hop, and it has a role in Israel-Palestine. The stories of Ghassan Kanafani, the deceased Palestinian writer, usually contain one stock Israeli character: the rifle-wielding soldier, as in the story "Going Back to Haifa" (1978). The imagery also appears in DAM's videos. This discourse of the enforcer-enforced pushes Ethiopian-Israelis into a category of those who need to be policed, as though they were themselves enemies of the state.

43. Native Tongues was a group of African American rappers in the 1980s and early 1990s performing conscious rap, such as DeLaSoul, Queen Latifah, and A Tribe Called Quest.

44. "Avadim Hayinu" is a centerpiece of the Passover seder, the ritual meal.

45. This is a riff on a right-wing political trope about population transfer, including that of '48 Palestinians to a future state of Palestine.

SIX *Levinski Street, Tel Aviv's Horn Mediascape*

1. Some examples from the Israeli press reveal that bias, and an Israeli fascination with the neighborhood, often framed by distaste: Danny Adeno Abebe, "The Dark Side of Tel Aviv," *Ynet News*, accessed July 28, 2017, www.ynet.com; Elon Gilad, "Tourist Tip #199 / The Underbelly of Tel Aviv Neve Sha'anan Street," *Haaretz*, accessed July 28, 2017, www.haaretz.com; Ben Hartman, "Drugs, Prostitutes and Renewal in South Tel Aviv," *Jerusalem Post*, accessed July 28, 2017, www.jpost.com.

2. The street name is often spelled Levinsky in English. I have found this phonetically challenging for non-Hebrew speakers, so I spell it Levinski throughout.

3. For an outstanding synthesis of theoretical issues surrounding soundscapes in Israel, see Wood (2014), as well as Golan (2009) about the history of Tel Aviv's soundscape.

4. Tally Kritzman-Amri's edited volume about labor migration along Levinski is a major influence on this chapter, though it contains no material about music. In part, this chapter is a contribution to the scholarly understanding of Tel Aviv's emerging underclass from the perspective of music and nation.

5. Shirly Seidler, "After Tel Aviv and Jerusalem, More Anti-Police Brutality Protests Planned around Country," *Haaretz*, accessed July 28, 2017, www.haaretz.com.

6. Yaniv Kubovich, Almog Ben Zikri, and Ilan Lior, "Police to Investigate Asylum Seeker's Lynching in Be'er Sheva," *Haaretz*, accessed July 28, 2017, www haaretz.com.

7. "Cops Beat Ethiopian IDF Soldier in Alleged Racist Attack," YouTube, accessed July 28, 2017, www.youtube.com.

8. Meirav Arlosoroff, "Ethiopians in Israel: An Employment and Educational Success," *Haaretz*, accessed July 28, 2017, www.haaretz.com.

9. "Ethiopian-Israelis Clash with Police as Anti-Racism Rally Turns Violent," *The Guardian*, accessed July 28, 2017, www.theguardian.com/uk; Isabel Kershner, "Anti-Police Protest in Israel Turns Violent," *New York Times*, accessed July 28, 2017, www.nytimes.com; "Video: Israeli Ethiopians' Protest against Police Brutality Was Confronted Last Night with Harsh Police Brutality," Active Stills, accessed July 28, 2017, www.facebook.com.

10. In the first weeks of the protests, President Reuven Rivlin referred to Ethiopian integration as an "open wound": Jonathan Lis, "President Rivlin to Ethiopian-Israelis: We've Failed to Listen to You," *Haaretz*, accessed July 28, 2017, www.haaretz.com.

11. Anshel Pfeffer, "Interior Ministry Closes Down Ethiopian Aliyah Operation," *Haaretz*, accessed July 28, 2017, www.haaretz.com.

12. Ilene Prusher, "Netanyahu Resorts to Race-Baiting to Win Elections," *Haaretz*, accessed July 28, 2017, www.haaretz.com.

13. Peter Beaumont, "Israeli Police Chief Says It Is Natural to Suspect Ethiopians of Crime," *The Guardian*, accessed July 28, 2017, www guardian.co.uk.

14. The ongoing vigilance about a "suspicious object" (*ḥafetz ḥashood*) is part of everyday activity in Israel, and clearing an area to investigate one is not uncommon. When I was a teenager, we were evacuated en route to a speech by the Dalai Lama.

15. Arik Mirovsky, "Tel Aviv's Old Central Bus Station Goes from Grit to Glory," *Haaretz*, accessed July 28, 2017, www.haaretz.com.

16. Simone Wilson, "Tel Aviv's Half-Abandoned Central Bus Station Is Home to a Bat Cave and Six Underground Theaters," *Jewish Journal*, accessed July 28, 2017, www.jewishjournal.com.

17. Greater Tel Aviv is a metropolitan area of several million people, but the city of Tel Aviv-Jaffa has a population of just 400,000, many of whom are migrant workers. The total number of guest workers in Israel from Asia and Africa rises each year, with the total today equaling approximately 25,000 to 30,000 per year: "Entrants with Work Permits, 2010," Central Bureau of Statistics, accessed July 28, 2017, www.cbs.gov.il.

18. Z. Mor et al., "The Levinsky Walk-in Clinic in Tel Aviv: Holistic Services to Control Sexually Transmitted Diseases in the Community," National Center for Biotechnology Information, accessed July 28, 2017, www.ncbi.nlm.nih.gov.

19. "Zvuloon Dub System—Going to Zion (Official Video)," YouTube, accessed July 28, 2017, www.youtube.com.

20. "Zvuloon Dub System & Tigrinya Lilay—Going to Zion (Balcony TV)," YouTube, accessed July 28, 2017, www.youtube.com.

21. Businesses that have puns in their names are ubiquitous around Tel Aviv, from the optometrist "You & Eye" on Shenkin Street (in English) to the steakhouse "A place for meat" (*Makom shel basar*, creating a homonym-pun only in translation) in Neve Tsedek to the tool store *Kli vaḥomer* on Frishman Street (a Hebrew pun referring to the biblical rhetorical technique of "light and stringent" or *kal vaḥomer*) to Café Albi in Florentin (written in Arabic as "Kalbi," meaning "my heart," the *k* going unpronounced in Levantine dialect).

22. "Tigrinya Lilay," YouTube, accessed July 28, 2017, www.youtube.com.

23. These are three different ways of expressing anxiety over space and power in the Israeli-Palestinian conflict. Birth rates are important on both sides, with Palestinians and religious Israelis competing to secure a majority. Meanwhile the government regularly issues building permits in controversial areas like East Jerusalem or the E-1 zone of the West Bank as retaliation for diplomatic or security disappointments. Likewise, a planned disengagement from the West Bank is consistently undermined with the building of new infrastructure like roads and barriers, and the expansion of existing settlements (Goldscheider 2015: 4–6).

24. Patrick Kingsley, "It's Not at War, but up to 3% of Its People Have Fled. What Is

Going On in Eritrea?" *The Guardian*, accessed July 28, 2017, www.theguardian.com/uk; David Smith, "Inside Eritrea: Conscription and Poverty Drive Exodus from Secretive African State," *The Guardian*, accessed July 28, 2017, www.theguardian.com/uk.

25. In a meeting at a rape crisis center in Tel Aviv, I learned that among Eritrean female immigrants who have come up through Sinai, a conservative estimate for cases of sexual assault would be 99% (personal communication, December 8, 2008).

26. Ben Gittleson, "Inside Sinai's Torture Camps," *Atlantic*, accessed July 28, 2017, www.theatlantic.com.

27. The other city with a substantial Eritrean presence is Eilat, the southern city on the Red Sea. The mostly male population works predominantly in the tourism sector, in hotels and on the beach.

28. "Learn Tigrinya Dance—Eritrean Music: Lela Kuflom," YouTube, accessed July 28, 2017, www.youtube.com.

29. The system of supervision (*hashgaha*) operates on a basis of surprise visits. Proprietors must be prepared for a *mashgiah* to inspect up to multiple times per week, but most restaurants find that their efforts go wasted as supervisors only come by to pick up their monthly check. The backlash against this system is encapsulated in the pun-tagline *mashgiah lo ba* (the supervisor isn't coming), a play on "the messiah—*moshiah*—isn't coming." Consumer-protection scholars Timothy Lytton and Motti Talias write about the phenomenon: Timothy D. Lytton and Motti Talias, "Shaking Up Israel's Kosher Certification System," *Jewish Review of Books*, accessed July 28, 2017, www.jewishreviewofbooks.com.

Conclusion

1. The Orthodox Christianity practiced in Ethiopia traces back longer than any church besides the Armenian, the monastic tradition being a particular source of pride.

2. "Aster Aweke Live Concert in Tel Aviv 05.05.14," YouTube, accessed July 28, 2017, www.youtube.com.

3. Israeli food company Kesem has recently set up a sugar factory in Ethiopia in coordination with an Ethiopian enterprise: "Omo Kuraz I Sugar Factory to Start Production in February," *Ethiopian Broadcasting Corporation*, accessed July 28, 2017, www.ebc.et.

4. As of 2012, the Israeli ambassador to Ethiopia is Ethiopian-born: Barak Ravid, "Foreign Ministry Names First Israeli of Ethiopian Origin as Ambassador," *Haaretz*, accessed July 28, 2017, www.haaretz.com.

5. Abate Barihun joined him onstage. The venue was the elite Jerusalem Theatre: "Mahmoud Ahmed in Israel: I.E.T.V.," YouTube, accessed July 28, 2017, www.youtube.com.

6. Yaniv Kubovich, "Cases Closed against Ethiopian-Israeli Soldier, Cop Who Manhandled Him," *Haaretz*, accessed July 28, 2017, www.haaretz.com.

BIBLIOGRAPHY

Print resources

Abate, Ezra. 2007. "Ethiopian K'iñit (Scales): Analysis of the Formation and Structure of the Ethiopian Scale System." In *Proceedings of the 16th International Conference of Ethiopian Studies,* ed. Svein Ege, Harald Aspen, Birhanu Teferra, and Shiferaw Bekele. Wiesbaden: Otto Harrassowitz.

Abbink, J. 1983. "Seged Celebration in Ethiopia and Israel: Continuity and Change of a Falasha Religious Holiday." *Anthropos* 78(5–6): 789–810.

Abu-Lughod, Lila. 2004. *Dramas of Nationhood: The Politics of Television in Egypt.* Chicago: University of Chicago Press.

Aidi, Hisham. 2014. *Rebel Music: Race, Empire, and the New Muslim Youth Culture.* New York: Vintage Books.

Al-Taee, Nasser. 2002. "Voices of Peace and the Legacy of Reconciliation: Popular Music, Nationalism, and the Quest for Peace in the Middle East." *Popular Music* 21(1): 41–61.

Althusser, Louis. 1970. "Ideology and Ideological State Apparatuses (Notes toward an Investigation)." In *Lenin and Philosophy and Other Essays.* London: NLB Press.

Alvarez-Pereyre, F., and S. Ben-Dor. 1999. "The Formal Organisation of the Beta Israel Liturgy—Substance and Performance: Literary Structure." In *The Beta Israel in Ethiopia and Israel: Studies on Ethiopian Jews,* ed. Tudor Parfitt and Emanuela Trevisan Semi, 235–51. Richmond, Surrey, UK: Curzon.

Anderson, David, Susan Beckerleg, Degol Hailu, and Axel Klein. 2007. *The Khat Controversy: Stimulating the Debate on Drugs.* Oxford and New York: Berg.

Anteby-Yemini, Lisa. 2004. *Les Juifs éthiopiens en Israël: Les paradoxes du paradis.* Paris: CNRS Éditions.

Appadurai, Arjun. 1990. "Disjuncture and Difference in the Global Cultural Economy." *Public Culture* 2(2): 1–24.

Arom, Simha, and Olivier Tourny. 1999. "The Formal Organisation of the Beta Israel Liturgy —Substance and Performance: Musical Structure." In *The Beta Israel in Ethiopia and Israel: Studies on Ethiopian Jews,* ed. Tudor Parfitt and Emanuela Trevisan Semi, 252–56. Richmond, Surrey, UK: Curzon.

Aronson, Shlomo. 2003. "The Post-Zionist Discourse and Critique of Israel: A Traditional Zionist Perspective." *Israel Studies* 8(1): 105–29.

Askew, Kelly. 2003. "As Plato Duly Warned: Musical, Political, and Social Change in Coastal East Africa." *Anthropological Quarterly* 76(4): 609–37.

Atar, Ron. 2005. "The Function of Musical Instruments in the Liturgy of the Ethiopian Jews." In *The Beta Israel in Ethiopia and Israel: Studies on Ethiopian Jews,* ed. Tudor Parfitt and Emanuela Trevisan Semi, 155–72. Richmond, Surrey, UK: Curzon.

Avineri, Shlomo. 1981. *The Making of Modern Zionism: Intellectual Origins of the Jewish State.* London: Basic Books.

———. 2013. *Herzl: Theodor Herzl and the Foundation of the Jewish State.* London: Weidenfeld & Nicolson.

Azaryahu, Maoz. 2006. *Tel Aviv: Mythography of a City.* Syracuse, NY: Syracuse University Press.

Azaryahu, Maoz, and S. Ilan Troen (eds). 2012. *Tel-Aviv, the First Century: Visions, Designs, Actualities.* Bloomington: Indiana University Press.

Baker, Ejima. 2005. "A Preliminary Step in Exploring Reggaeton." In *Critical Minded: New Approaches to Hip Hop Studies,* ed. Ellie M. Hisama and Evan Rapport, 107–24. Brooklyn, NY: Institute for Studies in American Music, 2005.

Baker, Geoffrey. 2005. "¡ Hip Hop, Revolucion! Nationalizing Rap in Cuba." *Ethnomusicology* 49(3): 368–402.

———. 2011. *Buena Vista in the Club: Rap, Reggaetón, and Revolution in Havana.* Durham, NC: Duke University Press.

Bakrania, Falu. 2013. *Bhangra and Asian Underground: South Asian Music and the Politics of Belonging in Britain.* Durham, NC: Duke University Press.

Ballantine, Christopher. 1991. "Concert and Dance: The Foundations of Black Jazz in South Africa between the Twenties and Early Forties." *Popular Music* 10(2): 121–45.

———. 2004. "Re-thinking 'Whiteness'? Identity, Change and 'White' Popular Music in Post-Apartheid South Africa." *Popular Music* 23(2): 105–31.

Ben-Dor, Shoshana. 1987. "The Sigd of Beta Israel: Testimony to a Community in Transition." In *Ethiopian Jews and Israel,* ed. Michael Ashkenazi and Alex Weingrod, 140–63. New Brunswick, NJ: Transaction Books.

Ben-Eliezer, Uri. 2008. "Multicultural Society and Everyday Cultural Racism: Second Generation of Ethiopian Jews in Israel's 'Crisis of Modernization.'" *Ethnic and Racial Studies* 31(5): 935–61.

BenEzer, Gadi. 2002. *The Ethiopian Jewish Exodus: Narratives of the Migration Journey to Israel 1977-1985.* London: Routledge.

————. 2005. "The Ethiopian Jewish Exodus: A Myth in Creation." In *The Beta Israel in Ethiopia and Israel: Studies on Ethiopian Jews,* ed. Tudor Parfitt and Emanuela Trevisan Semi, 122–30. Richmond, Surrey, UK: Curzon.

Benjamin, Walter. 1933. "On the Mimetic Faculty." *New German Critique* 17: 65–69.

————. 1936. "The Work of Art in the Age of Mechanical Reproduction." In *Illuminations,* ed. Hannah Arendt, 217–51. New York: Schocken.

Ben-Rafael, Eliezer. 2007. "Mizrahi and Russian Challenges to Israel's Dominant Culture: Divergences and Convergences." *Israel Studies* 12(3): 68–91.

Blackman, Lisa. 2012. *Immaterial Bodies: Affect, Embodiment, Mediation.* London: Sage.

Bohlman, Philip V. 2004. *The Music of European Nationalism: Cultural Identity and Modern History.* Santa Barbara, CA: ABC-CLIO.

Boyarin, Jonathan, and Daniel Boyarin. 1993. "Diaspora: Generation and the Ground of Jewish Identity." *Critical Inquiry* 19(4): 693–725.

Boym, Svetlana. 1998. "On Diasporic Intimacy: Ilya Kabakov's Installations and Immigrant Homes." *Critical Inquiry* 24(2): 498–524.

Brenner, Michael. 2003. *Zionism: A Brief History.* Princeton, NJ: Marcus Wiener.

Brinkerhoff, Jennifer A. 2011. "Being a Good Ethiopian Woman: Participation in the 'Buna' (Coffee) Ceremony and Identity." PhD diss., Arizona State University, Phoenix.

Brinner, Benjamin. 2009. *Playing across a Divide: Israeli-Palestinian Musical Encounters.* Oxford: Oxford University Press.

Buck-Morss, Susan. 1989. *The Dialectics of Seeing: Walter Benjamin and the Arcades Project.* Cambridge, MA: MIT Press.

Burkhalter, Thomas. 2013. *Local Music Scenes and Globalization: Transnational Platforms in Beirut.* New York: Routledge.

Burnim, Mellonie V., and Portia Maultsby (eds). 2006. *African American Music: An Introduction.* New York: Routledge.

Campbell, Joseph. 1978 (1940). *The Hero with a Thousand Faces.* New York: HarperCollins.

Carmel, Alex. 2011. *Ottoman Haifa: A History of Four Centuries under Turkish Rule.* London: I. B. Tauris.

Chang, Jeff. 2005. *Can't Stop Won't Stop: A History of the Hip-Hop Generation.* London: Ebury Press.

————. 2007. "It's a Hip-Hop World." *Foreign Policy* 163: 58–65.

Charry, Eric (ed.). 2012. *Hip Hop Africa: New African Music in a Globalizing World.* Bloomington: Indiana University Press.

Chivallon, Christine. 2011. *The Black Diaspora of the Americas: Experiences and Theories out of the Caribbean.* Kingston: Ian Randle.

Citron, Marcia. 1993. *Gender and the Musical Canon.* Cambridge: Cambridge University Press.

Clifford, James. 1994. "Diasporas." *Cultural Anthropology* 9(3): 302–38.

————. 1997. *Routes: Travel and Translation in the Late Twentieth Century.* Cambridge, MA: Harvard University Press.

Cohen, Nahoum. 2003. *Bauhaus Tel Aviv: An Architectural Guide.* London: Anova Books.

Cohen, Stuart A. 2008. *Israel and Its Army: From Cohesion to Confusion.* London: Routledge.

Collins, Edmund John. 1987. "Jazz Feedback to Africa." *American Music* 5(2): 176–93.

Danino, Dikla, and Zohar Amar. 2009. "Little Ethiopia: An Ethnopharmacological Study of the Ethiopian Community in Israel." *International Journal of Ethiopian Studies* 4(1–2): 105–34.

Davids, Jennifer Phillips. 1999. "Fertility Decline and Changes in the Life Course among Ethiopian Jewish Women." In *The Beta Israel in Ethiopia and Israel: Studies on Ethiopian Jews,* ed. Tudor Parfitt and Emanuela Trevisan Semi, 137–59. Richmond, Surrey, UK: Curzon.

Dixon Gottschild, Brenda. 2003. *The Black Dancing Body: A Geography from Coon to Cool.* New York: Palgrave Macmillan.

Djerrahian, Gabriella. 2010. "Eléments d'une négritude mondialisée: Le hip-hop et la conscience raciale chez les jeunes Israéliens d'origine éthiopienne." *Cahiers de Recherches Sociologiques* 49: 17–45.

Doty, William G. 1996. "Joseph Campbell's Myth 'and/versus' Religion." *Soundings: An Interdisciplinary Journal* 79(3–4): 421–45.

Du Bois, W. E. B. 1904. *The Souls of Black Folk.* New York: Penguin.

Durand, Alain-Philippe (ed.). 2002. *Black, Blanc, Beur: Rap Music and Hip-Hop Culture in the Francophone World.* Lanham, MD: Scarecrow.

Eisenberg, Andrew J. 2012. "Hip-Hop and Cultural Citizenship on Kenya's 'Swahili Coast.'" *Africa* 82(4): 556–78.

Elflein, Dietmar. 1998. "From Krauts with Attitudes to Turks with Attitudes: Some Aspects of Hip-Hop History in Germany." *Popular Music* 17(3): 255–65.

Elias, Nelly, and Adriana Kemp. 2010. "The New Second Generation: Non-Jewish *Olim,* Black Jews and Children of Migrant Workers in Israel." *Israel Studies* 15(1): 73–94.

Ellwood, Robert. 1999. *The Politics of Myth: A Study of C. G. Jung, Mircea Eliade, and Joseph Campbell.* Albany: State University of New York Press.

Erlmann, Veit. 1996. *Nightsong: Performance, Power and Practice in South Africa.* Chicago: University of Chicago Press.

Ewing, Adam. 2014. *The Age of Garvey: How a Jamaican Activist Created a Mass Movement & Changed Global Black Politics.* Princeton, NJ: Princeton University Press.

Eyal, Gil. 2008. *The Disenchantment of the Orient: Expertise in Arab Affairs and the Israeli State.* Palo Alto, CA: Stanford University Press.

Falceto, Francis. 2002. *Abyssinie Swing: A Pictorial History of Modern Ethiopian Music.* Addis Ababa: Shama Books.

Farnell, Brenda. 1994. "Ethno-Graphics and the Moving Body." *MAN, Journal of the Royal Anthropological Institute* 29(4): 929–74.

Feinstein International Center. 2012. *Refugee Livelihoods in Urban Areas: Identifying Program Opportunities. Case Study Israel.* Feinstein International Center, Friedman School of Nutrition Science and Policy, Tufts University.

Feld, Steven. 1996. "Pygmy POP: A Genealogy of Schizophonic Mimesis." *Yearbook for Traditional Music* 28: 1–35.

———. 2000. "A Sweet Lullaby for World Music." *Public Culture* 12(1): 145–71.

———. 2012. *Jazz Cosmopolitanism in Accra: Five Musical Years in Ghana.* Durham, NC: Duke University Press.

Feldstein, Ruth. 2013. *How It Feels to Be Free: Black Women Entertainers and the Civil Rights Movement.* New York: Oxford University Press.

Fenster, Tovi, and Ilan Vizel. 2007. "Belonging and Deportation: African Churches in Tel Aviv (Globalizatsia, Shayakhut veKehilat Mehagarei haAvodah haAfrikaim beTel Aviv-Yafo)." *Israeli Sociology* 8(2): 301–21.

Fernandes, Sujatha. 2003. "Fear of a Black Nation: Local Rappers, Transnational Crossings, and State Power in Contemporary Cuba." *Anthropological Quarterly* 76(4): 575–608.

Fredrickson, George M. 1995. *Black Liberation: A Comparative History of Black Ideologies in the United States and South Africa.* New York: Oxford University Press.

Friesel, Evyatar. 2006. "Zionism and Jewish Nationalism: An Inquiry into an Ideological Relationship." *Journal of Israeli History* 25(2): 285–312.

Fryer, Peter. 2000. *Rhythms of Resistance: African Musical Heritage in Brazil.* London: Pluto Press.

Gaunt, Kyra. 2006. *The Games Black Girls Play: Learning the Ropes from Double-Dutch to Hip-Hop.* New York: New York University Press.

Gertz, Nurith. 2000. *Myths in Israeli Culture: Captives of a Dream.* London: Vallentine Mitchell.

Gilroy, Paul. 1993. *The Black Atlantic: Modernity and Double Consciousness.* Cambridge, MA: Harvard University Press.

Golan, Arnon. 2009. "Soundscapes of Urban Development: Tel-Aviv in the 1920s and 1930s." *Israel Studies* 14(3): 120–36.

Goldblatt, Hadass, and Sara Rosenblum. 2011. "'There' to 'Here': The Values, Needs and Dreams of Immigrant Jewish Ethiopian Youth in Israel." *Megamot* 47(3–4): 593–615.

Goldscheider, Calvin. 2015. *Israeli Society in the 21st Century: Immigration, Inequality, and Religious Conflict.* Waltham, MA: Brandeis University Press.

Grant, Colin. 2010. *Negro with a Hat: The Rise and Fall of Marcus Garvey and His Dream of Mother Africa.* New York: Oxford University Press.

Greene, Paul. 2001. "Mixed Messages: Unsettled Cosmopolitanisms in Nepali Pop." *Popular Music* 20(2): 169–87.

Greenwald, Jeff. 2002. "Hip-Hop Drumming: The Rhyme May Define, but the Groove Makes You Move." *Black Music Research Journal* 22(2): 259–71.

Grupper, Emmanuel, and Anita Nudelman. 1995. "Cross-Cultural Pluralism in Action: The Case of 'Segd' Celebration of Ethiopian Jews in Youth Aliyah's Residential Institutions in Israel." In *Between Africa and Zion: Proceedings of the First International Congress of the Society for the Study of Ethiopian Jewry,* ed. Steven Kaplan, Tudor Parfitt, and Emanuela Trevisan Semi, 160–65. Jerusalem: SOSTEJE, Ben-Zvi Institute.

Habermas, Jürgen. 1994. "Citizenship and National Identity." In *The Condition of Citizenship,* ed. Bart van Steenbergen, 20–35. London: Sage.

Hahn, Tomie. 2007. *Sensational Knowledge: Embodying Culture through Japanese Dance.* Middletown, CT: Wesleyan University Press.

Hall, Stuart (ed.). 1997. *Representation: Cultural Representations and Signifying Practices.* London: Sage.

Hankins, Sarah. 2013. "Multi-Dimensional Israeliness and Tel Aviv's Tachanah Merkazit: Hearing Culture in a Polyphonic Traffic Hub." *City and Society* 25(3): 282–303.

———. 2015. "Black Musics, African Lives, and the National Imagination in Modern Israel." PhD diss., Harvard University, Cambridge, MA.

Hebdige, Dick. 1987. *Cut 'n' Mix: Culture, Identity and Caribbean Music.* London: Routledge.

Hellier-Tinoco, Ruth. 2011. *Embodying Mexico: Tourism, Nationalism & Performance.* New York: Oxford University Press.

Herman, Marilyn. 2012. *Gondar's Child: Songs, Honor and Identity among Ethiopian Jews in Israel.* Trenton, NJ: Red Sea Press.

Herskovits, Melville. 1961. *The Myth of the Negro Past.* Boston: Beacon.

Hertzberg, Arthur. 1960. *The Zionist Idea: A Historical Analysis and Reader.* Philadelphia: Jewish Publication Society.

Herzfeld, Michael. 1997. *Cultural Intimacy: Social Poetics in the Nation-State.* London: Routledge.

Hisama, Ellie M., and Evan Rapport (eds.). 2005. *Critical Minded: New Approaches to Hip Hop Studies.* Brooklyn, NY: Institute for Studies in American Music.

Ho, Wai-Chung. 2003. "Between Globalization and Localization: A Study of Hong Kong Popular Music." *Popular Music* 22(2): 143–57.

Hoffmann, Daniel. 2005. "West-African Warscapes: Violent Events as Narrative Blocs: The Disarmament at Bo, Sierra Leone." *Anthropological Quarterly* 78(2): 328–53.

Horowitz, Amy. 2010. *Mediterranean Israeli Music and the Politics of the Aesthetic.* Detroit: Wayne State University Press.

Hutchinson, Sydney. 2006. "*Merengue Tipico* in Santiago and New York: Transnational Regionalism in a Neo-Traditional Dominican Music." *Ethnomusicology* 50(1): 37–72.

Jackson, Michael D. 2013. *The Politics of Storytelling: Variations on a Theme by Hanna Arendt*. Copenhagen: Museum Musculanum Press.

Kanafani, Ghassan. 1978. "Returning to Haifa." In *Palestine's Children*. London: Heinemann Educational.

Kang, Jaeho. 2014. *Walter Benjamin and the Media: The Spectacle of Modernity*. London: Polity Press.

Kapchan, Deborah. 2009. "Learning to Listen: The Sound of Sufism in France." *The World of Music* 51(2): 65–89.

———. 2017. "Listening Acts: Witnessing the Pain (and Praise) of Others." In *Theorizing Sound Writing*, ed. Deborah Kapchan. Middletown, CT: Wesleyan University Press.

Kaplan, Steven. 1992. *The Beta Israel (Falasha) in Ethiopia, from the Earliest Times to the Twentieth Century*. New York: New York University Press.

———. 1999a. "Can the Ethiopian Change His Skin? The Beta Israel (Ethiopian Jews) and Racial Discourse." *African Affairs* 98: 535–50.

———. 1999b. "Everyday Resistance and the Study of Ethiopian Jews." In *The Beta Israel in Ethiopia and Israel: Studies on Ethiopian Jews*, ed. Tudor Parfitt and Emanuela Trevisan Semi, 113–27. Richmond, Surrey, UK: Curzon.

———. 2005. "Tama Galut Etiopiya: The Ethiopian Exile Is Over." *Diaspora: A Journal of Transnational Studies* 14(2–3): 381–96.

———. 2010. "Ethiopian Immigrants in the United States and Israel: A Preliminary Comparison." *International Journal of Ethiopian Studies* 5(1): 71–92.

Kaplan, Steven, Tudor Parfitt, and Emanuela Trevisan Semi (eds). 1995. *Between Africa and Zion: Proceedings of the First International Congress of the Society for the Study of Ethiopian Jewry*. Jerusalem: SOSTEJE, Ben-Zvi Institute.

Karadawi, Ahmed. 1991. "The Smuggling of the Ethiopian Falasha to Israel through Sudan." *African Affairs* 90(358): 23–49.

Kartun-Blum, Ruth. 1999. *Profane Scriptures: Reflections on the Dialogue with the Bible in Modern Hebrew Poetry*. Cincinnati: Hebrew Union College Press.

Katz, Mark. 2012. *Groove Music: The Art and Culture of the Hip-Hop DJ*. New York: Oxford University Press.

Kawase, Itsushi. 2010. "Intercultural Dialogue on the Visualization of Local Knowledge: Films on Hereditary Singers in Ethiopia." In *African Study Monographs* Suppl. 41: 101–109.

Kebede, Ashenafi. 1967. "The Krar." *Ethiopia Observer* 11: 154–61.

———. 1975. "The 'Azmari,' Poet-Musician of Ethiopia." *Musical Quarterly* 61(1): 47–57.

———. 1977. "The Bowl-Lyre of Northeast Africa. Krar: The Devil's Instrument." *Ethnomusicology* 21(3): 379–95.

Keil, Charles, and Steven Feld. 1994. "Respecting Aretha: A Letter Exchange." In *Music Grooves: Essays and Dialogues*, 218–26. Chicago: University of Chicago Press.

Kemp, Adriana, and Rebecca Rajiman. 2004. "'Tel Aviv Is Not Foreign to You': Urban Incorporation Policy on Labor Migrants in Israel." *International Migration Review* 38(1): 26–51.

Keyes, Cheryl. 1996. "At the Crossroad: Rap Music and Its African Nexus." *Ethnomusicology* 40(2): 223–48.

Kidron, Carol A. 2011. "Sensorial Memory." In *A Companion to the Anthropology of the Body and Embodiment*, ed. Frances E. Mascia-Lees, 451–66. Chichester, UK: Wiley-Blackwell.

Kimberlin, Cynthia Tse. 1978. "The Bägänna of Ethiopia." *Ethiopianist Notes* 2(2): 13–29.

———. 2009. "Diverse Connections as a Model for the 21st Century Yared School of Music." In *Proceedings of the 16th International Conference of Ethiopian Studies*, ed. Svein Ege, Harald Aspen, Birhanu Teferra, and Shiferaw Bekele. Wiesbaden: Otto Harrassowitz.

Kirschenblatt-Gimblett, Barbara. 1995. "Theorizing Heritage." *Ethnomusicology* 39(3): 367–80.

Kritzman-Amir, Tally (ed.). 2015. *Where Levinksy Meets Asmara: Social and Legal Aspects of Israeli Asylum Policy (Levinsky Pinat Asmara)*. Jerusalem: Van Leer Jerusalem Institute.

Laqueur, Walter. 1972. *A History of Zionism: From the French Revolution to the Establishment of the State of Israel*. New York: Schocken.

Le Gendre, Kevin. 2012. *Soul Unsung: Reflections on the Band in Black Popular Music*. London: Equinox.

Leitman, Eva, and Elisabeth Weinbaum. 1999. "Israeli Women of Ethiopian Descent: The Strengths, Conflicts and Successes." In *The Beta Israel in Ethiopia and Israel: Studies on Ethiopian Jews*, ed. Tudor Parfitt and Emanuela Trevisan Semi, 128–36. Richmond, Surrey, UK: Curzon.

Lemelle, Sidney, and Robin D. G. Kelley (eds). 1994. *Imagining Home: Class, Culture and Nationalism in the African Diaspora*. London: Verso.

Levine, Donald. 1965. *Wax and Gold: Tradition and Innovation in Ethiopian Culture*. Chicago: University of Chicago Press.

———. 2000 (1974). *Greater Ethiopia: The Evolution of a Multiethnic Society*. Chicago: University of Chicago Press.

———. 2004. "Reconfiguring the Ethiopian Nation in a Global Era." *International Journal of Ethiopian Studies* 1(2): 1–15.

Mann, Barbara. 2006. *A Place in History: Modernism, Tel Aviv, and the Creation of Jewish Urban Space*. Stanford, CA: Stanford University Press.

Manuel, Peter. 1993. *Cassette Culture: Popular Music and Technology in North India*. Chicago: University of Chicago Press.

———. 2000. "The Construction of a Diasporic Tradition: Indo-Caribbean 'Local Classical Music.'" *Ethnomusicology* 44(1): 97–119.

Marshall, T. H. 1949. "Citizenship and Social Class." In *Citizenship and Social Class and Other Essays*, 1–85. Cambridge: Cambridge University Press.

Mascia-Lees, Frances E. (ed.). 2011. *A Companion to the Anthropology of the Body and Embodiment*. Chichester, UK: Wiley-Blackwell.

Maultsby, Portia. 2006. "Chapter 12: Rhythm and Blues/R&B," "Chapter 13: Soul," "Chapter 14: Funk." In *African American Music: An Introduction,* ed. Mellonie V. Burnim and Portia Maultsby, 239–319. New York: Routledge.

McDonald, David A. 2009. "Poetics and the Performance of Violence in Israel/Palestine." *Ethnomusicology* 53(1): 58–85.

———. 2010. "Geographies of the Body: Music, Violence and Manhood in Palestine." *Ethnomusicology Forum* 19(2): 191–214.

———. 2013. *My Voice Is My Weapon: Music, Nationalism, and the Poetics of Palestinian Resistance*. Durham, NC: Duke University Press.

McDonald, Emily. 2011. "Transnationalism." In *A Companion to the Anthropology of the Body and Embodiment*, ed. Frances E. Mascia-Lees, 504–20. Chichester, UK: Wiley-Blackwell.

McFarland, Pancho. 2013. *The Chican@ Hip Hop Nation: Politics of a New Millennial Mestizaje*. East Lansing: Michigan State University Press.

Meintjes, Louise. 1990. "Paul Simon's Graceland, South Africa, and the Mediation of Musical Meaning." *Ethnomusicology* 34(1): 34–73.

Mintz, Sidney W., and Richard Price. 1992. *The Birth of African-American Culture: An Anthropological Perspective*. New York: Beacon.

Mitchell, Tony (ed.). 2001. *Global Noise: Rap and Hip Hop outside the USA*. Middletown, CT: Wesleyan University Press.

Monterescu, Daniel. 2015. *Jaffa Shared and Shattered: Contrived Coexistence in Israel/Palestine*. Bloomington: Indiana University Press.

Morgan, Marcyliena. 2009. *The Real HipHop: Battling for Knowledge, Power, and Respect in the LA Underground*. Durham, NC: Duke University Press.

Morris, Benny. 1988. "The New Historiography: Israel Confronts Its Past." *Tikkun* 2 (November–December): 19–23, 99–102.

———. 2009. *1948: A History of the First Arab-Israeli War*. New Haven, CT: Yale University Press.

Muller, Carol A. 2006. "The New African Diaspora, the Built Environment and the Past in Jazz." *Ethnomusicology Forum* 15(1): 63–86.

Nooshin, Laudan. 2011. "Hip-Hop Tehran: Migrating Styles, Musical Meanings, Marginalized Voices." In *Migrating Music,* ed. Jason Toynbee and Byron Dueck, 92–111. New York: Routledge.

O'Brian Chang, Kevin, and Wayne Chen. 1998. *Reggae Routes: The Story of Jamaican Music*. Philadelphia: Temple University Press.

Pardue, Derek. 2004. "'Writing in the Margins': Brazilian Hip-Hop as an Educational Project." *Anthropology & Education Quarterly* 35(4): 411–32.

———. 2011. *Brazilian Hip Hoppers Speak from the Margins: We's on Tape.* London: Palgrave Macmillan.

Parfitt, Tudor. 1985. *Operation Moses: The Story of the Exodus of the Falasha Jews from Ethiopia.* London: Weidenfeld & Nicolson.

Parfitt, Tudor, and Emanuela Trevisan Semi (eds). 1999. *The Beta Israel in Ethiopia and Israel: Studies on Ethiopian Jews.* Richmond, Surrey, UK: Curzon.

———. 2005. *Jews of Ethiopia: The Birth of an Elite.* London: Routledge.

Perelson, Inbal. 1998. "Power Relations in the Israeli Popular Music System." *Popular Music* 17(1): 113–28.

Perullo, Alex. 2011. *Live from Dar es Salaam: Popular Music and Tanzania's Music Economy.* Bloomington: Indiana University Press.

Poole, Amada. 2013. "Ransoms, Remittances, and Refugees: The Gatekeeper State in Eritrea." *Africa Today* 60(2): 67–82.

Powne, Michael. 1968. *Ethiopian Music, an Introduction: A Survey of Ecclesiastical and Secular Ethiopian Music and Instruments.* London: Oxford University Press.

Pratt, Mary Louise. 1991. "Arts of the Contact Zone." *Profession* 91: 33–40.

Quirin, James. 1992. *The Evolution of the Ethiopian Jews: A History of the Beta Israel (Falasha) to 1920.* Philadelphia: University of Pennsylvania Press.

———. 1995. "Ayhud and Falasha: Oral and Written Traditions concerning the Reign of King Yeshaq in Fifteenth Century Ethiopia." In *Between Africa and Zion: Proceedings of the First International Congress of the Society for the Study of Ethiopian Jewry,* ed. Steven Kaplan, Tudor Parfitt, and Emanuela Trevisan Semi, 55–71. Jerusalem: SOS-TEJE, Ben-Zvi Institute.

Rabinowitz, Dan, and Daniel Monterescu. 2008. "Reconfiguring the 'Mixed Town': Urban Transformations of Ethnonational Relations in Palestine and Israel." *International Journal of Middle East Studies* 40(2): 195–226.

Raboteau, Emily. 2007. "Searching for Zion." *Transition* 97: 52–89.

———. 2014. *Searching for Zion: The Quest for Home in the African Diaspora.* New York: Atlantic Monthly Press.

Rahaim, Matthew. 2012. *Musicking Bodies: Gesture and Voice in Hindustani Music.* Middletown, CT: Wesleyan University Press.

Ram, Uri. 2005. "Jerusalem, Tel Aviv, and the Bifurcation of Israel." *Journal of Politics, Culture and Society* 19(2): 1–33.

Rasmussen, Anne. 1992. "'An Evening in the Orient': The Middle Eastern Nightclub in America." *Asian Music* 23(2): 63–88.

Ratner, David. 2015. *Black Sounds: Black Music and Identity among Young Israeli Ethio-*

pians (*Shomim Shachor: Muziqah Shechorah uZehut beKerev Tseirim Yotsei Etyopia beYisrael*). Tel Aviv: Resling.

Raz-Krakotzkin, Amnon. 2013. "Exile, History, and the Nationalization of Jewish Memory: Some Reflections on the Zionist Notion of History and Return." *Journal of Levantine Studies* 3(2): 37–70.

Regev, Motti. 1996. "Musica Mizrakhit, Israeli Rock and National Culture in Israel." *Popular Music* 15(3): 275–84.

Regev, Motti, and Edwin Seroussi. 2004. *Popular Music & National Culture in Israel.* Berkeley: University of California Press.

Resnik, Julia. 2006. "Alternative Identities in Multicultural Schools in Israel: Emancipatory Identity, Mixed Identity and Transnational Identity." *British Journal of Sociology of Education* 27(5): 585–601.

Roman-Velazquez, Patria. 1999. "The Embodiment of Salsa: Musicians, Instruments and the Performance of a Latin Style and Identity." *Popular Music* 18(1): 115–31.

Rose, Tricia. 1994. *Black Noise: Rap Music and Black Culture in Contemporary America.* Middletown, CT: Wesleyan University Press.

———. 2008. *The Hip Hop Wars: What We Talk about When We Talk about Hip Hop — and Why It Matters.* New York: Basic Books.

Rosen, Chaim. 1987. "Core Symbols of Ethiopian Identity and Their Role in Understanding the Beta Israel Today." In *Ethiopian Jews and Israel,* ed. Michael Ashkenazi and Alex Weingrod, 55–62. New Brunswick, NJ: Transaction Books.

Rotbard, Sharon. 2005. *Ir Levana, Ir Shehora* [White City, Black City]. Tel Aviv: Bavel Books.

Salamon, Hagar. 1995. "Reflections of Ethiopian Cultural Patterns on the Beta Israel Absorption in Israel: The 'Barya' Case." In *Between Africa and Zion: Proceedings of the First International Congress of the Society for the Study of Ethiopian Jewry,* ed. Steven Kaplan, Tudor Parfitt, and Emanuela Trevisan Semi, 126–30. Jerusalem: SOSTEJE, Ben-Zvi Institute.

———. 1999. *The Hyena People: Ethiopian Jews in Christian Ethiopia.* Berkeley: University of California Press.

———. 2002. "Between Conscious and Subconscious: Depth-to-Depth Communication in the Ethnographic Space." *Ethos* 30(3): 249–72.

———. 2003. "Blackness in Transition: Decoding Racial Constructs through Stories of Ethiopian Jews." *Journal of Folklore Research* 40(1): 3–32.

———. 2010. "Misplaced Home and Mislaid Meat: Stories Circulating among Ethiopian Immigrants in Israel." *Callaloo* 33(1): 165–76.

———. 2011. "The Floor Falling Away: Dislocated Space and Body in the Humour of Ethiopian Immigrants in Israel." *Folklore* 122(1): 16–34.

Sanga, Imani. 2010. "Postcolonial Cosmopolitan Music in Dar es Salaam: Dr. Remmy Ongala and the Traveling Sounds." *African Studies Review* 53(3): 61–76.

Schloss, Joseph. 2004. *Making Beats: The Art of Sample-Based Hip-Hop*. Middletown, CT: Wesleyan University Press.

———. 2006. "'Like Old Folk Songs Handed Down from Generation to Generation': History, Canon, and Community in B-Boy Culture." *Ethnomusicology* 50(3): 411–32.

Seeman, Don. 1999. "All in the Family: 'Kinship' as a Paradigm for the Ethnography of Beta Israel." In *The Beta Israel in Ethiopia and Israel: Studies on Ethiopian Jews,* ed. Tudor Parfitt and Emanuela Trevisan Semi, 94–112. Richmond, Surrey, UK: Curzon.

———. 2009. *One People, One Blood: Ethiopian-Israelis and the Return to Judaism*. New Brunswick, NJ: Rutgers University Press.

———. 2015. "Coffee and the Moral Order: Ethiopian Jews and Pentecostals against Culture." *American Ethnologist* 42(4): 734–48.

Segal, Robert A. 1999. *Theorizing about Myth*. Boston: University of Massachusetts Press.

———. 2002. "Myth and Politics: A Response to Robert Ellwood." *Journal of the American Academy of Religion* 70(3): 611–20.

———. 2005. "The Function of 'Religion' and 'Myth': A Response to Russell McCutcheon." *Journal of the American Academy of Religion* 73(1): 209–13.

Segev, Tom. 1986. *1949: The First Israelis*. London: Collier Macmillan.

———. 2002. *Elvis in Jerusalem: Post-Zionism and the Americanization of Israel*. New York: Metropolitan Books.

Seroussi, Edwin. 1986. "Politics, Ethnic Identity, and Music in Israel: The Case of the Moroccan Bakkashot." *Asian Music* 17(2): 32–45.

Shabtay, Malka. 1999. "Identity Reformulation among Ethiopian Immigrant Soldiers: Processes of Interpretation and Struggle." In *The Beta Israel in Ethiopia and Israel: Studies on Ethiopian Jews,* ed. Tudor Parfitt and Emanuela Trevisan Semi, 169–80. Richmond, Surrey, UK: Curzon.

———. 2001. *Between Reggae and Rap: The Integration Challenge of Ethiopian Youth in Israel*. Tel Aviv: Cherikover.

———. 2003. "'RaGap': Music and Identity among Young Ethiopians in Israel." *Critical Arts: A South-North Journal of Cultural & Media Studies* 17(1–2): 93–105.

Shafir, Gershon, and Yoav Peled. 2002. *Being Israeli: The Dynamics of Multiple Citizenship*. Cambridge: Cambridge University Press.

Shapira, Anita. 1992. *Land and Power: The Zionist Resort to Force, 1881–1948*. Stanford, CA: Stanford University Press.

———. 2012. *Israel: A History*. London: Weidenfeld & Nicolson.

Shelemay, Kay Kaufman. 1980–81. "Seged: A Falasha Pilgrimage Festival." *Musica Judaica* 3: 42–62.

———. 1986. *Music, Ritual, and Falasha History.* East Lansing: Michigan State University Press.

———. 1991. *A Song of Longing: An Ethiopian Journey.* Urbana: University of Illinois Press.

———. 2006a. "Ethiopian Musical Invention in Diaspora: A Tale of Three Musicians." *Diaspora* 15(2–3): 303–20.

———. 2006b. *Soundscapes: Exploring Music in a Changing World,* 2nd ed. New York: W. W. Norton.

———. 2009. "Musical Scholarship and Ethiopian Studies: Past, Present, Future." *Journal of Ethiopian Studies* 42(1–2): 175–90.

Shokeid, Moshe. 2015. "Newcomers at the Israeli National Table: Transforming Urban Landscapes and the Texture of Citizenship." *City and Society* 27(2): 208–230.

Slobin, Mark. 1992. "Micromusics of the West: A Comparative Approach." *Ethnomusicology* 36(1): 1–87.

Smith, Anthony. 2004. *Chosen Peoples: Sacred Sources of National Identity.* Oxford: Oxford University Press.

———. 2008. *The Cultural Foundations of Nations: Hierarchy, Covenant, and Republic.* London: Wiley-Blackwell.

Smooha, Sammy. 1997. "Ethnic Democracy: Israel as Archetype." *Israel Studies* 2(2): 198–241.

Solomon, Thomas. 2005. "'Living Underground Is Tough': Authenticity and Locality in the Hip-Hop Community in Istanbul, Turkey." *Popular Music* 24(1): 1–20.

Stanislawski, Michael. 2001. *Zionism and the Fin de Siècle: Cosmopolitanism and Nationalism from Nordau to Jabotinsky.* Berkeley: University of California Press.

Starr, Deborah. 2006. "Sensing the City: Representations of Cairo's Harat al-Yahud." *Prooftexts* 26(1–2): 138–62.

Sternhell, Zeev. 2002. *The Founding Myths of Israel: Nationalism, Socialism, and the Making of the Jewish State.* Princeton, NJ: Princeton University Press.

Stokes, Martin. 1992. *The Arabesk Debate: Music and Musicians in Modern Turkey.* Oxford: Clarendon Press.

———. 2004. "Music and the Global Order." *Annual Review of Anthropology* 43: 37–72.

———. 2010. *The Republic of Love: Cultural Intimacy in Turkish Popular Music.* Chicago: University of Chicago Press.

Strenski, Ivan. 1992. *Malinowski and the Work of Myth.* Princeton, NJ: Princeton University Press.

Stround, Sean. 2008. *The Defence of Tradition in Brazilian Popular Music: Politics, Culture and the Creation of* Musica Popular Brasileira. Aldershot, UK: Ashgate.

Swedenburg, Ted. 1997. "Saida Sultan/Danna International: Transgender Pop and the Polysemiotics of Sex, Nation, and Ethnicity on the Israeli-Egyptian Border." *Musical Quarterly* 81(1): 81–108.

————. 2013. "Palestinian Rap: Against the Struggle Paradigm." In *Popular Culture in the Middle East and North Africa: A Postcolonial Outlook,* ed. Walid El-Hamamsy and Mounira Soliman, 1–13. London: Routledge.

Tang, Patricia. 2007. *Masters of the Sabar: Wolof Griot Percussionists of Senegal.* Philadelphia: Temple University Press.

————. 2012. "The Rapper as Modern Griot: Reclaiming Ancient Traditions." In *Hip Hop Africa: New African Music in a Globalizing World,* ed. Eric Charry, 79–91. Bloomington: Indiana University Press.

Taussig, Michael. 1993. *Mimesis and Alterity: A Particular History of the Senses.* New York: Routledge.

Taylor, Timothy D. 1997. *Global Pop: World Music, World Markets.* New York: Routledge.

Teferi, Amaleletch. 2005. "About the Jewish Identity of the Beta Israel." In *The Beta Israel in Ethiopia and Israel: Studies on Ethiopian Jews,* ed. Tudor Parfitt and Emanuela Trevisan Semi, 173–92. Richmond, Surrey, UK: Curzon.

Terkourafi, Marina (ed.). 2010. *Languages of Global Hip-Hop.* London: Continuum.

Tourny, Olivier (ed.). 2007. *Annales d'Éthiopie: Musiques traditionelles d'Éthiopie* 23.

————. 2010. *Le chant liturgique juif éthiopien: Analyse musicale d'une tradition orale.* Paris: Éditions Peeters.

Tourny, Olivier, and Simha Arom. 1999. "The Formal Organisation of the Beta Israel Liturgy—Substance and Performance: Musical Structure." In *The Beta Israel in Ethiopia and Israel: Studies on Ethiopian Jews,* ed. Tudor Parfitt and Emanuela Trevisan Semi, 252–56. Richmond, Surrey, UK: Curzon.

Trevisan Semi, Emanuela. 2004. "Jacques Faitlovitch." *Pe'amim: Revon L'kheker Kehilot Yisrael Bamizrach* 100: 91–112.

Turino, Thomas. 2000. *Nationalists, Cosmopolitans, and Popular Music in Zimbabwe.* Chicago: University of Chicago Press.

————. 2003. "Are We Global Yet? Globalist Discourse, Cultural Formations and the Study of Zimbabwean Popular Music." *British Journal of Ethnomusicology* 12(2): 51–79.

Turner, Terence. 2011. "Bodiliness." In *A Companion to the Anthropology of the Body and Embodiment,* ed. Frances E. Mascia-Lees, 102–18. Chichester, UK: Wiley-Blackwell.

Ullendorff, Edward. 1968. *Ethiopia and the Bible.* London: Oxford University Press.

Van Steenbergen, Bart. 1994. "The Condition of Citizenship: An Introduction." In *The Condition of Citizenship,* ed. Bart van Steenbergen, 1–9. London: Sage.

Vertovec, Steven. 2003. "Migration and Other Modes of Transnationalism: Towards Conceptual Cross-Fertilization." *International Migration Review* 37(3): 641–65.

Wagaw, Teshome G. 1991. "The International Ramifications of Falasha Emigration." *Journal of Modern African Studies* 29(4): 557–81.

Walser, Robert. 1995. "Rhythm, Rhyme, and Rhetoric in the Music of Public Enemy." *Ethnomusicology* 39 (2): 193–217.

Wardhaugh, Ronald. 2009. *An Introduction to Sociolinguistics*. Chichester, UK: Blackwell.

Washburne, Christopher. 1997. "The Clavé of Jazz: A Caribbean Contribution to the Rhythmic Foundation of an African-American Music." *Black Music Research Journal* 17(1): 59–80.

Waterman, Christopher. 1998. "Chop and Quench." *African Arts* 31(1): 1, 4, 6–9.

Webster-Kogen, Ilana. 2011. "The Azmari Paradox: Ethnicity, Identity, and Migration in Ethiopian-Israeli Music." PhD diss., University of London, London.

———. 2013. "Engendering Homeland: Migration, Diaspora and Feminism in Ethiopian Music." *Journal of African Cultural Studies* 12(2): 156–69.

———. 2014. "Song Style as Strategy: Nationalism, Cosmopolitanism and Citizenship in the Idan Raichel Project's Ethiopian-Influenced Songs." *Ethnomusicology Forum* 23(1): 27–48.

———. 2016. "Bole to Harlem via Tel Aviv: Networks of Ethiopia's Musical Diaspora." *African and Black Diaspora* 9(2): 274–29.

Weil, Shalva. 1995. "'It Is Futile to Trust in Man': Methodological Difficulties in Studying Non-Mainstream Populations with Reference to Ethiopian Jews in Israel." *Human Organization* 54(1): 1–9.

———. 2004. "Ethiopian Jewish Women: Trends and Transformations in the Context of Transnational Change." *Nashim: A Journal of Jewish Women's Studies & Gender Issues* 8: 73–86.

Weisser, Stéphanie, and Francis Falceto. 2013. "Investigating Qəñət in Amhara Secular Culture: An Acoustic and Historical Study." *Annales d'Éthiopie* 28: 299–322.

Weitz, Yechiam. 2007. "Dialectical versus Unequivocal." In *Making Israel*, ed. Benny Morris, 278–98. Ann Arbor: University of Michigan Press.

Werbner, Pnina. 2006. "Vernacular Cosmopolitanism." *Theory, Culture & Society* 23(2): 496–98.

Westheimer, Ruth, and Steven Kaplan. 1992. *Surviving Salvation: The Ethiopian Family in Transition*. New York: New York University Press.

White, Bob. 2002. "Congolese Rumba and Other Cosmopolitanisms." *Cahiers d'Études Africaines* 42(168): 663–86.

Wilder, Gary. 2015. *Freedom Time: Negritude, Decolonization, and the Future of the World*. Durham, NC: Duke University Press.

Wood, Abigail. 2014. "Soundscapes of Pilgrimage: European and American Christians in Jerusalem's Old City." *Ethnomusicology Forum* 23(3): 285–305.

Woubshet, Dagmawi. 2009. "Tizita: A New World Interpretation." *Callaloo* 32(2): 628–35.

Yiftachel, Oren, and Avinoam Meir. 1998. *Ethnic Frontiers and Peripheries: Landscapes of Development and Inequality in Israel*. Boulder, CO: Westview Press.

Yuval-Davis, Nira. 1997. *Gender & Nation*. London: Sage.

Select Discography

Aga, Alemu. 2002. "Tew Semagn Hagere." Éthiopiques *11: The Harp of King David*. Buda Musique, 82232–2.

Ahmed, Mahmoud. 1975. "Tezeta." *Ere Mela Mela*. Kaifa Records, LPKF 20. Axum.

Axum. 2008. "Ma Im Hakesef." *Axum*. JDub Records (no number).

Aweke, Aster. 1990. "Tizita." *Aster*. CBS Records, CT 46848.

———. 1991. *Kabu*. Sony Music Entertainment. Columbia Records, CK 47846.

Barihun, Abate, and Yitzhak Yedid. 2005. *Ras Deshen: From Ethiopian Music to Contemporary Jazz*. Treasure Ltd. (no number).

Cafe Shahor Hazak. 2015. "Ihiya Beseder." *Rak Laalot*. Not on label, no number.

Haza, Ofra. 1984. *Yemenite Songs*. Hed-Arzi, ANP 15110.

Idan Raichel Project. 2002. *Idan Raichel's Project*. Helicon, HL 8202.

———. 2002. "Bo'ee." *Idan Raichel's Project*. Helicon, HL 8202.

———. 2002. "Brachot Lashana Hachadasha." *Idan Raichel's Project*. Helicon, HL 8202.

———. 2005. *Mima'amakim*. Helicon, HL 8245.

———. 2008. *Within My Walls*. Helicon, HL 8295.

———. 2011. *Traveling Home*. Helicon, HL 02–8310.

———. 2013. *Quarter to Six*. Helicon, HSIR4TH13.

Ilanit. 1973. "Eretz Eretz." *The Best of Ilanit*. Hed-Arzi, BAN 14719.

Jeremy Kol Habash. 2010. "Hotsaot Gedolot Hakhnasot Ktanot Lemi Ikhpat." Not on label, no number.

Kafé Shahor Hazak (Cafe Shahor Hazak), featuring Eli Luzon. 2008. "Eizo Medina." Not on label, no number.

Luzon, Eli. 1987. *Eizo Medina*. Ben Mosh Records, BM 1050.

Manchlot, Dejen. 2007. *Dejen Traditional Instruments*. Vol. 1. NRI (Nahum Records Israel). No number.

Melesse, Muluken. 1975 (1999). "Nanu Nanu Ney." *Muluken Melesse*. Vol. 1. AIT Records, AIT021.

Menilek and Avi. 2009. *Songs from Habesh* (unpublished field recordings). Recorded by Ilana Webster-Kogen.

Orchestra Ethiopia. 2007 (recorded 1963–1975). *Éthiopiques 23: Orchestra Ethiopia*. Buda Musique, 860152.

Rada, Ester. 2013. *Life Happens*. Not on label (no number).

———. 2014. *Ester Rada*. Fit Fit Records, The Eighth Note, and Afficoman (no number). Distributed in France by Discograph, SP 6107755.

———. 2015. *I Wish*. Not on label.

———. 2017. *Different Eyes*. Fit Fit Records (number forthcoming).

Seyum, Aklilu. 2013. *Yechaw Mededgna*. No label (no number).

Simon, Paul. 1986. *Graceland*. Warner Bros. Records, 9 25447-2.

Simone, Nina. 1967. "Four Women." *Ne me quitte pas*. Decca International, 30 CV 1205.

Teddy Afro. 2017. *Ethiopia*. Teddy Afro, 191061615965.

Werqu, Asnaqetch. 2003. *Éthiopiques 16: The Lady with the Krar*. Buda Musique, 82265-2.

Zfirah, Bracha, and Nahum Nardi at the Piano. 1937. *Palestine Folk Song* (in Hebrew). Columbia Phonograph 4199-M (CO 21428).

Zvuloon Dub System. 2014. *Anbessa Dub*. Medtone Records, MTR-CD-002.

[Various artists.] 2002 (tracks recorded 1970–1974 for Amha Records). *Éthiopiques 10: Tezeta—Ethiopian Blues & Ballads*. Buda Musique, 82222-2.

———. 2004. *Éthiopiques 18: Asguèbba!* Buda Musique, 82289-2.

Web Resources

Abebe, Dabby Adeno. "The Dark Side of Tel Aviv," Ynet News, accessed July 28, 2017, www.ynet.com.

"Aklilu Seyoum," Facebook, accessed July 28, 2017, www.facebook.com.

"אלי לחזן ויצפאן - איזו מדינה," YouTube, accessed July 28, 2017, www.youtube.com.

"Anbessa Dub," Zvuloon Dub System Bandcamp, accessed July 28, 2017, www.zvuloon dubsystem.bandcamp.com.

Arlosoroff, Meirav. "Ethiopians in Israel: An Employment and Educational Success," *Haaretz*, accessed July 28, 2017, www.haaretz.com.

"Aster Aweke Live Concert in Tel Aviv 05.05.14," YouTube, accessed July 28, 2017, www.youtube.com.

"Axum, Ma Im Hakesef," YouTube, accessed July 28, 2017, www.youtube.com.

"Axum—Pocket Full of Money (official video)"—"אקסום," YouTube, accessed July 28, 2017, www.youtube.com.

"Balezena—New Ethiopian Eskista Music 2015," YouTube, accessed July 28, 2017, www.youtube.com.

Beaumont, Peter. "Israeli Police Chief Says It Is Natural to Suspect Ethiopians of Crime," *The Guardian*, accessed July 28, 2017, www.theguardian.com/uk.

"Beta Dance Troupe—Opus for Heads," YouTube, accessed July 28, 2017, www.youtube.com.

"Black over White—Tomer Heymann Film Trailer," YouTube, accessed July 28, 2017, www.youtube.com.

"Cabra Casay in Paris at the Cirque d'hiver with Yannick Noah, Yael Naim, Ayo, Oxmo Puccino, Fefe, Mathieu Chedid, abd EL Malik," Facebook, accessed July 28, 2017, www.facebook.com.

"Cafe Shachor Chazak in San Francisco—My Baby," YouTube, accessed July 28, 2017, www.youtube.com.

"Chai Eurovision Song Contest 1983—Ofra Haza," YouTube, accessed July 28, 2017, www .youtube.com.

"Common—The Game," YouTube, accessed July 28, 2017, www.youtubecom.

"Cops Beat Ethiopian IDF Soldier in Alleged Racist Attack," YouTube, accessed July 28, 2017, www.youtube.com.

"DAM, 'Born Here', Hebrew/Arabic with English subtitles," YouTube, accessed July 28, 2017, www.youtube.com.

"Entrants with Work Permits, 2010," Central Bureau of Statistics, accessed July 28, 2017, www.cbs.gov.il.

"Ester Rada—Four Women (Official Video)," YouTube, accessed July 28, 2017, www .youtube.com.

"Ester Rada—Four Women—Montreal Jazz Festival 2014," YouTube, accessed July 28, 2017, www.youtube.com.

"Ester Rada—Life Happens (Official Video)," YouTube, accessed July 28, 2017, www .youtube.com.

"Ester Rada vs Nina Simone—Four Women," YouTube, accessed July 28, 2017, www .youtube.com.

"The Ethiopian Community in Israel," Israeli Ministry of Foreign Affairs, accessed July 28, 2017, www.mfa.gov.il.

"Ethiopian Israelis Clash with Police as Anti-Racism Rally Turns Violent," *The Guardian*, accessed July 29 2017, www.theguardian.com/uk.

"The Ethiopian Population in Israel," Central Bureau of Statistics, accessed July 28, 2017, www.cbs.gov.il.

"The Ethiopian Population of Israel: Basic Demographic Details," Central Bureau of Statistics, accessed July 28, 2017, www.cbs.gov.il.

Gilad, Elon. "Tourist Tip #199 / The Underbelly of Tel Aviv: Neve Sha'anan Street," *Haaretz*, July 28, 2017, www.haaretz.com.

"Gili Yalo—Tenesh Kelbe Lay," YouTube, accessed July 28, 2017, www.youtube.com.

Gittleson, Ben. "Inside Sinai's Torture Camps," *The Atlantic*, accessed July 28, 2017, www .theatlantic.com.

Harel, Amos. "Hot, Black Israeli Rap Duo Bubbles Over on YouTube," *Haaretz*, accessed July 28, 2017, www.haaretz.com.

Hartman, Ben. "Drugs, Prostitutes and Renewal in South Tel Aviv," *Jerusalem Post*, accessed July 28, 2017, www.jpost.com.

Hebblethwaite, Cordelia, "World Music Israeli Style: Idan Raichel Project," *BBC News*, accessed July 28, 2017, www.bbc.co.uk.

"Hip Hop Wars," YouTube, accessed July 28, 2017, www.youtube.com.

"Interview with Artist Aklilu Seyoum part 1," Ethiotube, accessed July 28, 2017, www .ethiotube.com.

"Israel Celebrates Ethiopian Jewish Holiday," YouTube, accessed July 28, 2017, www .youtube.com.

"Israel Music History Singer Bracha Zefira the Mother of the Composer & Singer Ariel Zilber," YouTube, accessed July 28, 2017, www.youtube.com.

"איכפת למי קטנות הכנסות גדולות הוצאות \ חבש קול גרמי," YouTube, accessed July 28, 2017, www .youtube.com.

Kershner, Isabel. "Anti-Police Protest in Israel Turns Violent," *New York Times*, accessed July 28, 2017, www.nytimes.com.

Kingsley, Patrick. "It's Not at War, but up to 3% of Its People Have Fled: What Is Going on in Eritrea?" *The Guardian*, accessed July 28, 2017, www.theguardian.com/uk.

Kubovich, Yaniv. "Cases Closed against Ethiopian-Israeli Soldier, Cop Who Manhandled Him," *Haaretz*, accessed July 28, 2017, www.haaretz.com.

Kubovich, Yaniv, Almog Ben Zikri, and Ilan Lior. "Police to Investigate Asylum Seeker's Lynching in Be'er Sheva," *Haaretz*, July 28, 2017, www.haaretz.com.

"Learn Tigrinya Dance—Eritrean Music: Lela Kuflom," *YouTube*, accessed July 28, 2017, www.youtube.com.

Lior, Ilan. "Father of Israeli Soldiers Faces Deportation Despite Being Eligible for Residency," *Haaretz*, accessed July 28, 2017, www.haaretz.com.

———. "Immigration Authority Freezes Deportation of Father to IDF Soldiers," *Haaretz*, accessed July 28, 2017, www.haaretz.com.

Lis, Jonathan. "President Rivlin to Ethiopian Israelis: We've Failed to Listen to You," *Haaretz*, accessed July 28, 2017, www.haaretz.com.

Lytton, Timothy D., and Motti Talias. "Shaking Up Israel's Kosher Certification System," *Jewish Review of Books*, accessed July 28, 2017, www.jewishreviewofbooks.com.

"Mahmoud Ahmed in Israel: I.E.T.V.," YouTube, accessed July 28, 2017, www.youtube .com.

"Mima'amakim," the Idan Raichel Project, accessed July 28, 2017, www.idanraichelproject .com.

Mirovsky, Arik. "Tel Aviv's Old Central Bus Station to Go from Grit to Glory," *Haaretz*, accessed July 28, 2017, www.haaretz.com.

Mor, Z., et al. "The Levinsky Walk-In Clinic in Tel Aviv: Holistic Services to Control Sexually Transmitted Diseases in the Community," National Center for Biotechnology Information, accessed July 28, 2017, www.ncbi.nlm.nih.gov.

"Ofra Haza—Live in Japan 1989_behind the Scenes," YouTube, accessed July 28, 2017, www.youtube.com.

"Ofra Haza—The Prince of Egypt Film Clip—Deliver Us," YouTube, accessed July 28, 2017, www.youtube.com.

"Old School Guragna and Amharic Song by Dejen Manchilot Live from Israel," YouTube, accessed July 28, 2017, www.youtube.com.

"Omo Kuraz I Sugar Factory to Start Production in February," *Ethiopian Broadcasting Corporation*, accessed July 28, 2017, www.ebc.et.

Pfeffer, Anshel. "Interior Ministry Closes Down Ethiopian Aliyah Operation," *Haaretz*, accessed July 28, 2017, www.haaretz.com.

Prusher, Ilene. "Netanyahu Resorts to Race-Baiting to Win Elections," *Haaretz*, accessed July 28, 2017, www.haaretz.com.

Ravid, Barak. "Foreign Ministry Names First Israeli of Ethiopian Origin as Ambassador," *Haaretz*, accessed July 28, 2017, www.haaretz.com.

"Research" (*meḥkar*—in Hebrew), Israel Association for Ethiopian Jews, accessed July 28, 2017, www.iaej.co.il.

Seidler, Shirly. "After Tel Aviv and Jerusalem, More Anti-Police Brutality Protests Planned around Country," *Haaretz*, July 28, 2017, www.haaretz.com.

Shalev, Ben. "Israeli Soul Sister Chooses to Sing in English," *Haaretz*, accessed July 28, 2017, www.haaretz.com.

———. "You Have to Listen to Israeli Soul Singer Ester Rada's New Album," *Haaretz*, accessed August 24, 2017, www.haaretz.com.

Sheffer, Gabi. "Listen to American Jews' Stand on Israel," *Haaretz*, accessed July 28, 2017, www.haaretz.com.

Shilon, Avi. "The Double Life of Ofra Haza," *Haaretz,* accessed July 28, 2017, www.haaretz.com.

"Sigd 2013: Un film en noir et en couleurs," YouTube, accessed July 28, 2017, www.youtube.com.

Smith, David. "Inside Eritrea: Conscription and Poverty Drive Exodus from Secretive African State," *The Guardian*, accessed July 28, 2017, www.theguardian.com/uk.

Sontag, Deborah. "A Pop Diva, a Case of AIDS and an Israeli Storm," *New York Times*, accessed July 28, 2017, www.nytimes.com.

"Sorries—Ester Rada—Indie City," YouTube, accessed July 28, 2017, www.youtube.com.

"Tigrinya Lilay," YouTube, accessed July 28, 2017, www.youtube.com.

"Video: Israeli Ethiopians' Protest against Police Brutality Was Confronted Last Night with Harsh Police Brutality," Active Stills, accessed July 28, 2017, www.facebook.com.

Wilson, Simone. "Tel Aviv's Half-Abandoned Central Bus Station Is Home to a Bat Cave and Six Underground Theaters," *Jewish Journal*, accessed July 28, 2017, www.jewishjournal.com.

"Zvuloon Dub System—Going to Zion (Official Video)," *YouTube*, accessed July 28, 2017, www.youtube.com.

"Zvuloon Dub System & Tigrinya Lilay—Going to Zion (Balcony TV)," YouTube, accessed July 29, 2017, www.youtube.com.

INDEX

Page numbers in *italics* refer to illustrations.

and, 111; fieldwork use of, 18; Habash use of,
157–58; at Inyalinya performances, 125–26;
IRP use of, 82, 85, 90, 92, 95–96; at Nahum
Records, 174; Rada use of, 44, 46–47; in
Sigd recitations, 119; wax-and-gold and, 8
ancestry claims, 10
anchihoy mode, 19, 58, 67
anti-anti-essentialism, 39–40
antisemitism, 7, 88
appropriation, 28, 102
Aragai, Reuben ("Tedross"), 134, 141
Arba Lijotch, 45
Arom, Simha, 5
Ashkelon, 17–18, 126–28
Ashkenazi Judaism: Ashkenazi Orthodox
Judaism, 2; Beta Israel history and, 15;
dominance in Israel, 203–4n15; IRP musical
style and, 82, 89; safe-haven narrative and,
98; Tel Aviv neighborhoods and, 166–67;
views of immigrants, 149; Zionism and, 95,
198n20
Askew, Kelly, 203n12
assimilation. *See* integration
Astatke, Mulatu, 65, 67–68, 192n5
Atar, Ron, 5
Avineri, Shlomo, 88–89
Awad, Mira, 83
Aweke, Aster, 26, 65, 67, 70–71, 108–9, 114–15,
183–84
Axum, 26, 134, 140, 150–51, 159–61, 187. *See also*
"Ma Im Hakesef"
Ayhud, 14–15
Azmari music: *Azmari-bet* (music house)
traditions, 55, 64, 73–74, 77, 100, 128,
180–81, 195n8; Beta Dance Troupe use of,
114–15; black Atlantic references in, 40;
Ethio-jazz and, 45; Ethiopianist myth and,
106; as everyday resistance, 75; genealogical
transmission of, 60, 62; hip-hop influence,
138, 203n10; massenqo as symbol of,
59–60, 63; ornamentation, 57; performance
practice, 62, 75; *qignit* modal system, 19,
57–59, 61–62, 107; self-taught musicians

and, 56–57; as Sigd component, 122–23;
"Tezeta" versions in, 67. *See also* "Tezeta"/
tezeta; wax-and-gold principle
Azmaris: Azmari citizenship, 7–11, 135, 166,
188; egalitarian society, 63; Ethiopian
Jews as, 60; Manchlot as advocate for, 133;
overview, 4

"Back to Jerusalem" (Idan Raichel Project),
99–100
"Bad Guy" (Rada), 25
Barihun, Abate, 124, 180, 183, 188, 194n4
batti mode, 19, 58
"Bazi" (Rada), 39–42
BDS movement (Boycott, Divestment, and
Sanctions), 49
beganna ("Harp of King David"), 61, 96
Beit Gordon Absorption Center, 112, 126–29
Belaw, Eshet, 108
belonging, 7, 12, 23–24, 169. *See also*
citizenship; integration
Ben-Dor, Shoshana, 5, 122, 202n33
Ben-Eliezer, Uri, 84
BenEzer, Gadi, 83, 112–13
Benjamin, Walter, 199n3
"Berakhot Leshanah Hadasha" ("Blessings for
the New Year," Idan Raichel Project), 90,
99–100
Beta Dance Troupe (later Beta Dance
Company), 106–7, 111–14, 130–32. *See also*
Eskesta
Beta Israel: Beta Israel studies, 9–10, 16;
Christian prejudice against, 15, 202n33;
"discovery" of, 15; Ethiopian prejudice
against, 74, 77; *Etyopim* collective status
and, 202n33; extended family importance,
16; as immigrants, 16; Jewish lineage,
79–80; liturgy and religious practices, 5,
202n3; as "lost tribe of Israel," 16, 112, 173;
Operation Moses's importance for, 116,
199n8; religious legitimacy and, 15–17,
69–70, 80; secular music tradition, 60; self-
identification as, 14–15, 129–31, 191n1; Sigd

pertinence to, 119–21. *See also* Ethiopian-Israelis

Bialik, Hayim Nahman, 146–48, 151, 204n21

black Atlantic: Afrodiasporic myth and, 23, 29, 106; public sphere, 6; Ethiopian historical connection to, 141–42; Ethio-soul and, 30; global black minorities and, 13–14; *musiqa shehorah* and, 138–39; Rada compositional style and, 39–40. *See also* Afrodiasporic myth; race

Blackman, Lisa, 110, 116

black music (*musiqa shehorah*): Afro-shop sales outlet, 172; as club scene genre, 138–39, 165–66; as integration device, 24, 141–42; Rada as proponent of, 32. *See also* Afrodiasporic myth; race

"blood affair" of 1996, 1–2, 26, 169, 191n2

B'nei Akiva, 30

"Bo'ee" ("Come with Me," Idan Raichel Project), 90, 95–97, *97*, 182–83

Bolel music, 176

Boym, Svetlana, 81

Brinner, Benjamin, 167

Buda Musique, 45

Cafe Shahor Hazak (CSH), 140, 152–54, 159–61, 184, 205n37

Campbell, Joseph, 192n9

Capoeira, 75

Casay, Cabra, 82–83, 91, 100, 102, 186, 196n19

Chanukah, 15

chat, 52

Christianity: African American Christians, 28, 35; Amhara Christians, 55; Beta Israel liturgy influences, 201n28; Ethiopian-Israeli Pentecostalism, 74, 129, 189, 196n22, 202n33; Ethiopianist myth and, 78; Jerusalem's significance in, 182–83; prejudice against Beta Israel, 15. *See also* Falash Mura

citizenship: Afrodiasporic myth and, 29–30; Azmari, 7–11, 135, 166, 188; belonging as component of, 169; cultural intimacy and, 135; dialectical engagement of myth and,

87–88; ecological citizenship, 7; embodied formation of, 24–25, 105–6, 109–10, 131–32; entry interrogations and, 48–50; Ethiopian-Israeli compromised, 6; Ethiopianist myth and, 78; as ethnomusicology interest, 6; as hip-hop theme, 152–53; as integration device, 6–7; IRP cosmopolitanism and, 84–85; Levinski Street citizenship model, 181; Mizrahi immigrants and, 149; obedience as precondition, 9; post-Soviet citizenship models, 7; quantitative citizens, 149; Rada narratives of belonging, 39; religious legitimacy and, 10, 80, 121–22; safe-haven narrative and, 96–98; soundworlds as alternative framework, 4–5. *See also* belonging; integration

Citron, Marcia, 199n2

class: Bauhaus architecture and, 142; class-conscious rap, 134, 136–38, 142–48, 150–51, 153–54; Eritrean service sector in Tel Aviv, 18, 178–79, 186; Ethiopian-Israeli class convergence, 130; Ethiopian-Israeli poverty, 4, 195n7; hip-hop as commercial opportunity, 158–59; IRP class differences, 84, 197n10; Israeli minorities and, 18; labor migrants, 154–55; Labor Zionism and, 146–48, 150; public transportation and, 127–28; race as class barrier, 140, 187; Tel Aviv neighborhoods and, 22–23, 53, 162–63, 167; transnational class solidarity, 136–39; wedding work financial mobility, 176

Clifford, James, 81, 85–86, 98

Common, 67, 68

cosmopolitanism: cosmopolitan hybridity, 84; cosmopolitanism from below, 101; cosmopolitan utopia in IRP, 85–86, 89–90, 94–95, 102–3; discrepant cosmopolitanism, 81–82, 85–86, 98; Ethiopian "golden era" cosmopolitanism, 45; *Graceland* critiques and, 89; multicultural Zionism and, 81; vernacular cosmopolitanism, 91; world music and, 32. *See also* multiculturalism

critical discourse: Afrodiasporic critical

musical style, 42, 49; class-conscious rap, 134, 136–38, 142–48, 150–51, 153–54; counternarrative in Ester Rada, 24, 26–27, 41–42; Eskesta embodied formations and, 109–10, 116, 131–32; Ethiopian-Israeli advocacy groups, 111–12; everyday resistance, 74–75; in funk, 42; identity politics and, 38–39; IRP avoidance of, 85–87; Israeli protest music, 38; limits on success of, 192n8; musicians as agents of integration, 185–86; political unrest of 2015 and, 168–70; RSA (Repressive State Apparatus) depiction, 157–61, 205n42; style as political discourse, 41; "Tezeta" nostalgia mode and, 19, 55, 65–71, 74, 194n6; wax-and-gold principle and, 8–11, 72–74, 76–77

cultural citizenship, 7

cultural intimacy: citizenship and, 135; diasporic, 81, 83, 90, 99, 102; hip-hop appeal to, 140, 161; home/exile myth and, 83; IRP nationalism and, 90; national, in hybrid cultures, 197n6

cultural restaurants, 55, 73, 77

cut 'n' mix principle, 27, 39–40, 42

DAM, 203n9, 205n42

Damari, Shoshana, 83

Dana International (Saida Sultana), 198n13

Darfur, asylum seekers from, 168

Davis, Miles, 48

diaspora: diasporic intimacy, 81, 83, 90, 99, 102; exile narrative and, 25, 27; music as heritage and, 62; return narrative and, 13. See also Afrodiasporic myth; Jewish diaspora

Dixon Gottschild, Brenda, 107, 109–10

Djerrahian, Gabriella, 134

Doty, William, 192n9

dreadlocks, 12, 23, 32, 50, 157

dub, 24, 39

Du Bois, W. E. B., 73, 146

"Eizo Medinah" ("What a Country/State," Cafe Shahor Hazak), 140, 152–56, 158–61

English language: Azmari taunting and, 73; CD retail sales and, 176; Haza use of, 150; IRP use of, 82, 100–101; Rada use of, 3, 19, 24, 25, 28, 32, 38–39, 49; SLI translations, 80; ZDS use of, 172–73

"Ere Mela Mela" (Ahmed), 67–68

"Eretz Eretz Eretz" ("Land, Land, Land," Paikov/Ilanit), 94–95

Eritreans: asylum status in Israel and, 20, 164–66, 168–69, 178–79, 186; chat rituals and, 52; as Habesha people, 53; importance in Tel Aviv, 20, 164–65, 168, 177; service sector jobs and, 18, 178–79, 186; vulnerability of, 168–69

Eshel, Ruth, 105, 113–14, 116, 122–23, 131

Eshete, Alemayehu, 44, 64, 192n5

Eskesta (Ethiopian national dance): accessibility of, 123; as audience participation facilitator, 75; as embodied memory, 106, 109–10, 118, 131–32; Ethiopian-Israeli fondness for, 85; Inyalinya performances, 128–29; music, 107–8; performance media tastes and, 108–9; performance practice and, 105; physical virtuosity as integration device, 20; as Sigd component, 1–2, 119, 122–23; in Tel Aviv, 53, 73–74; wax-and-gold and, 7–8. See also Beta Dance Troupe

Eskesta Dance Theater, 113–14

Ethio-jazz: Afrodiasporic music and, 29, 48; Derg immigration period and, 195n8; Ethiopian-Israeli fondness for, 108; Ge'ez liturgy similarity to, 201n28; history, 44–45, 66; IRP arrangements, 92; as mainstream genre, 188; musical training and, 31; "Nanu Nanu Ney" versions, 44; as Rada influence, 19, 24–25, 32, 33t, 37–38, 40–41; as Sigd component, 122, 124; Tel Aviv gigging and, 183–84; "Tezeta" arrangements in, 65, 67–68; as world music, 192n5

Ethiopia: as anticolonial site, 13; antisemitism in, 7; Axum/Aksum as national symbol, 141; Beta Israel as minority in, 74, 77,

196n18; as black Zion, 40–41, 69, 78, 172–73; chat rituals, 52; Ethio-jazz origin and, 44–45; Ethiopian Afrodiasporic music, 29; Ethiopian diaspora, 65; Ethiopian-Israeli visits to, 71, 196n19; ethnoreligious diversity, 70–71; Israeli political relationship with, 183; *Kebra Negast* national epic, 32, 53, 68–71, 77–78, 173, 194n3; Mengistu "Derg" military regime, 16, 45, 66–67, 108–9, 116, 195n8; "Nanu Nanu Ney" provenance and, 47–48; Orthodox Christianity in, 55, 189, 202n33, 208n1; racial identification in, 139; in Rastafarian myth, 23, 28–29, 32, 141–42, 172; Sigd festival in, 120; in Solomonic narrative, 28–29; Swinging Addis period, 41, 44, 45–46, 64; wax-and-gold response to repression, 72–73

Ethiopia — Judaism: Ark of the Covenant narrative and, 69, 141, 194n3; liturgical and ritual traditions, 15–16, 121; Nahum Records selections and, 177; New Year's blessings, 99–101; slavery (*barya*) and, 10; terms for, 14. *See also* Beta Israel

Ethiopia — music: African American influence, 26; anti-anti-essentialism in, 39–40; anti-synthesizer purism, 194n4; collage style, 41; cut 'n' mix principle, 27, 39–40, 42; Ethiopian pop, 108; Israeli brass bands and, 45, 66; modal system, 19, 115; musical style, 33t; ornamentation, 57; polyrhythmic effects, 31; *qignit* modal system, 19, 57–59, 61–62, 107, 194n5, 195n10; secular music tradition, 60–61; as Sigd component, 119; versioning, 40. *See also* Azmari music; Ethio-jazz; wax-and-gold principle

Ethiopian-Israelis: advocacy groups, 111–12; "blood affair" of 1996, 1–2, 26, 169, 191n2; class status, 195n7; collective subgroups, 129–30; Ethiopian prejudice against, 74; *Etyopim* collective status, 14, 16–17, 129, 202n33; "honorary" Ethiopians, 156–57; IRP as representation of, 79–80; Israeli-born generation, 9, 130, 189, 196n19; Israeli prejudice/

exclusion, 26, 69–70, 84–85, 111, 168–69, 177, 185–86; as "new Mizrahim," 149, 153–54, 160–61, 168–69; paradigm of exile and, 1, 7, 25; restaurants and social places, 51–53, 55, 73, 77, 199n7; settlement areas, 153–54

Ethiopian-Israelis — Judaism: adoption of rabbinic Orthodoxy, 121; Beta Israel Jewish lineage, 79–80; Ethiopian Jewish legitimacy, 4, 7, 10, 16, 70, 80–84, 101–2, 121, 185; history, 14–15; Qessim regulation and licensing, 2, 188, 200–201n23; Rada representation of, 3–4; self-identification and, 129–30; Sigd festival as Jewish practice, 119–20; soundworlds and, 4–5; state administration of, 111; wax-and-gold principle and, 73. *See also* Beta Israel

Ethiopian-Israelis — music: "Bo'ee" as representative of, 95; club scene, 18, 23, 82, 138–41; Ethiopianist myth and, 55–57, 59–60, 63–64; Ethiopian musical style, 26; fondness for recorded music, 108, 199n3; Habesh as music site, 54–55; IRP effect on, 79; IRP musical style, 82; as Jewish liturgy, 15; Levinski Street musical representation, 166; music economy, 18; musicians (*muziqa'im*) distinction, 56–57; performance practices, 56, 105; schizophonic references, 8, 12, 21, 89; self-taught musicians and, 56–57, 60–61; sonic myth references, 11–13; "Tezeta" functions for, 68–71; U.S. tours, 152–53, 204–5n31; visual references, 59–60, 63–64; wax-and-gold principle and, 8–11; wedding work, 176

Ethiopianist myth: Afrodiasporic-Ethiopianist-Zionist myth tension, 11–14, 87–89, 102, 158; Azmari music and, 106; Ethiopian-Israeli identity and, 19; Habesha performances and, 55–57, 59–60, 63–64, 74; Judaic/Semitic roots and, 77–78; multicultural utopia in, 106; ZDS appeal to, 173

Éthiopiques, 24, 44, 45–46, 59, 65–68, 184, 192n5

Ethio-pop, 65, 107–8

Ethio-soul, 25, 30, 37

ethnic democracy, 7

Etyopim, 14, 16–17, 129, 202n33

exile narrative (*shelilat hagalut*): African
American embrace of, 28; African diaspora
as alternative, 25, 27; Ethiopian-Jewish
identification with, 1, 7, 25, 28–29; as
fundamental to Judaism, 193n10; Operation
Moses journey and, 115–17; return to Israel
motif in, 13; as Zionist myth, 88–89, 198n20

Faitlovitch, Jacques, 10, 15–16

Falasha, 14–15

Falash Mura: Beta Israel and, 117; Ethiopianist
myth and, 77–78; Habesh clientele and,
56; immigration and, 80, 84, 122, 169, 188;
Israeli prejudice against, 70, 160; origin of
term, 14; Pentecostalism as resistance, 74,
189; return to Judaism of, 9–10, 17, 169; self-
identification as, 129–30; Sigd festival and,
121. *See also* Christianity

Falceto, Francis, 5, 24, 45, 195n10

Farnell, Brenda, 105, 107

Feder, Dege, 113

"Feeling Good" (Rada cover of Nina Simone),
34, 38

Fekadeh, Demas, 168–69, 185

Feld, Steven, 8, 81–82, 85–86, 89, 99–102

Feldstein, Ruth, 35

fieldwork and methodology: at Beit Gordon
Absorption Center, 126–28; at the Central
Bus Station, 170–71; fieldwork sites, 17–18;
food traditions and, 51, 99, 194n1; Habesh
encounter, 56; interview techniques, 71–72;
IRP fieldwork, 196–97n23; massenqo
lessons, 57–58; semilegal restaurants and,
52; statistical sources, 192n10; wax-and-gold
principle and, 9–11, 72

Filipino/a-Israelis, 154

"Four Women" (Rada cover of Nina Simone),
26, 33t, 34–39, 43t

Franklin, Aretha, 30

Fredu, Shai, 120

Friesel, Evyatar, 99

funk, 24, 31, 33t, 38, 40–42, 46

fusion, 7–8

Garvey, Marcus, 28–29, 48, 142

Gedaref Refugee Camp, 16, 113

Ge'ez language: IRP use of, 82, 85, 95–96; as
Kebra Negast language, 32, 53; as liturgical
language, 15, 141, 188–89; Sigd prayer ritual
and, 120, 122–23, 188–89, 200–201n23,
201n28

Geffen, Aviv, 3

gender: chat rituals and, 52; "Four Women"
as women's song, 34–35, 37; labor
responsibilities and, 76, 196n23; mixed
dancing, 2; "Tezeta" performance and, 66;
violence against Eritrean women, 178–79;
vulnerability of Ethiopian-Israeli men, 75;
women in music and dance, 108, 199n2

Gessesse, Tilahoun, 44, 108

Gigi, 108

Gilroy, Paul, 6, 39–40, 43

Ginsberg, Asher, 87–88

global citizenship, 7

"Going to Mount Zion" (Zvuloon Dub
System), 173

Gondar region, 16, 54, 56–57, 59, 100, 113, 115,
124, 195n12, 202n33

gospel, 31, 33t

Graceland (Simon), 46–47, 79, 89, 102–3

Greenwald, Jeff, 139

Gronich, Shlomo, 197n2

Gurage, 45–46, 176

Habermas, Jürgen, 6–7

Habesh: *Azmari-bet* traditions and, 55, 64,
73–74, 77; Eskesta as celebratory trigger, 75;
fieldwork at, 52, 156–57; musical style at, 19;
performance practices at, 56–57; as support
network site, 76–77; as Tel Aviv gathering
place, 19, 52–54, 54, 180; "Tezeta" popularity
at, 66–67, 69; wax-and-gold principle in,
55, 73–74

Habesha, 53, 55–57, 59–60, 63–64, 74

Hahn, Tomie, 106, 116

Haifa, 16–18, 107, 112–13, 117

Haile Selassie, 28–29, 45, 66, 68

Hamasa (BenEzer), 113–14, 115–18

hardship narrative, 29–32, 115–17, 200n10

Haza, Ofra, 149–51

Hebdige, Dick, 27, 39–40, 139

Hebrew language: CSH use of, 152; Eritrean migrant use of, 178; in Ethiopia, 14; in Ethiopian-Israeli hip-hop, 20, 138; Ethiopian-Israeli use of, 15; *Etyopim* term and, 16; as fieldwork language, 18, 56; at *Hamasa* launch, 117; at Inyalinya performances, 125–26; IRP use of, 85, 90, 92, 100–101; Levinski Street languages, 163; Mizrahi music and, 149; necessity for employment, 126, 150; Rada use of, 24, 31, 34, 38; refusal to learn, as resistance, 74; SLI use of, 89, 93–94, 149

Hellier-Tinoco, Ruth, 110

Herman, Marilyn, 61–62, 197–98n11

Herzl, Theodor, 87–88

Hess, Moses, 87

hip-hop: advocacy for global migrant minorities, 136–38, 193n6; appeal to cultural intimacy, 135, 140; Azmari music and, 138, 203n10; citizenship narratives and, 152–53; Ethiopian-Israeli popular taste for, 64, 85, 134, 202–3n4; Ethiopian-Israeli vernacular and, 138; Ethiopian popular taste for, 107–8; griot tradition and, 133, 138, 195n9; Hip-Hop studies, 136; Israeli multicultural narrative in, 20; occupation-of-urban-space theme, 154; as Rada influence, 26; U.S. confrontational style of, 134, 139, 153, 158–61, 205n42; wax-and-gold strategies, 7–8, 135, 152; white reception of, 139

Hoffman, Daniel, 116

Holiday, Billie, 30

Horowitz, Amy, 168

Huldai, Ron, 3

Hulugeb festival, 34, 38

Hutchinson, Sydney, 89–90

hybridity, 45, 84, 89–90

Idan Raichel Project (IRP): Aga as musician cited by, 182–83; discrepant cosmopolitanism of, 81–82, 85–86, 89–90; effect on Ethiopian-Israeli musicians, 79; English language use, 82, 100–101; Ethiopian-Israeli adoption of, 157; Ethiopian Jewish legitimacy and, 185; Hebrew language use, 85, 90, 92, 100–101, 197n3; pop music influences, 80–81, 89–95; Zionist myth and, 19–20, 87–89, 94–95, 102, 187. Songs and albums: "Back to Jerusalem," 99–100; "Berakhot Leshanah Hadasha," 90, 99–100; "Bo'ee," 90, 95–97, 97; *The Idan Raichel Project*, 82; "Mima'amakim," 44, 46–48, 81, 90–95; *Mima'amakim*, 46–48, 80–82; "Nanu Nanu Ney," 46–48, 92; *Quarter to Six*, 82; *Traveling Home*, 82; *Within My Walls*, 82

immigration: absorption centers, 17–18, 56, 111–12, 126–29, 159, 186; ancestry claims, 10; Eritrean asylum in Israel, 20, 164–66, 168–69, 178–79; Falash Mura immigration, 80, 84, 122, 169, 188; first wave (1984–1985), 16; "hitchhikers" (*trempistim*), 117, 130; influences on Israeli music, 92; Israeli policy, 202n34; labor migrants, 154–55; Mizrahi, 148–51; rabbinical recognition and, 16–17; religious authenticity and, 80; Sigd Scouts stage representation, 122–24, 131–32, 201n27; Tel Aviv guest workers, 207n17; as Zionist return journey, 87, 115–17

"Im Ninalu" (Haza), 149–50

integration: Aḥ Boger program, 126–28, 131, 201n32; "Bo'ee" musical references to, 97–98; citizenship as integration device, 6–7; as CSH theme, 152; Eritrean, in Tel Aviv, 186–89; failed Ethiopian-Israeli, 4–5; generational difference in, 117, 130; Israeli-born generation and, 189; journey narrative and, 112–13, 130; loss of cultural identity and, 118, 130–31; military service as key to, 6–7, 18, 49–50; musicians as agents of, 185–86; *musiqa shehorah* and, 141–42; non-Ethiopian advocacy for, 117–18; obedience as precondition, 9; paradox of belonging, 12; state top-down approach, 7–9, 13, 21, 102, 107, 111–13, 116–18, 121–22. *See also* belonging; citizenship

Inyalinya, 108–9, 111–12, 125–31, 188

Iraqi-Israelis, 149

Israel: Beta Israel settlements, 16; ethnic political alignments, 150; international isolation and, 184–85; kosher certification, 51–53, 179, 208n29; military service, 6–7, 18, 49–50; racial delineation in, 30; role in Operation Moses/Solomon, 16, 60, 115–16; Sigd festival and, 119–20; two-part religious/civic observances, 123, 201n29. *See also* citizenship

Israeli popular music: historical immigrant influences on, 92; *Kokhav Nolad* contest, 188; Mizrahi music, 92–93; Rada influence by, 30–31, 47; religious legitimacy and, 81, 185. *See also* SLI

"I Wish" (Rada cover of Nina Simone/Bill Taylor), 34

Jackson, Michael, 12

jazz-funk, 48

Jeremy Kol Habash, 140, 157–61, 188

Jerusalem: Ethiopian touring performers in, 70–71; as fieldwork site, 17–18; Jerusalem Sacred Music Festival, 3, 182–83; Rada Old City performance, 3, 40–41, 192n4. *See also* Sigd

Jewish diaspora: civic celebration and, 201n29; Ethiopian-Israeli identification with, 7; IRP recognition in, 85–86; political and cultural Zionism and, 87–88; safe-haven narrative and, 82, 88, 96–98; support for Operation Moses, 116

Jung, Carl, 192n9

Kalkidan, 134

Kanafani, Ghassan, 205n42

Kapchan, Deborah, 191n3

Kaplan, Steven, 74–75, 140, 193n9, 196n18, 202n3

Kassa, Getatchew, 66, 68

Kawase, Itsushi, 11

Kebede, Ashenafi, 4, 61

Kebra Negast national epic, 32, 53, 68–71, 77–78, 173, 194n3

Keyes, Cheryl, 203n10

"Kezira" (Aweke), 114–15

kibbutz movement, 146

Kidane, Tesfa-Maryam, 67

Kidron, Carol, 106

krar (plucked lyre): Avi facility with, 60–63; in *Azmari-bet* performances, 73–74; Azmari rhythmic function of, 68; in Eskesta performance, 107; as fieldwork interest, 57; as Habesh feature, 54, 58; *qignit* modal system and, 58; Tigrinya Lilay as proponent, 176; Western audiences and, 195n11; ZDS use of, 173–74

Kuti, Fela, 45

Le Gendre, Kevin, 31

"Lemi Ikhpat?" (Habash), 140, 157–58

Levine, Donald, 8–9, 55, 69–70, 194n3

Levinski Street Ethiopian district (Tel Aviv): citizenship model, 181; Eritrean immigrants and, 20, 164–65, 168, 177; as fieldwork site, 22, 104; languages in, 163; Levinski/Florentin delineation and, 23; Nahum Records, 22, 57, 64, 128, 158, 165, 174–77, *175*; Tel Aviv social geography and, 104–5, 162–63; Tenät restaurant, 22, 165, 179–80, *180*; vegan restaurants, 179

"Life Happens" (Rada), 25, 33t, 39–41, 43t

Lilay, Tigrinya ("Yaakov"), 173–74, 176

Luzon, Eli, 140, 153–54

Maharo (Beta Dance Troupe), 115

"Ma Im Hakesef" ("What about the Money," Axum): appeal to cultural intimacy, 135;

cityscape visuals for, 142; class consciousness in, 134, 136–38, 142–48, 150–51, 153–54,
203n8; "Eizo Medinah" similarity, 155–56;
Ethiopian-Israeli Afrodiasporic performers, 140; multicultural narrative in, 20;
popularity of, 134, 141, 151, 153, 161; style
and structure of, 142–45; wax-and-gold
principle in, 145–46
Malinowski, Bronisław, 12
Manchlot, Dejen, 57, 61, 63, 124, 126, 133,
173–74, 180, 183
Manor, Ehud, 71
Marshall, T. H., 6
Maryam Wodet, 17
massenqo (Azmari one-string): in *Azmari-
bet* performances, 73–74; in Eskesta
performance, 107; as fieldwork interest, 18,
51; at Habesh, 54; in IRP arrangements, 99;
qignit modal system and, 57–59, 61–62, 63;
Rada use of, 41, 43t; in Sigd performances,
124; as visual symbol, 59–60, 63; Western
audiences and, 195n11
Maultsby, Portia, 38
McDonald, David A., 110
Mekurya, Getatchew, 67
Melesse, Muluken, 44, 46, 92, 124
Menilek: on Ethiopian-Israeli music, 59–60,
62–63; at Habesh, 54, 56, 73–77, 156–57; on
Idan Raichel, 79, 84
Menilek, King of Ethiopia, 69, 182–83
Middle Passage theme, 13–14, 23, 29–30, 32
"Mima'amakim" (Idan Raichel Project), 44,
46–48, 81, 90–95
Mizrahim: Beta Israel history and, 15; as
early Israeli minority, 150, 153; Ethiopian-
Israeli identification with, 121, 203–4n15;
Ethiopian-Israelis as "new Mizrahim," 149,
153–54, 160–61; IRP compositions and,
100–101; immigration, 148–51; music, 92–
93, 149–51, 154, 167–68; social advancement
of, 149–50, 155–56, 163–64, 167–68; Tel Aviv
neighborhoods and, 22, 166–68
Morad, Moshe, 44

Moroccan-Israelis, 125, 127, 140, 149
multiculturalism: citizenship and, 6; CSH
depiction of, 154–55; in hip-hop, 20;
identity politics and, 85, 197–98n11; IRP
melting-pot aesthetic, 89, 91; Israel as
white society and, 193n9; Israeli minorities,
18; multicultural Zionism, 81; Nahum
Records mediascape and, 175–77; race-
gender-ethnicity axis and, 196n23; Sigd
embodied otherness and, 124–25. *See also*
cosmopolitanism
music. *See* Azmari music; black music; dub;
Ethio-jazz; Ethiopia—music; Ethiopian-
Israelis—music; Ethio-soul; funk; hip-hop;
Israeli popular music; protest music; R&B;
reggae; soul; world music
musiqa sheḥorah. See black music
myth: citizenship and, 8, 87–88;
multidisciplinary approach to, 27–28; as
multisensory narrative, 188; overview,
11–13; scholarship on, 192n9. *See also*
Afrodiasporic myth; Ethiopianist myth;
exile narrative; hardship narrative; return
narrative; Zionist myth
myths of Abyssinian glory. *See* Ethiopianist
myth

Nahum Records, 22, 57, 64, 128, 158, 165,
174–77, *175*
"Nanu Nanu Ney" (Idan Raichel Project),
46–48, 92
"Nanu Ney" (Rada), 33t, 43t, 44–46, 92
Nardi, Nahum, 148
nationalism: alternative musical narratives
of, 21; Biblical references to, 94–95; IRP
cosmopolitan nationalism, 47, 81–86, 90,
94–95; Israel's national-religious party, 2;
progressive vernacular cosmopolitanism,
91; Rada alternative paradigm of exile and,
47, 49; safe-haven narrative and, 82, 88,
96–98; Zionist myth and, 87, 198n20. *See
also* Zionism
Native Tongues Collective, 158, 205n43

personal journey narrative, 30–31, 49; political critique of, 24, 26–27, 41–42, 49; recordings, 23–24; as Sheba Choir singer, 197n2; Sigd performance, 124; visits to Ethiopia, 196n19. Songs: "Bad Guy," 25; "Bazi," 39–42; "Feeling Good," 34, 38; "Four Women," 26, 33t, 34–39, 43t; "I Wish," 34; "Life Happens," 25, 33t, 39–41, 43t; "Nanu Ney," 33t, 43t, 44–46, 92; "Sinnerman," 34, 36; "Sorries," 33t, 34, 39–40, 43t

Rahaim, Matthew, 110

Raichel, Idan. *See* Idan Raichel Project

rap. *See* hip-hop

Rastafarian references, 28–30, 32, 39, 48, 70, 141–42, 172–74

Ratner, David, 20, 71–72, 85, 134, 158–59, 192–93n3, 202–3n4

Raz-Krakotzkin, Amnon, 88

Regev, Motti, 31, 148, 150, 198n16

reggae: as Afrodiasporic identity resource, 29, 39–40, 106; Max Romeo Old City performance, 3; as *musiqa sheḥorah*, 138–39; as Rada influence, 24, 31, 33t, 39; rap vs. reggae in Israel, 85, 202–3n4; reconfiguration of Zion in, 39; as Tel Aviv hipster genre, 23; wax-and-gold strategies, 7–8; white reception of, 139; as ZDS specialty, 23, 172–74

return narrative (*shivat Tziyon*): Beta Israel immigration and, 202n33; Cabra Casay Exodus narrative, 83; diasporic solidarity and, 13, 197n5; Ethiopian-Israeli advocacy and, 112–13, 117–18, 130; Falash Mura journey as, 117; integration as component of, 124–25; as IRP theme, 82, 86–87, 100–102; *kibbutz galuyot* (ingathering of exiles) principle, 99–102, 106, 113, 120; Law of Return provisions, 122; Operation Moses journey and, 116–17; performance presentation of, 118; race as integration barrier, 146; Sigd prayer ritual and, 120–22; as Zionist myth, 20, 28, 88–89, 198n20

Roman-Velazquez, Patria, 110

Romeo, Max, 3

Rose, Tricia, 133–34, 137, 139

Rotbard, Sharon, 167

safe haven (*eretz miklat*), 96

Sahalu, Ilak, 152

Salamon, Hagar, 4, 10–11, 55

Schloss, Joseph, 137

Seeman, Don, 9–11, 15, 80, 191n2, 202n3

Segal, Robert, 12

Sephardic Judaism. *See* Mizrahim

Seroussi, Edwin, 31, 148, 150, 198n16

settler movement, 2, 30, 148, 193n12, 201n26

sexuality, 41–42

Seyoum, Aklilu, 59–60

Shabazi, Shalom, 149–50

Shabtay, Malka, 127, 202–3n4

Shafir, Gershon, 149

Shakur, Tupac, 26, 134, 172, 193n6

Shapira, Anita, 88–89

Sheba Choir, 197n2

Shelemay, Kay Kaufman, 5–6, 10, 15, 124, 177, 191n3

Shirei Eretz Yisrael. *See* SLI

"Shir Ha'avodah Vehamelakha" ("The song of work and toil," Bialik), 146–48

Sigd (Ethiopian-Israeli festival): description, 119–20; Eskesta role in, 119, 122; Ethiopian-Israeli integration and, 123–25; Ethiopian Jewish legitimacy and, 119, 121; Ge'ez prayer ritual, 120, 122–23, 188–89, 200–201n23; musical influences on, 111; overview, 1–2; as public sphere event, 121–23; Scouts stage, 122–24, 131–32, 201n27; state endorsement of, 119, 121–22; as Yom Tov, 118

Simon, Paul, 46–47

Simone, Nina, 3–4, 24, 26, 30, 34–39

"Sinnerman" (Rada cover of Nina Simone), 34, 36

slavery (*barya*), 10, 29–30

SLI (Shirei Eretz Yisrael / Songs of the Land of Israel), 33t, 80–81, 89–95, 149, 151, 198n16

social citizenship, 6–7

Marié Abe

*Resonances of Chindon-ya:
Sounding Space and Sociality
in Contemporary Japan*

Frances Aparicio

*Listening to Salsa: Gender, Latin Popular
Music, and Puerto Rican Cultures*

Paul Austerlitz

*Jazz Consciousness:
Music, Race, and Humanity*

Harris M. Berger

*Metal, Rock, and Jazz: Perception and the
Phenomenology of Musical Experience*

Harris M. Berger

*Stance: Ideas about Emotion, Style, and
Meaning for the Study of Expressive
Culture*

Harris M. Berger and Giovanna P. Del
Negro

*Identity and Everyday Life:
Essays in the Study of Folklore, Music,
and Popular Culture*

Franya J. Berkman

*Monument Eternal:
The Music of Alice Coltrane*

Dick Blau, Angeliki Vellou Keil,
and Charles Keil

*Bright Balkan Morning: Romani Lives and
the Power of Music in Greek Macedonia*

Susan Boynton and Roe-Min Kok, editors

*Musical Childhoods and the
Cultures of Youth*

James Buhler, Caryl Flinn,
and David Neumeyer, editors

Music and Cinema

Thomas Burkhalter, Kay Dickinson,
and Benjamin J. Harbert, editors

*The Arab Avant-Garde:
Music, Politics, Modernity*

Patrick Burkart

Music and Cyberliberties

Julia Byl

*Antiphonal Histories: Resonant Pasts
in the Toba Batak Musical Present*

ABOUT THE AUTHOR

Ilana Webster-Kogen is an assistant professor and the Joe Loss Lecturer in Jewish Music at SOAS, University of London. Her work has appeared in *African and Black Diaspora: An International Journal, Ethnomusicology Forum,* and the *Journal of African Cultural Studies.*